Advance Praise for *The Wonder Weeks*:

"Vanderijt and Plooij's work on infant development has enormous value for clinical use and scientific application. Not only have they explained the periods of puzzling, difficult behavior in infancy which so worry parents, they have also shown how these behaviors mark developmental leaps and have described the stages in the infant's understanding. Together, this gives parents and professionals soundly based insight into babies' developing minds. What's more, Vanderijt and Plooij have described the play and communication that work best with babies at different ages and thus helped parents understand and connect sensitively with their babies. This parent-child connection is the major prerequisite for the development of secure, well-adjusted children. *The Wonder Weeks* is essential reading for everyone who works with infants—pediatricians, social workers, psychologists, and, of course, parents."

—John Richer, Ph.D., Dip. Psych., principal clinical psychologist, department of pediatrics, John Radcliffe Hospital, Oxford, England

"Vanderijt and Plooij will help you see the world the way an infant sees it. As the child grows, displays of emotion (such as crying) tell us the child is summoning reserves of energy and is calling out for help in finding new ways to perceive the changing world. Because Vanderijt and Plooij have discovered predictable stages in the widening of the infant's perceptions and skills, they can enable you, with their superb examples, to recognize the onset of these stressful episodes and to join your child in coping with them. So rich, indeed, are the implications of finding new perceptions and new skills in the midst of stress that whether or not you are a parent, it can never be too early or too late to profit from this book."

—Philip J. Runkel, Ph.D., professor emeritus of psychology and education, University of Oregon

the Wonder
Weeks

the Wonder Weeks

How to Turn Your Baby's
8 Great Fussy Phases
into Magical Leaps Forward

Hetty Vanderijt, Ph.D.,
and
Frans Plooij, Ph.D.

RODALE

© 2003 by Kiddy World Promotions B.V.

First published in 1992 as *Oei, ik groei!* by Kosmos-Z & K Uitgevers, Utrecht and Antwerp

Kiddy World Promotions B.V. 1992, 2003

Hetty Vanderijt and Frans Plooij assert the moral right to be identified as the authors of this work.

Printed in the United States of America
Rodale Inc. makes every effort to use acid-free ∞, recycled paper ♺.

Book design by Leanne Coppola
Illustrations by John Coulter

Library of Congress Cataloging-in-Publication Data

Vanderijt, Hetty.
    [Oei, ik groei! English]
    The wonder weeks : how to turn your baby's eight great fussy phases
into magical leaps forward / Hetty Vanderijt and Frans Plooij.
        p.   cm.
    Includes index.
    ISBN 1–57954–645–5 paperback
    1. Infant psychology.   2. Infants (Newborn)—Psychology.
3. Infants—Development.   4. Child rearing.   I. Plooij, Frans X.   II. Title.
BF719 .V3613   2003
649'.122—dc21   2002014537

Distributed to the book trade by St. Martin's Press

2   4   6   8   10   9   7   5   3   1   paperback

RODALE

WE **INSPIRE** AND **ENABLE** PEOPLE TO IMPROVE
THEIR LIVES AND THE WORLD AROUND THEM

FOR MORE OF OUR PRODUCTS
WWW.RODALESTORE.COM
(800) 848-4735

To our children, Xaviera and Marco,
and to our grandchildren, Thomas and Victoria,
from whom we have learned so much

Contents

introduction

Jolted from a deep sleep, the new mother leaps from her bed and runs down the hall to the nursery. Her tiny infant, red-faced, fists clenched, screams in his crib. On instinct, the mother picks up the baby, cradling him in her arms. The baby continues to shriek. The mother nurses the baby, changes his diaper, then rocks him, trying every trick to ease his discomfort, but nothing seems to work. "Is there something wrong with the baby?" the mother wonders. "Am I doing something wrong?"

Parents commonly experience worry, fatigue, aggravation, guilt, and sometimes even aggression toward their inconsolable infants. The baby's cries may cause friction between the parents, especially when they disagree on how to deal with it. Well-meant but unwelcome advice from family, friends, and even strangers only makes things worse. "Let him cry, it's good for his lungs" is not the solution mothers wish to hear. Disregarding the problem does not make it go away.

The Good News: There Is a Reason

For the past 25 years, we have studied the development of babies and the way mothers and other caregivers respond to their changes. Our research was done in homes, where we observed the daily activities of mothers and children. We gleaned further information from more formal interviews.

Our research has shown that from time to time all parents are plagued by a baby who won't stop crying. In fact, we found that, surprisingly, all normal, healthy babies are more tearful, troublesome, demanding, and fussy at the same ages, and when this occurs they may drive the entire household to despair. *From our research, we are now able to predict, almost to the week, when parents can expect their babies to go through one of these "fussy phases."*

During these periods, a baby cries for a good reason. She is suddenly undergoing drastic changes in her development, which are upsetting to her. These changes enable the baby to learn many new skills and should therefore be a reason for celebration. After all, it's a sign that she is making wonderful progress. But as far as the baby is concerned, these changes are bewildering. She's taken aback—everything has changed overnight. It is as if she has entered a whole new world.

It is well known that a child's physical development progresses in what we commonly call "growth spurts." A baby may not grow at all for some time, but then she'll grow a quarter inch in just one night. Research has shown that essentially the same thing happens in a child's mental development. Neurological studies have shown that there are times when major, dramatic changes take place in the brains of children younger than 20 months. Shortly after each of them, there is a parallel leap forward in mental development.

This book focuses on the eight major leaps that every baby takes in her first 14 months of life. It tells you what each of these developments mean for your baby's understanding of the world about her and how she uses this understanding to develop the new skills that she needs at each stage in her development.

What This Means for You and Your Baby

Parents can use this understanding of their baby's developmental leaps to help them through these often confusing times in their new lives. You will better understand the way your baby is thinking and why he acts as he does at certain times. You will be able to choose the right kind of help to give him when he needs it and the right kind of environment to help him make the most of every leap in his development.

This is not a book about how to make your child into a genius, however. We firmly believe that every child is unique and intelligent in his own way. It is a book on how to understand and cope with your baby when he is difficult and how to enjoy him most as he grows. It is about the joys and sorrows of growing with your baby.

All that's required to use this book is:
- One (or two) loving parent(s)
- One active, vocal, growing baby
- A willingness to grow along with your baby
- Patience.

How to Use This Book

This book grows with your baby. You can compare your experiences with those of other mothers during all stages of your baby's development. Over the years, we've asked many mothers of new babies to keep records of their babies' progress and also to record their thoughts and feelings as well as observations of their babies' behavior from day to day. The diaries we've included in this book are a sample of these, based on the weekly reports of mothers of 15 babies—eight girls and seven boys. We hope you will feel that your baby is growing alongside those in our study group and that you can relate your observations of your baby to those of other mothers.

However, this book is not just for reading. Each section offers you the opportunity to record the details of your baby's progress. By the time a baby has grown into middle childhood, many mothers yearn to recall all of the events and emotions of those first all-important years. Some mothers keep diaries, but most mothers—who are not particularly fond of writing or who simply lack the time—are convinced they will remember the milestones and even the minor details in their babies' lives. Unfortunately, later on these mothers end up deeply regretting the fact that their memories faded faster than they could ever have imagined.

You can keep a personal record of your baby's interests and progress in the "My Diary" sections provided throughout this book. They offer space for you to record your thoughts and comments on your child's growth and budding personality, so that you can easily turn this book into a diary of the development of your baby. Often, a few key phrases are enough to bring memories flooding back later on.

The next chapter, "Growing Up: How Your Baby Does It" explains some of the research on which this book is based and how it applies to your baby. You will learn how your baby grows by making "leaps" in her mental development and how these are preceded by stormy periods when you can expect her to be fussy, cranky, or temperamental.

"Chapter 2: Newborn: Welcome to the World" describes what a newborn's world is like and how she perceives the new sensations that surround her. You will learn how nature has equipped her to deal with the challenges of life and how important physical contact is to her future development. These facts will help you get to know your new baby, to learn about her wants and needs, and to understand what she is experiencing when she takes the first leap forward.

Subsequent chapters discuss the Wonder Weeks—the eight big changes your baby undergoes in the first 14 months of life, at around 5, 8, 12, 19, 26, 37, 46, and 55 weeks. Each chapter tells you the signs that will let you know that a major leap is occurring. Then they explain the new perceptual changes your baby experiences at this time and how your baby will make use of them in his development.

Each leap is discussed in a separate chapter, consisting of four sections:

"This Week's Fussy Signs" describes the clues that your baby is about to make a developmental leap. Reflections from other mothers about their babies' troublesome times offer sympathetic support as you endure your baby's stormy periods.

In this section, you'll also find a diary section titled "Signs My Baby Is Growing Again." Check off the signs you've noticed that indicate your baby is about to experience a big change.

"The Magical Leap Forward" discusses the new abilities your baby will acquire during the current leap. In each case it's like a new world opening up, full of observations she can make and skills she can acquire.

In this section, you will find a diary section, "How My Baby Explores the New World," which lists the skills that babies can develop once they have made this developmental leap. As you check off your baby's skills on the lists, remember that no baby will do everything listed. Your baby may exhibit only a few of the listed skills at this time, and you may not see other skills until weeks or months later. How much your baby does is not important—your baby will choose the skills best suited to her at this time. Tastes differ, even among babies! As you mark or highlight your own baby's preferences, you will discover what makes your baby unique.

"What You Can Do to Help" gives you suggestions for games, activities, and toys appropriate to each stage of development which will increase your baby's awareness and satisfaction—and enhance your playtime together.

"After the Leap" lets you know when you can expect your baby to become more independent and cheerful again. This is likely to be a delightful time for parents and babies, when both can appreciate the newly acquired skills that equip the baby to learn about and enjoy her world.

This book is designed to be picked up at any point in your baby's first year when you feel you need help understanding her current stage of development. You do not have to read it from cover to cover. If your baby is a little older, you can skip the earlier chapters.

What This Book Offers You

We hope that you will use this knowledge of your child's developmental leaps to understand what he is going through, help him through the difficult times, and encourage him as he takes on the momentous task of growing into a toddler. Also, we hope that this book helps provide the following.

Support in times of trouble. During the times that you have to cope with crying problems, it helps to know that you are not alone, that there is a reason for the crying, and that a fussy period never lasts more than a few weeks, and sometimes no longer than several days. This book tells you what other mothers experienced when their babies were the same age as yours. You will learn that all mothers struggle with feelings of anxiety, aggravation, and a whole range of other emotions. You will come to understand that these feelings are all part of the process, and that they will help your baby progress.

Self-confidence. You will learn that you are capable of sensing your baby's needs better than anyone else. You are the expert, the leading authority on your baby.

Help in understanding your baby. This book will tell you what your baby endures during each fussy phase. It explains that he will be difficult when he's on the verge of learning new skills, as the changes to his nervous system start to upset him. Once you understand this, you will be less concerned about and less resentful of his behavior. This knowledge will also give you more peace of mind and help you to help him through each of these fussy periods.

Hints on how to help your baby play and learn. After each fussy period, your baby will be able to learn new skills. He will learn faster, more easily, and with more pleasure if you help him. This book will give you insight into what is preoccupying him at each age. On top of that, we supply a range of ideas for different games, activities, and toys so that you can choose those best suited to your baby.

A unique account of your baby's development. You can track your baby's fussy phases and progress throughout the book and supplement it with your own notes, so that it charts your baby's progress during the first 14 months of his life.

We hope that you will use this knowledge of your child's developmental leaps to understand what he is going through, help him through the difficult times, and encourage him as he takes on the momentous task of growing into a toddler. Also, we hope you will be able to share with him the joys and challenges of growing up.

Most of all, we hope you will gain peace of mind and confidence in your ability to bring up your baby. We hope this book will be a reliable friend and an indispensable guide in the crucial first year of your baby's life.

chapter 1

Growing Up: How Your Baby Does It

Watching their babies grow is, for many parents, one of the most interesting and rewarding experiences of their lives. Parents love to record and celebrate the first time their babies sit up, crawl, say their first words, feed themselves, and a myriad of other precious "firsts."

But few parents stop to think about what's happening in their babies' minds that allows them to learn these skills when they do. We know that a baby's perception of the world is growing and changing when she suddenly is able to play peek-a-boo or to recognize Grandma's voice on the telephone. These moments are as remarkable as the first time she crawls, but even more mysterious because they involve things happening inside her brain that we cannot see. They're proof that her brain is growing as rapidly as her chubby little body.

But every parent discovers sooner or later that the first year of life can be a bumpy road. While parents revel in their children's development and share their joy as they discover the world around them, parents also find that at times baby joyfulness can suddenly turn to abject misery. A baby can seem as changeable as a spring day.

At times, life with baby can be a very trying experience. Inexplicable crying bouts and fussy periods are likely to drive both mother and father to desperation, as they wonder what's wrong with their little tyke and try every trick to soothe her or coax her to happiness, to no avail.

Crying and Clinging Can Simply Mean He's Growing

For 25 years, we have been studying interactions between mothers and babies. We have documented—in objective observations, from personal records, and on videotape—the times at which mothers report their babies to be "difficult." These difficult periods are usually accompanied by the three C's: clinginess, crankiness, and crying. We now know that they are the telltale signs of a period in which the child makes a major leap forward in his development.

It is well known that a child's physical growth progresses in what are commonly called "growth spurts." A child's mental development progresses in much the same way.

Recent neurological studies on the growth and development of the brain support our observations of mother and baby interactions. Study of the physical events that accompany mental changes in the brain is still in its infancy. Yet, at six of the ten difficult ages we see take place in the first 20 months, major changes in the brain have been identified by other scientists. Each major change announces a leap forward in mental development of the kind we are describing in this book. We expect that studies of other critical ages will eventually show similar results.

It is hardly surprising, when you think of the number of changes that your baby has to go through in just the first year of life, that he should occasionally feel out of sorts. Growing up is hard work!

The Fussy Signs that Signal a Magical Leap Forward

In this book, we outline the eight major developmental leaps that all babies go through in the first 60 weeks of their lives. Each leap allows your baby to assimilate information in a new way and use it to advance the skills she needs to grow, not just physically but also mentally, into a fully functioning, thinking adult.

Each leap is invariably preceded by what we call a fussy phase or clingy period, in which the baby demands extra attention from her mother or other caregiver. The amazing and wonderful thing is that all babies go through these difficult periods at exactly the same time, give or take a week or two, during the first 60 weeks of their lives.

These eight developmental leaps that infants undergo are not necessarily in synch with physical growth spurts, although they may occasionally coincide. Many of the common milestones for a baby's first year of development, such as cutting teeth, are also unrelated to these leaps in mental development.

Milestones in mental development may, on the other hand, be *reflected* in physical progress, although they are by no means limited to that.

Signs of a Leap

Shortly before each leap, a sudden and extremely rapid change occurs within the baby. It's a change in the nervous system, chiefly the brain, and it may be accompanied by some physical changes as well. In this book we call this a "big change." Each big change brings the baby a new kind of perception and alters the way that she perceives the world. And each time a new kind of perception swamps your baby, it also brings the means of learning a new set of skills appropriate for that world. For instance, at approximately 8 weeks, the big change in the brain enables the baby to perceive simple patterns for the first time.

During the initial period of disturbance that the big change always brings, you may already notice new behaviors emerging. Shortly thereafter, you most certainly will. In the 8-week example, your baby will suddenly show an interest in visible shapes, patterns, and structures, such as cans on a supermarket shelf or the slats on her crib. Physical developments may be seen as well. For example, she may start to gain some control over her body, since she now recognizes the way her arms and legs work in precise patterns and is able to control them. So, the big change alters the perception of sensations inside the baby's body as well as outside it.

The major sign of a big change is that the baby's behavior takes an inexplicable turn for the worse. Sometimes it will seem as if your baby has become a changeling. You will notice a fussiness that wasn't there in the previous weeks and often there will be bouts of crying that you are at a loss to explain. This is very worrisome, especially when you encounter it for the first time, but it is perfectly normal. When their babies become more difficult and demanding, many mothers wonder if their babies are becoming ill. Or they may feel annoyed, not understanding why their babies are suddenly so fussy and trying.

The Timing of the Fussy Phases

Babies all undergo these fussy phases at around the same ages. During the first 14 months of a baby's life, there are eight developmental leaps with their corresponding fussy periods at onset. The fussy periods come at 5, 8, 12, 15, 23, 34, 42, and 51 weeks. The onsets may vary by a week or two, but you can be sure of their arrival.

In this book, we confine ourselves to the developmental period from birth to just past the first year of your baby's life. This pattern does not end when your baby becomes a toddler, however. Two more leaps will occur before your baby reaches 20 months—at 64 and 75 weeks—and several more have been documented throughout childhood.

The initial fussy phases your baby goes through as an infant do not last long. They can be as short as a few days—although they often seem longer

Your Baby's 8 Great Fussy Phases

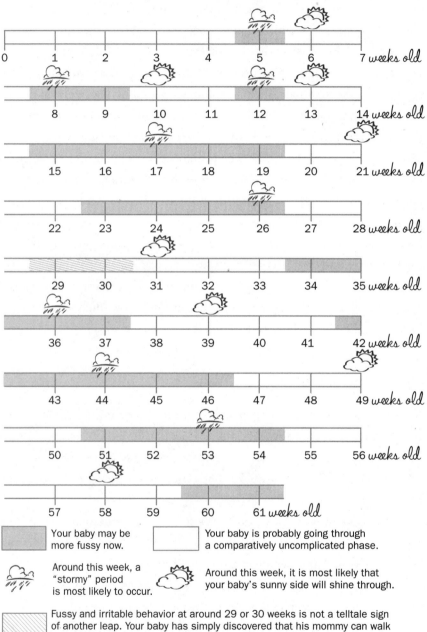

▓	Your baby may be more fussy now.	
□	Your baby is probably going through a comparatively uncomplicated phase.	

Around this week, a "stormy" period is most likely to occur.

Around this week, it is most likely that your baby's sunny side will shine through.

Fussy and irritable behavior at around 29 or 30 weeks is not a telltale sign of another leap. Your baby has simply discovered that his mommy can walk away and leave him behind. Funny as it may sound, this is progress. It is a new skill: He is learning about distances.

Not a Single Baby Gets Away

All babies experience fussy periods when big changes in their development occur. Usually calm, easygoing babies will react to these changes just as much as more difficult, temperamental babies do. But not surprisingly, temperamental babies will have more difficulty in dealing with them than their calmer counterparts. Mothers of "difficult" babies will also have a harder time as their babies already require more attention and will demand even more when they have to cope with these big changes. These babies will have the greatest need for mommy, the most conflict with their mothers, and the largest appetite for learning.

to parents distressed over an infant's inexplicable crying. The intervals between these early periods are also short—3 or 4 weeks, on average.

Later, as the changes your infant undergoes become more complex, they take longer for her to assimilate and the fussy periods may last from 1 to 6 weeks. Every baby will be different, however. Some babies find change more distressing than others, and some changes will be more distressing than others. But every baby will be upset to some degree while these big changes are occurring in her life.

Every big change is closely linked to changes in the developing infant's nervous system, so nature's timing for developmental leaps is actually calculated from the date of conception. In this book, we use the more conventional calculation of age from a baby's birth date. Therefore, the ages given at which developmental leaps occur are calculated for full-term babies. If your baby was premature or very late, you should adjust the ages accordingly. For example, if your baby was born 2 weeks late, her first fussy phase will probably occur 2 weeks earlier than we show here. If she was 4 weeks early, it will occur 4 weeks later. Remember to make allowances for this with each of the eight developmental leaps.

The Magical Leap Forward

To the baby, these big changes always come as a shock, as they turn the familiar world he has come to know inside out. If you stop to think about this, it makes perfect sense. Just imagine what it would be like to wake up and find yourself on a strange planet where everything was different from the one you were used to. What would you do?

You wouldn't want to calmly eat or take a long nap. Neither does your baby.

All she wants is to cling tightly to someone she feels safe with.

To make matters more challenging for you and your baby, each developmental leap is different. Each gives the baby a new kind of perception that allows him to learn a new set of skills that belong to the new developmental world—skills he could not possibly have learned at an earlier age, no matter how much encouragement you gave him.

We will describe the perceptual changes your baby undergoes in each developmental leap, as well as the new skills that then become available to him. You will notice that each world builds upon the foundations of the previous one. In each new world, your baby can make lots of new discoveries. Some skills he discovers will be completely new, while others will be an improvement on skills he acquired earlier.

No two babies are exactly the same. Each baby has his own preferences, temperament, and physical characteristics, and these will lead him to select things in this new world that he, personally, finds interesting. Where one baby will quickly sample everything, another will be captivated by one special skill. These differences are what makes babies unique. If you watch, you will see your baby's unique personality emerging as he grows.

What You Can Do to Help

You are the person your baby knows best. She trusts you more and has known you longer than anyone else. When her world has been turned in-

Quality Time: An Unnatural Whim

When a baby is allowed to decide for himself when and what sort of attention he prefers, you'll notice this differs from one week to the next. When a big change occurs within a baby he will go through the following phases.

• A need to cling to mommy

• A need to play and learn new skills with mommy

• A need to play on his own.

Because of this, planned playtimes are unnatural. If you want your baby's undivided attention, you have to play when it suits him. It is impossible to plan having fun with a baby. In fact, he may not even *appreciate* your attention at the time you had set aside for "quality time." Gratifying, tender, and funny moments simply *happen* with babies.

side out, she will be completely bewildered. She will cry, sometimes incessantly, and she will like nothing better than to be simply carried in your arms all day long. As she gets older, she will do anything to stay near you. Sometimes she will cling to you and hold on for dear life. She may want to be treated like a tiny baby again. These are all signs that she is in need of comfort and security. This is her way of feeling safe. You could say that she is returning to home base, clinging to mommy.

When your baby suddenly becomes fussy, you may feel worried or even irritated by her troublesome behavior. You will want to know what's wrong with her, and you will wish that she would become her old self again. Your natural reaction will be to watch her even more closely. It's then that you are likely to discover that she knows much more than you thought. You may notice that she's attempting to do things you have never seen her do before. It may dawn on you that your baby is changing, although your baby has known it for some time already.

As her mother, you are in the best position to give your baby things that she can handle and to meet her needs. If you respond to what your baby is trying to tell you, you will help her progress. Obviously, your baby may enjoy certain games, activities, and toys that you, personally, find less appealing, while you may enjoy others that she does not like at all. Don't forget that mothers are unique, too. You can also encourage her if she loses interest or wants to give up too easily. With your help, she will find the whole play-and-learn process more challenging and fun, too.

When your baby learns something new, it often means that she has to break an old habit. Once she can crawl, she is perfectly capable of fetching her own playthings, and once she can walk quite confidently on her own, she can't expect to be carried as often as before. Each leap forward in her development will make her more capable and more independent.

This is the time when mother and baby may have problems adjusting to one another. There is often a big difference in what baby wants and what mother wants or thinks is good for the baby, and this can lead to anger and resentment on both sides. When you realize what new skills your baby is trying to exercise, you will be better equipped to set the right rules for each developmental stage and alter them as needed as she grows.

After the Leap

The troublesome phase stops just as suddenly as it started. Most mothers see this as a time to relax and enjoy their babies. The pressure to provide constant attention is off. The baby has become more independent, and she is often busy putting her new skills into practice. She is more cheerful at this stage, too. Unfortunately, this period of relative peace and quiet doesn't last long—it's just a lull before the next storm. Nature does not allow babies to rest for long.

Place Photo Here

Name: _____

Date of birth: _____

Time: _____

Place: _____

Weight: _____

Height: _____

Reflections: _____

chapter 2

Newborn: Welcome to the World

Watch any new mother when she holds her baby for the first time. Chances are she'll follow this particular pattern: First she'll run her fingers through his hair. Then she'll run a finger around his head and over his face. After this, she'll feel his fingers and toes. Then she'll slowly move toward his middle, along his arms, legs, and neck. Finally, she'll touch his tummy and chest.

The *way* in which mothers generally touch their newborn babies is often very similar, too. First a new mother will touch her infant with her fingertips only, stroking and handling him very gently. Slowly but surely, as she becomes more comfortable, she'll use all of her fingers and may sometimes squeeze him. Finally, she'll touch him with the palm of her hand. When she eventually dares to hold him by the chest or tummy, the new mother will be so delighted that she may exclaim what a miracle it is that she has produced something as precious as this.

Ideally, this discovery process should happen as close to birth as possible. After a mother's first encounter with her baby, she will no longer be afraid to pick him up, turn him around, or put him down. She will know how her little one feels to the touch.

Every baby looks and feels different. Try picking up another baby if his mother will allow it, and you'll find that it's a strange experience. It will take a minute or two to get used to the other infant. This is because you have become so accustomed to *your* baby.

Those Important First Hours

A mother is usually extremely perceptive to her newborn baby in the first hours after birth. Try to have your baby with you at this critical time to get to know each other. Your newborn baby is often wide awake during this period. She is aware of her surroundings, she turns toward quiet sounds, and she fixes her gaze on the face that happens to hover above her. Most mothers love it if the father is there, too, so they can share this experience as a brand-new family.

Take Charge Early

The sooner a mother becomes confident handling her baby, the quicker she can begin responding sensitively to his needs. A baby shouldn't be dumped in his mother's arms; she should be allowed all the time she needs to take her baby into her arms herself. This sort of tuning-in to the new baby is easily interrupted if others don't give the mother space at the birth. If the new mother feels that things are not under her control, she may feel powerless and even afraid to handle her baby.

Take control of the situation as soon as you are able, and get to know your baby as soon as you can. Even if the baby has to be placed in an incubator, spend as much time with him as you can and look after as many aspects of his care as you are able. Talk to him to let him know you are there when you are not able to touch him.

Be sure to speak up. If you want to have your baby near you, or if you want to be alone with him for a while, say so. *You* decide how often you want to pick him up and cuddle him.

The majority of mothers whose early contact with their newborns was thwarted by hospital procedures or others around them say that they regret not having spent more time alone with their babies during this period. Many mothers feel resentful about this for quite some time. The maternity period wasn't like they imagined. Instead of enjoying a well-earned rest, they felt harassed. They had wanted to have their babies near them all the time, especially when the little ones were crying. If they were not allowed to hold their babies, the new mothers felt disappointed and annoyed. They felt as if they were being treated like immature, helpless children who were incapable of deciding for themselves what was best for them and their babies. These feelings have also been expressed by fathers, too, who felt overwhelmed by hospital rules and frustrated by meddling from others.

"I had to do as I was told. I wasn't just told *how* to sit during nursing, but also when I could nurse, and for how long. I also had to allow my baby to cry whenever it wasn't "his time" yet. I was annoyed most of the time, but I didn't want to be rude, so I nursed him in secret. I just couldn't stand hearing him cry, and I wanted to comfort him. My breasts kept swelling and shrinking all day long. I'd really had more than I could take. I was the one who had given birth, and I wanted my baby. I was so angry that I just started crying. But of course they had a name for that, too—"maternity tears." That was the last straw. All I wanted was my baby and a bit of peace and quiet."

Paul's mom

"I had a long delivery. Our baby was taken away from us immediately. For hours, we assumed we'd had a baby boy. When I got my baby back later on, it turned out to be a girl. We were shocked. It wasn't that we didn't want a girl, but we had started getting used to the idea that we had a son."

Jenny's mom

"When I nursed my baby, I liked to snuggle up to her and get nice and close. But the maternity nurse wouldn't let me. She made me lean back into the cushions on the sofa. It felt so unnatural—detached and unemotional."

Nina's mom

When mothers have problems with their babies shortly after the birth, they often say this is because they don't feel completely confident. They are afraid of dropping them or holding them too tightly. They haven't learned to assess their babies' needs and responses to certain situations. They feel they are failing as mothers.

Some mothers think this has to do with the fact that they saw so little of their babies just after the birth. They would have loved to have spent more time with their babies back then, but now they feel relieved when the babies are back in their cribs. They've become afraid of motherhood.

 Do Remember

Cuddle, rock, caress, and massage your baby when she is in a good mood, since this is the best time to find out what suits her and what relaxes her most. When you know her preferences, you will be able to use these methods to comfort her later on when she is upset. If you cuddle, rock, caress, and massage her only when she is in a bad mood, the "comfort" will cause her to cry even longer and louder.

"Because I had a difficult birth, we had to stay in the hospital for 10 days. I was only allowed to see my baby during the day, at nursing times. Nothing was the way I had imagined it would be. I'd planned to breastfeed, but sometimes the staff gave my baby a bottle on the sly, to make things easier for themselves. At night, they always gave her bottles. I wanted to have her near me more often, but they wouldn't allow it. I felt helpless and angry. When I was allowed to go home, I felt that they might as well keep her. By that time, she felt like a stranger, like she wasn't mine."

Juliette's mom

"The maternity nurse was a nuisance. She stayed when I had company, did most of the talking, and went on and on telling everyone about every case she'd been on that had ever gone just the slightest bit wrong. For some reason, she was overly concerned that my healthy baby would turn yellow. She would check on her every hour, sometimes every 15 minutes, and tell me she thought she'd seen the first signs of jaundice. It made me so nervous. When I tried to breastfeed, the nurse kept interrupting by whisking my hungry baby off to be weighed. This upset me every time, and my baby didn't seem too pleased about it, either. She wriggled around on the scales, so it would take even longer for the nurse to see whether she had taken 1.4 or 1.5 ounces of milk. Meanwhile, my baby's desperate screams made me even more nervous, so I finally decided to stop breastfeeding. When I look back on it, I feel terrible. I would have liked so much to nurse my little girl."

Emily's mom

"With my second child, we were determined to do everything exactly the way we wanted. When the baby started crying, I would simply feed her a little. For nearly 2 weeks, we had been told to let our eldest cry and go hungry—for no reason, as it later turned out. With the first baby, you tend to take advice from everyone. The second time, I listened only to myself."

Eve's mom

Getting to Know and Understand Your Baby

In some ways, you already know your baby. After all, she was with you day and night for 9 months. Before she was born, you wondered what kind of baby you would have and whether you would recognize any traits you thought she had while in your womb. But once she's born it's different—totally different, in fact. You see your baby for the first time, and your baby also finds herself in completely new surroundings.

Most mothers look for familiar traits in their tiny newborns. Is she the peaceful little person she expected her to be? Does she kick at certain times of the day like she did before she was born? Does she have a special bond with her Dad? Does she recognize his voice?

Often mothers want to "test" their babies' reactions. They want to find out what makes their children happy and contented. They will appreciate advice, but not rules and regulations. They want to get to know their babies and see how their babies respond to them. They want to find out for themselves what is best for their children. If they're right about their likes and dislikes, they feel pleased with themselves, as it shows how well they know their babies. This increases their self-confidence and will make them feel they are perfectly able to cope after they take their infants home.

Seeing, hearing, smelling, and feeling your baby during those first few days has a tremendous impact on your relationship with your baby. Most mothers instinctively know how important these intimate "parties" are. They want to experience everything their babies do. Just looking at them gives them enormous pleasure. They want to watch them sleep and listen to them breathe. They want to be there when they wake up. They want to caress them, cuddle them, and smell them whenever they feel like it.

> "My son's breathing changes whenever he hears a sudden noise or sees a light. When I first noticed this irregular breathing, I was really concerned, but then I realized he was just reacting to sound and light. Now I think it's wonderful when his breathing changes, and I don't worry about it anymore."
>
> Bob's mom

Your Baby Gets to Know and Understand You

When a new parent gazes down into her baby's face, it often seems as if the baby, gazing steadily back with wide, astonished eyes, is thinking, "What a strange and wonderful world this is!"

Indeed, a newborn baby's world is an astonishing place of new and strange sensations. Light, sound, motion, smells, the sensations on his soft skin—it is all so new that he can't even separate them one from another yet. Sometimes, snuggled tightly up against his mother's breast, it all feels so wonderfully good. He feels full, warm, sleepy, and soothed by the softness around him.

At other times, his whole world seems utterly shattered, and he can't figure out what's making him feel so miserable. *Something* is wet, cold, hungry, noisy, blindingly bright, or just desperately unhappy, and all he can do is wail.

During the first 5 weeks of your baby's life, he will slowly become familiar with the world around him. You and he will get to know each other more intimately than anyone else in your shared world at this time. Soon he will make the first major leap in his development.

But before you are able to understand what your baby will experience when he is 5 weeks old and takes his first leap forward, you need to know what your newborn baby's world is like now and how he is equipped to deal with it. Also, to help him meet his new challenges, you need to know how important physical contact is and how to use it.

Your New Baby's World

Babies are interested in the world around them from the moment they are born. They look and listen, taking in their surroundings. They try very hard to focus their eyes as sharply as possible, which is why babies frequently look cross-eyed as they strain to get a better look. Sometimes they tremble and gasp from sheer exhaustion in the effort. A newborn often looks at you as if he is staring, transfixed with interest.

Your new baby has an excellent memory, and he is quick to recognize voices, people, and even some toys, such as an especially colorful stuffed animal. He also clearly anticipates regular parts of his daily routine, such as bath-time, cuddle-time, and nursing-time.

Even at this age, a baby mimics facial expressions. Try sticking your tongue out at him while you sit and talk to him, or open your mouth wide as if you are going to call out. Make sure that he's really looking at you when you try this, and give him plenty of time to respond. Most of your baby's movements are very slow by adult standards, and it will take him several seconds to react.

A young baby is able to tell his mother just how he feels—whether he is happy, angry, or surprised. He does this by slightly changing the tone of his murmuring, gurgling, and crying and by using body language. You will rapidly get to know what he means. Besides, the baby will make it perfectly clear that he expects to be understood. If he isn't, he will cry angrily or sob as if heartbroken.

Your newborn baby has preferences even at this tender age. Most babies prefer to look at people, rather than toys. You will also find that if

(continued on page 29)

Your New Baby's Senses

Young babies can already see, hear, smell, taste, and feel a variety of things, and they are able to remember these sensations. However, a newborn baby's perception of these sensations is very different from the way she will experience them as she gets older.

WHAT BABIES SEE

Until recently, scientists and doctors believed that new babies were unable to see. This is not true. Mothers knew all along that newborns love to look at faces, although it is true that vision is the last sense to reach full capacity. Your newborn can see most clearly up to a distance of about a foot. Beyond this, her vision is probably blurred. Sometimes she will also have difficulty focusing both eyes on whatever she is looking at, but once she has, she can stare at the object intently. She will even stop moving briefly. All her attention will be focused on the object. If she is very alert, she will sometimes be able to follow a moving toy by moving her eyes, turning her head, or sometimes by doing both together. She can manage to do this whether the object is moved horizontally or vertically. The important thing is that the object must be moved very slowly and deliberately. If she loses track after a few moments, pick up her gaze again and try it even more slowly.

The object that your baby will follow best is a simple pattern with the basic characteristics of a human face—two large dots at the top for the eyes and one below for the mouth. Babies are able to do this within an hour of birth. Many of them have their eyes wide open and are very alert. Fathers and mothers are often completely fascinated by their newborn baby's big, beautiful eyes. It is possible that babies are attracted to anything that even vaguely resembles a human face when they are this young.

Your baby will be particularly interested in sharp contrasts—red and white stripes will probably hold her attention longer than green and blue ones. The brighter the color contrasts, the more interested she will be. Black and white stripes actually hold a baby's attention longest because the contrast is strongest.

WHAT BABIES HEAR

At birth, your new baby can already clearly distinguish between different sounds. She will recognize your voice shortly after birth. She may like music, the hum of an engine, and soft drumming. This makes sense, because these sounds are already familiar to her. In the womb, she was surrounded by the constant thump, rustle, grumble, wheeze, and squeak of heart, veins, stomach, lungs, and intestines. She also has a built-in interest in people's voices and finds them soothing. By and large babies will feel comfortable in environments similar to those that they were used to in the womb. For example, a baby whose mother spent a lot of time in noisy surroundings while she was pregnant may be quite upset by a room that is too quiet.

Your baby recognizes the difference between deep and high-pitched voices. High-pitched sounds will draw her attention more quickly. Adults sense this and speak to babies in high-pitched voices, so there is no need to be ashamed of your "oochy-koochy-cooing." Your baby is also able to differentiate between soft and loud sounds and does not like sudden, loud noises. Some babies are easily frightened, and if this is so for your baby, it is important that you do nothing that will frighten her.

WHAT BABIES SMELL

Your new baby is very sensitive to smells. She does not like pungent or sharp odors. These smells will make her overactive. She will try to turn away from the source of the smell, and she may start to cry, too.

(continued)

Your New Baby's Senses (cont.)

Your baby can smell the difference between your body scent and breast milk and those of other mothers. If she is presented with several items of worn clothing, she will turn toward the article that you have worn.

WHAT BABIES TASTE

Your baby can already distinguish between several different flavors. She has a distinct preference for sweet things and will dislike anything that tastes sour or acidic. If something tastes bitter, she will spit it out as fast as she can.

WHAT BABIES FEEL

Your baby can sense changes in temperature. She can feel heat, which she puts to good use when searching for a nipple if it is not put in her mouth, since the nipple is much warmer than the breast. She simply moves her head in the direction of the warmest spot. Your baby can also sense cold. But if she is allowed to become cold, she will be unable to warm herself, because at this age she can't shiver to get warm as a means of controlling her own body temperature. Her parents need to consider her bodily warmth. For instance, it's not very sensible to take a baby for a long walk through snow and ice, no matter how well wrapped up she is, because she may become too cold and show signs of hypothermia. If your baby shows distress of any kind, hurry inside where it is warm.

Your baby is extremely sensitive to being touched. Generally, she loves skin contact, whether it's soft or firm. Find out what your baby prefers. She will usually enjoy a body massage in a nice warm room, too. Physical contact is simply the best possible comfort and amusement for her. Try to find out what kind of contact makes your baby sleepy or alert, since you can put this knowledge to good use in troublesome times.

presented with two playthings, he is able to express a preference by fixing his gaze on one of them.

Your new baby is quick to react to encouragement. He will adore being praised for his soft baby fragrance, his looks, and his achievements. You will hold his interest longer if you shower him with compliments!

Even though your baby's senses are in complete working order, he is unable to process the signals his senses send to his brain in the same way adults do. This means that he isn't able to distinguish among his senses. Babies experience their world in their own way, and it's quite different from ours. We *smell* a scent, *see* the flower spreading it, *touch* its soft, velvety petals, *hear* a bee buzzing toward it, and know we are *tasting* honey when we put it into our mouths. We understand the difference among each of our senses, and so we are able to distinguish the differences.

Your new baby is not yet able to make this distinction, however. He experiences the world as all one universe—a mish-mash of sensation that changes drastically as soon as a single element changes. He receives all these impressions but cannot distinguish among them. He does not yet realize that his world is made up of signals from individual senses and that each sense conveys messages about a single aspect of it.

To make matters even more confusing for your infant, he cannot yet make a distinction between himself and his surroundings, and he is not yet aware of being an independent person. Because of this, he also is unable to make a distinction between sensations that have their origin within his own body and those that come from outside it. As far as he is concerned, the outside world and his body are one and the same. To him, the world is one big color-cuddle-smell-and-sound sensation. What his body feels, he assumes everyone and everything else feels.

Because a newborn baby perceives the world and himself as one and the same, it is often difficult to discover the reason why he is crying. It could be anything inside or outside of him. No wonder his crying fits can drive his parents to distraction.

Your New Baby's Tool Kit

If you were to experience the world in the same way your baby does, you too would be incapable of acting independently. You would not know that you have hands to grasp things with and a mouth to suck with. Only when you understand these things will you be able to do things deliberately.

This does not mean, however, that newborn babies are completely incapable of reacting to the world. Fortunately, your baby comes equipped with several special features to compensate for these shortcomings and help him survive this initial period.

His Reflexes Tell Him What to Do

Babies have several reflex reactions to keep them safe. For example, a newborn baby will automatically turn his head to one side to breathe freely when lying face down. In some ways, this reflex is similar to the way a puppet reacts to its strings being pulled. He does not stop to think, "I'm going to turn my head." It simply happens. As soon as a baby learns to think and respond, this reflex disappears. It is a perfect system. (Of course, when it's time for your baby to go to sleep, be sure to place him on his back.)

Newborn babies also turn their heads toward sound. This automatic reaction ensures that a baby will shift his attention to the place of interest closest by. For many years, doctors overlooked this reaction because the newborn's response to sound is delayed. It takes 5 to 7 seconds before the baby starts to move his head, and it takes another 3 to 4 seconds to complete the movement. This reflex disappears somewhere between the 5th and 8th week after birth.

Here are some of your baby's other reflexes.

As soon as the mouth of a hungry newborn comes in contact with an object, his mouth will close around it, and he will start to suck. This reflex provides the baby with an incredibly strong sucking ability. It disappears as soon as a baby no longer needs to suckle.

Babies also have a strong gripping reflex. If you want your baby to grasp your finger, just stroke the palm of his hand. He will automatically

Babies Get Bored, Too

Your tiny infant is not yet able to amuse herself. Lively, temperamental babies in particular make no secret about wanting some action as soon as they are awake.

Here are some ways to keep your baby entertained.

- Explore the house with her. Give her the opportunity to see, hear, and touch whatever she finds interesting. Explain the items you come across while exploring. No matter what it is, she will enjoy listening to your voice. Pretty soon, she will start recognizing objects herself.

- Have a quiet "chat." Your baby enjoys listening to your voice. But if you also have a radio playing in the background, she will have difficulty in concentrating on your voice only. Although young babies are able to make a distinction between different voices when they hear them one at a time, they cannot distinguish one from the other when hearing them simultaneously.

- Place interesting objects in convenient places for your baby to look at when she is awake. At this age she won't be able to search for them herself, so for her it's "out of sight, out of mind."

- Experiment with music. Try to discover her favorite music and play it to her. She may find it to be very soothing.

In all activities, let your baby's responses guide you.

grab your finger. If you do the same with his feet, he'll use his toes to grab your finger. This gripping reflex is thought to date back to prehistoric times, when hominid mothers were covered with thick body hair. Because of this reflex, babies were able to cling to their mothers' hair shortly after birth. A baby will use this gripping reflex during the first 2 months of life, especially if he senses you want to put him down when he would much rather stay with you!

A baby shows a reaction called the *Moro reflex* when he is frightened. He looks as if he is trying to grab at something during a fall. He arches his back, throws his head back, and waves his arms and legs about, outward at first, then inward, before crossing them across his chest and stomach.

All of these baby reflexes disappear when they are replaced by voluntary responses. But there are other automatic reflexes that remain for life, such as breathing, sneezing, coughing, blinking, and jerking back a hand from a hot surface.

His Cries Get Your Attention

The reflexes mentioned above are your new baby's way of restoring an uncomfortable situation to normal. Sometimes these reflexes are not enough—for instance, if he is too hot or cold, if he is not feeling well, or if he is bored. In these cases, the baby employs another strategy: He wails until *someone else* rectifies the situation. If no one helps him, the baby will cry incessantly until he is completely exhausted.

> "My son's crying fits started in his second week. He yelled day and night, even though he was nursing well and growing steadily. When I took him to the clinic for his regular checkup, I mentioned that perhaps he was bored. But the pediatrician said that was impossible because babies keep their eyes closed for the first 10 days, and even if my baby had his eyes open, he still wouldn't be able to see anything. Last week, I put a rattle in his crib anyway. It seems to be helping. He's certainly crying less. So he was bored after all!"
>
> **Paul's mom, 4th week**

His Appearance Melts Your Heart

In order to survive, your baby has to rely on someone else to attend to his every need, morning, noon, and night. Therefore, nature has supplied him with a powerful weapon that he continually puts to use—his appearance.

Nothing is cuter than a baby. His extraordinarily large head makes up almost one third of his total length. His eyes and forehead are also "too big," and his cheeks are "too chubby." Furthermore, his arms and legs are "too short and too plump." His cute looks are endearing. Designers of dolls, cuddly toys, and cartoons are quick to copy them. This look sells! This is exactly how your baby sells himself, too. He is sweet, tiny, and helpless—a little cutie, just begging for attention. He will charm you into picking him up, cuddling him, and taking care of him.

Throughout the world, babies have been seen smiling before they are 6 weeks old. Smiling babies have even been filmed in the womb. Even so, this is a very rare occurrence in babies this young. Nevertheless, you may be one of the lucky parents who has witnessed an early smile. Newborn babies smile when touched, when a breath of fresh air brushes their cheeks, when they hear human voices or other sounds, when they see faces hovering over their cribs, or simply when they are full of milk and feeling content. Sometimes they even smile in their sleep.

Your New Baby's Biggest Need

Even before she was born, your baby perceived her world as one whole. At birth, she left her familiar surroundings and for the first time was exposed to all kinds of unknown, completely new things. This new world was made up of many new sensations. Suddenly, she's able to move freely, sense heat and cold, hear a whole range of different and louder noises, see bright lights, and feel clothes wrapped around her body. Besides these impressions, she also has to breathe by herself and get used to drinking milk, and her digestive organs have to process this new food, too. All these things are new to her. Because she suddenly has to cope with these enormous changes in lifestyle, it's easy to understand why she needs to feel safe and secure.

Close human contact is the best way of imitating your baby's secure

Touch: Simply the Best Comfort

Besides food and warmth, nothing is more important to your infant than snuggling close to you during the first 4 months of her life. As long as she experiences lots of physical contact, her development will not be delayed, even if you don't have much opportunity to play with her.

A young baby generally loves lying close to you and being carried around. At the same time, this is also a good opportunity for her to learn to control her body.

Another idea is to give her a relaxing massage. Make sure the room is warm. Pour some baby oil into your hands and softly massage every part of her naked body. This is a nice way of helping her to grow accustomed to her body, and it will make her wonderfully drowsy.

At this age, a baby loves to be picked up, cuddled, caressed, and rocked. She may even enjoy soft pats on her back. She cannot get enough physical contact now. Don't worry about whether you're doing the right thing—she'll soon let you know what she likes best and what comforts her most. In the meantime, she is learning that she has a wonderful home base to which she can safely return when she is upset.

world inside the womb. It makes her feel safe. After all, your womb hugged her body, and your movements kneaded it, as far back as she can remember. It was her home. She was part of whatever took place in there—the rhythmical beating of your heart, the flow of your blood, and the rumbling of your stomach. Therefore, it makes perfect sense that she will enjoy feeling the old, familiar physical contact and hearing those well-known sounds once more. It is her way of "touching base."

Place Photo Here

Before the First Leap

Age: _____

Reflections: _____

chapter 3

Wonder Week 5:
The World of Changing Sensations

For much of the last 4 or 5 weeks, you have watched your infant grow rapidly. You have become acquainted with each other, and you have learned all of his little ways. His world at this time is hard for adults to imagine. It's in soft focus and its qualities are undefined—in some ways it has not been so different from his life in your womb.

Now, before the mists that envelop his infant world part and allow him to start making sense of all the impressions that he has been busy absorbing in the last few weeks, he will need to go through his first major developmental leap. At about 5 weeks, and sometimes as early as 4, your baby will begin to take the first leap forward in his development.

New sensations bombard your baby inside and out, and he is usually bewildered by them. Some of these new things have to do with the development of his internal organs and his metabolism. Others are a result of his increased alertness—his senses are more sensitive than they were immediately after birth. So it is not so much the sensations themselves that are changing, but rather the baby's perceptions of them.

Do Remember

If your baby is fussy, watch him closely to see if he is attempting to master new skills.

This rapidly changing world is very disturbing at first. Your baby's first reaction will be to want to return to the safe, warm, familiar world he so recently left, a world with mommy at its center. Suddenly, your infant may seem to need more cuddles and attention than he did before. While eating and sleeping and being well-looked after physically were enough to lull him with a sense of well-being before, he now seems to need something more from you. Although your baby has been very close to you since his birth, this may be the first time you think of him as fussy or demanding. This period may last only a day, but with some babies it lasts a whole week.

As this clinginess begins to ease, you will notice that your baby is just a little more grown-up in some way that you find it hard to put your finger on. He seems more alert and aware of the world around him.

Even very young babies of 5 weeks can sense the changes occurring inside their tiny bodies. Having so newly gotten used to a world outside the warm embrace of your body, your baby is now finding her world changing for a second time. It's important to understand that although everything seems the same to you, to her everything she sees, feels, hears, smells, or tastes is different somehow. She may like some of these changes, but she may dislike others because she doesn't yet know how to cope with them. She is still too young to turn to you for help, and she certainly can't ask you what is going on.

How You Know It's Time to Grow

Even though your baby can't form the words to tell you what's going on, she is able to communicate quite a bit. Here are some signs that she is preparing to make her first leap.

She May Be Highly Upset

At this time, it's very likely your baby will yell, cry, scream, and refuse to go to sleep in her crib until she has driven the entire household crazy. These are the clues that your baby is about to make her first leap! With a bit of luck, her distress will make you run toward her, pick her up, hold her tight, and let her snuggle up.

She May Crave Closeness with You

If she's even luckier, after you pick her up, you may also let her nurse. Sometimes she will drift off to sleep only if she's snuggled up to mommy in the closest way possible—latched onto the breast. Providing this sort of physical comfort with breast or bottle may be the only way to create the safe world she is so desperate for at this time.

"Normally, my baby is very easy, but she suddenly started crying non-stop for almost 2 days. At first I thought it was just stomach cramps. But then I noticed she stopped whenever I had her on my lap, or when I let her lie in between us. She fell asleep right away then. I kept asking myself if I was spoiling her too much by allowing it. But the crying period stopped just as suddenly as it started, and now she's as easygoing as she was before."

— Eve's mom, 5th week

How This Leap May Affect You

As these major changes in your baby affect her, they're bound to have an affect on you as well. Here are some emotions you may feel.

You May Feel Insecure

All mothers want to find out why their babies are being troublesome and restless so that they can make it better for them. Usually, they will first try to see if the baby is hungry. Then they look for loose pins that may be sticking into her. They change her diaper. They try to comfort her with all the love and soothing they can muster in those trying moments. But it isn't easy. Pretty soon they discover that all the best care and comfort doesn't really stop the little bundle from resuming her relentless crying.

Most mothers find a sudden change in their babies' behavior to be a miserable experience. It undermines their confidence and is very distressing.

"My son wanted to be with me all of the time, and I either held him against my chest or on my lap, even when we had company. I was terribly concerned. One night I hardly slept at all. I just spent the whole night holding and cuddling him. Then my sister came and took over for a night. I went in the other bedroom and slept like a log the whole night. I felt reborn when I woke up the next day."

— Bob's mom, 5th week

You May Feel Very Concerned

Often, mothers are afraid that something is wrong with their tiny screamers. They think that she's in pain, or that she may be suffering from some abnormality or disorder that has gone undetected until now. Others worry that the milk supply from breastfeeding alone is not sufficient. This is because the baby seems to crave the breast constantly and is always hungry. Some mothers take their babies to doctors for checkups. Of course, most babies are pronounced perfectly healthy and the mothers are sent home to worry alone. (When in doubt, always consult your family doctor or go to the childcare clinic.)

"My daughter was crying so much that I was afraid something was terribly wrong. She wanted to breastfeed constantly. I took her to see the pediatrician, but he couldn't find anything wrong with her. He said she just needed time to get used to my milk and that many infants went through a similar crying phase at 5 weeks. I thought that it was a strange thing to say, because she hadn't had any problems with my milk until then. Her cousin, who was the same age, kept crying, too, but he was being bottle-fed. When I told the doctor that, he pretended he hadn't heard. I didn't push the subject, though. I was happy enough just knowing it wasn't anything serious."

Juliette's mom, 5th week

Because your baby senses something changing, she feels insecure and has a greater need for close skin-to-skin contact. This close embrace seems to be the most powerfully calming type of physical contact when she is upset. Give her all the cuddling she needs and all the contact you feel you can handle at times like these. She needs time to adjust to these new changes and grow into her new world. She's accustomed to your body scent, warmth, voice, and touch. With you, she will relax a little and feel contented again. You can provide the tender loving care she really needs during this trying period.

"Sometimes my daughter will nurse for half an hour and refuse to come off the breast. 'Just take her off after 20 minutes, and let her scream. She'll soon learn,' is the advice people give me. But secretly I think, 'They can say what they like; I decide what's best.'"

Nina's mom, 5th week

You may notice that close physical contact will help during these crying fits, and that a noisy little creature will respond better and quicker when she is with you. Try carrying your baby around in a sling if you can while you go about your chores, or keep her on your lap while you read or do other sedentary activities. A gentle massage or stroking can be helpful, too.

Soothing Tips

When you want to comfort a tiny baby, a gentle rhythm can play a very important role. Hold your baby close to you, with his bottom resting on one arm while your other arm supports his head resting against your shoulder. When he's in this position, he can feel the soothing beat of your heart.

Here are a few other mom-recommended methods to soothe a tiny screamer.

• Cuddle and caress him.

• Rock him gently in your arms, or sit in a rocking chair with him.

• Walk around slowly with him.

• Talk or sing to him.

• Pat him gently on the bottom.

Not all of these ideas will suit your baby personally, so if you don't succeed at first, keep trying until you find out what works for him. The most successful way of comforting a crying baby is to do the things he enjoys most when he's in a cheerful mood.

"When my baby was crying all the time, she seemed so lost. I had to massage her for a long time before she calmed down a bit. I felt exhausted but extremely satisfied. Something changed after that. It doesn't seem to take as long to soothe her now. When she cries now, I don't find it such an effort to put her world to rights again."

Nina's mom, 4th week

Mothers who carry their babies around whenever they are in a fussy mood may label them "extremely dependent." These babies like nothing

How to Make a Sling

Slings are extremely easy to make and cozy for you and your new baby. A sling will help to give your arms a break by supporting your baby's weight and make your baby feel safe and secure. Plus, they cost only a few dollars to make. Your baby can use a sling almost immediately after birth since it allows him to lie flat. Here's how to make one.

Use a sturdy piece of material, 1 yard by 3 ½ yards. Drape the cloth over your left shoulder if you are right-handed, or over your right shoulder if you are left-handed, and knot the ends together at the opposite hip. Turn the knot toward your back. Check to see if the length of the sling feels right. If it does, the sling is ready for use. Pop your baby inside and support her with your hands. It's that easy!

better than lying quietly against their mothers and being stroked, rocked, or cuddled. They may fall asleep on their mothers' laps, but start to cry again as soon as furtive attempts are made to sneak them back into their cribs.

Mothers who stick to feeding and sleeping schedules often notice that their babies fall asleep during feeding. Some wonder if this is because the babies are so exhausted from crying and lack of sleep that they have no energy left to nurse. This may seem logical, but it may not be the whole story. It's more likely that the baby falls asleep because she's where she wants to be. She's finally with mommy, and she's content, so she is able to fall asleep.

"The first 2 days my son cried so much. I was doing my best to stick to the proper bedtimes, but it turned out to be a total disaster. It drove us both up the wall. Now I keep him on my lap for as long as he wants without feeling guilty. I feel good about it. It's nice and warm and cozy. It's obvious he loves it. The feeding schedule's gone out the window, too. I didn't stick to it. Now he just lets me know when he's hungry. Sometimes he nurses for a long time, but sometimes he doesn't. He's much more contented now, and I am, too."

Steven's mom, 5th week

A number of indications in babies of approximately 4 to 5 weeks show that they are undergoing enormous changes that affect their senses, metabolism, and internal organs. This is when the first leap occurs—the

Sleeping Tips

A baby with sleeping problems will often fall asleep more quickly when he is with you. The warmth of your body, your gentle movements, and your soft sounds will help to soothe him. Here are some tips on the best ways to get him to sleep.

- Give him a warm bath, put him on a warm towel, and then massage him gently with baby oil.

- Breast or bottle-feed him, since sucking will help to relax and soothe him.

- Walk around with him, either in a sling or baby carrier.

- Push him around in his stroller.

- Take him for a ride in the car.

- Pop him into bed beside you.

baby's alertness in the world of sensations increases dramatically. At this point your baby is losing some of his newborn skills. He will no longer follow a face with his eyes or turn toward a sound. There are signs that these early skills were controlled by primitive centers in the lower brain, and that they disappear to make way for developments in the higher levels of the brain. Soon you will see similar behaviors emerge, but this time they will seem to be much more under your baby's control. At this age, your baby is also likely to outgrow problems that he may have had initially with his digestive system.

Between 4 and 5 weeks old, your baby goes through a whole set of changes that affect his senses—the way he experiences the world, the way he feels, even the way he digests his food. His whole world feels, looks, smells, and sounds different. Some of these changes have direct consequences that you can see. For example, this may be the first time that you notice him crying real tears. He may stay awake for longer periods and seem more interested in the world around him. Just after birth, he was only able to focus on objects that were up to a foot away, but now he can focus at a larger distance. It's not surprising, therefore, that a baby feels it's time for some action.

Five to six-week-old babies are even prepared to *work* in order to experience interesting sensations. In a laboratory experiment, babies showed that they could adjust the focus of a color movie by sucking harder on a pacifier. As soon as the baby stopped sucking, the picture blurred. Babies at this age have difficulty sucking and watching at the

Brain Changes

At approximately 3 to 4 weeks, there is a dramatic increase in a baby's head circumference. His glucose metabolism, which is the way a baby's digestive system processes food, also changes.

My Diary

How My Baby Explores the New World of Changing Sensations

Check off the boxes below as your baby changes. Stop filling this out once the next stormy period begins, heralding the next leap.

HIS INTEREST IN HIS SURROUNDINGS

❑ Looks at things longer and more often

❑ Listens to things more often and pays closer attention

❑ Is more aware of being touched

❑ Is more aware of different smells

❑ Smiles for the first time, or more often than before

❑ Gurgles with pleasure more often

❑ Expresses likes or dislikes more often

❑ Expresses anticipation more often

❑ Stays awake longer, and is more alert

HIS PHYSICAL CHANGES

❑ Breathes more regularly

❑ Startles and trembles less often

❑ Cries real tears for the first time, or more often than before

❑ Chokes less

❑ Vomits less

❑ Burps less

OTHER CHANGES YOU NOTICE

_____

_____

same time, so they could keep this up only for a few seconds. To check that this was really what they were trying to do, the babies were then required to *stop* sucking in order to bring the picture into focus. They could do this, too!

Babies can also start using their smile in social contact to influence their experiences. Your baby's smiles change from something superficial, almost robot-like, into social smiles around this age. Mothers and fathers become very excited when they see a smile at an earlier age, but once they have seen the "social smile," they will admit noticing a difference.

Your Baby's Choices: A Key to His Personality

The senses of all babies develop rapidly at this time, and they will all become clearly more interested in their surroundings. It may or may not seem obvious at first, but every baby will have his own preferences. Some bright-eyed infants really enjoy looking at and watching everything and everyone around them. Others will listen keenly to music and sounds around them and will find sound-producing objects such as rattles more appealing than anything else. Another group of babies will love to be touched, and they would like nothing better than to play games that involve being touched and caressed by someone. Some babies don't have any clear preference. Even at this very young age, you will find that every baby is different.

As you go through the "My Diary" list on page 45, you may want to mark or highlight the items that apply now to your baby. He may display only a few of the behaviors, and others may not appear for several weeks. An infant who is more interested in certain sensory experiences in his world than others is showing you that he is already an individual.

"I take my daughter along to my singing classes every day. During the first few weeks, she hardly reacted to sounds at all, and I felt quite concerned, to be honest. Now suddenly, she's totally preoccupied by noises of any kind when she is awake. If she wakes up in a bad mood and I sing to her, she stops crying immediately. She doesn't stop when my friends sing, though!"

Hannah's mom, 6th week

Rocky Times for Everyone

Going through a big change can be a stressful event for your baby and for you, and you may both find the strain unbearable at times. You may become exhausted from lack of sleep or because anxieties prevent you from sleeping well. Here's an example of how this vicious cycle can work.

The baby is confused and cries.

Constant crying makes her mother feel insecure and anxious.

Tension builds, and mother finds herself unable to cope.

The baby senses the extra tension, becomes even more fussy, and cries even louder than before.

The cycle repeats, again and again.

When the strain gets to be too much, remember that it is normal to feel this way. Try to take time out to relax. Your baby will benefit from it as much as you will.

Use physical contact and attention to comfort your baby. This will make it easier for her to adapt to all the changes at her own pace, and it will also give her self-confidence. She will know that someone is there for her whenever she needs comfort.

As her mother, you need support, too, not criticism, from family and friends. While criticism will only undermine your already battered self-confidence, support will make you better able to cope with the difficult periods.

You Can Do to Help

The very best way to help your baby is to give her tender loving care and support. It is impossible to spoil her at this age, so never feel guilty about comforting her, especially when she cries.

Help your baby on her voyage of discovery. You'll find that she is usually more interested in the world around her now. She is more perceptive, and she is often awake for a longer time to enjoy her surroundings. Try to find out what activities she likes best by watching her reactions carefully. As small as she is, she is still able to let you know what pleases or displeases her. Once you know what your baby likes, you'll be able to introduce new activities, games, and toys gently.

How Can You Tell What She Likes Best?

Your baby will smile when given the things that she enjoys most. It can be something she sees, hears, smells, tastes, or feels. Because her senses have developed and she is now able to perceive a little more of her world, she will also smile more often. It will be very rewarding to experiment and discover which activities produce these wonderful smiles.

"I dance around with my baby, and when I stop, he smiles."

John's mom, 6th week

That's Just How Babies Are

Babies love anything new, and it is important that you acknowledge your baby's new skills and interests. He will enjoy it if you share these new discoveries, and his learning will progress more quickly with your encouragement.

"When I put my face close to my daughter's and smile and talk to her, she makes eye contact and grins. It's wonderful."

Laura's mom, 5th week

"My daughter smiles at her dolls and teddy bears."

Jenny's mom, 6th week

Help Your Baby Explore the New World through Sight

Your baby looks longer at objects that interest her now. The brighter the colors, the more fascinating she will find them. She also likes striped and angular objects. And your face, of course.

If you walk around with your baby, you'll automatically discover what she likes looking at best. Give her enough time to have a good look at things—and don't forget that her range of focus is not much more than a foot. Some babies like looking at the same objects time and time again, while others get bored if they are not shown something different each time. If you notice that your baby is getting bored, show her objects that are similar to the ones she likes but slightly different.

"My baby is much more aware of everything she sees now. Her favorites are the bars of her crib, which contrast with the white walls; books on the bookshelf; our ceiling, which has long wooden slats with a dark stripe in between; and a black-and-white ink drawing on the wall. At night, lights seem to interest her the most."

Emily's mom, 5th week

"My son stares right into my face and gazes at me for quite some time. He thinks it's funny when I eat. He looks at my mouth and watches me chew. He seems to think it's fascinating."

Kevin's mom, 6th week

"When I move a green and yellow ball slowly from left to right, my daughter turns her head to follow it. She seems to think it's great fun, although this proud mom probably enjoys it more than she does."

Ashley's mom, 5th week

Help Your Baby Explore the New World through Sound

Sounds usually fascinate babies. Buzzing, squeaking, ringing, rustling, or whizzing sounds are all interesting. Babies find human voices very intriguing, too. High-pitched voices are extremely interesting, although nothing can beat the sound of mother's voice, even if she's not a natural soprano.

Even at 5 weeks old, you can have cozy little chats with your baby. Pick a comfortable place to sit and put your face close to hers. Chat to her about how beautiful she is, everyday events, or whatever comes to mind. Stop talking once in a while to give her a chance to "reply."

"I really think my son is listening to me now. It's remarkable."

Matt's mom, 5th week

"Sometimes my baby chats back to me when I'm talking to her. She talks longer now, and sometimes it seems as if she's really trying to tell me something. It's adorable. Yesterday, she chatted to her rabbit in her crib."

Hannah's mom, 5th week

Help Your Baby Explore the New World through Touch

All babies become more aware of being touched at this age. Too many cuddling visitors may suddenly become "too much" for one baby, whereas another one may enjoy the attention tremendously. Every baby is different! You may hear your baby laughing out loud for the very first time now,

 **Baby Care**

Don't Overdo It

Let your baby's responses guide you. Your baby has become more sensitive, so you need to be careful not to overstimuate him. Bear this in mind when you play with him, cuddle him, show him things, or let him listen to things. *You* have to adapt to *him*. Stop as soon as you notice something is getting to be too much for him.

Your baby is still unable to concentrate for a long period of time, so he'll need short rest breaks. You may think he's lost interest, but he hasn't. Be patient. Usually he'll be raring to go again if you let him rest for a short while.

perhaps when she is being tickled. But for most babies of this age, tickling is something that they will not yet particularly appreciate.

"My daughter laughed out loud, really roared, when her brother started tickling her. Everyone was startled, and it went dead quiet."

Emily's mom, 5th week

Let Her Know You Understand Her

Your baby may use a greater range of crying and gurgling sounds than before, and she may produce these sounds more frequently at this age. She may have different sounds for different situations. Babies will often make a whimpering sound before falling asleep. If a baby is really upset, you'll be able to tell by the way she cries, because it's a totally different sound. It's telling you that something is wrong. Your baby may also make other noises, such as gurgling sounds to show she is happy, especially when she is looking at or listening to something. These sounds will help you to understand her better. If you understand what your baby is trying to tell you, let her know. Babies adore interaction.

"I know exactly when my baby is gurgling with pleasure or grumbling because she's angry. Sometimes she gurgles with pleasure when she sees her mobile, and she loves it when I imitate the sounds she makes."

Hannah's mom, 6th week

At around 6 weeks, the leap has ended, and a period of comparative peace dawns. Babies are more cheerful, more alert, and more preoccupied with looking and listening at this time. Many mothers claim that their eyes seem brighter. Babies are also capable of expressing their likes and dislikes at this age. In short, life seems a little less complicated than before.

"We communicate more now. Suddenly, the hours that my son is awake seem more interesting."

Frankie's mom, 6th week

"I feel closer to my baby. Our bond is stronger."

Bob's mom, 6th week

Place Photo Here

After the Leap

Age: _____

Reflections: _____

chapter 4

Wonder Week 8: The World of Patterns

Sometime around 8 weeks, your baby will begin to experience the world in a new way. He will become able to recognize simple patterns in the world around him and in his own body. Although it may be hard for us to imagine at first, this happens in all the senses, not just vision. For example, he may discover his hands and feet and spend hours practicing his skill at controlling a certain posture of his arm or leg. He'll be endlessly fascinated with the way light displays shadows on the wall of his bedroom. You might notice him studying the detail of cans on the grocery store shelf or listening to himself making short bursts of sounds, such as *ah, uh, ehh*.

Any of these things—and a whole lot more—signal a big change in your baby's mental development. This change will enable him to learn a new set of skills that he would have been incapable of learning at an earlier age, no matter how much help and encouragement you gave him. But just as in his previous developmental leap, adjusting to this new world will not come easily at first.

The change in the way your baby perceives the world around him will initially make him feel puzzled, confused, and bewildered as his familiar world is turned upside down. He suddenly sees, hears, smells, tastes, and feels in a completely new way, and he will need time to adjust. To come to terms with what is happening to him, he needs to be somewhere safe and familiar. Until he begins to feel more comfortable in this new world, he will want to cling to his mommy for comfort. This time, the fussy phase could last anywhere from a few days to 2 weeks.

If you notice your baby is more cranky than usual, watch him closely. It's likely he's attempting to master new skills.

Once you're over the hump, however, you will probably experience this second leap as a real milestone in your child's development. As he begins to learn to control his body and use his senses to explore what interests him, he will start to express his own preferences. You'll learn what he likes and doesn't like, whether he listens more keenly to particular kinds of sounds, which colors he prefers, what kinds of toys or activities he enjoys, and whose face makes him light up most—beside yours, of course. These are the first signs of your baby's newly emerging personality.

Sometime between 7 and 9 weeks of age, your baby may become more demanding. She may cry more often, as this is her way of expressing how stressful these changes are to her. At this age, crying is the most effective way to show she feels lost and needs attention. More sensitive babies will sob and scream even more now than they did before and drive their mothers and fathers to distraction. Even when everything possible is done to console these tiny screamers, they may still continue to wail.

Most babies will calm down, however, when they experience close physical contact, although for some babies it can never be close enough. If such a tiny cuddler had her way, she would crawl right back into her mommy. She would like to be totally enveloped in her mother's arms, legs, and body. She may demand her mother's undivided attention and will protest as soon as it wanders.

How You Know It's Time to Grow

It's time to change again! Here are some clues that this leap is approaching.

She May Demand More Attention

Your baby may want you to spend more time amusing her. She may even want you to be totally absorbed in her, and only her. At this time, many babies no longer want to lie in their cribs or on blankets on the floor, even if they had always been happy to do so until now. They may not object to lying in baby chairs, just as long as their mothers are close by. But their ultimate goal is to be with their mommies. They want their mothers to look at them, talk to them, and play with them.

> "Suddenly, my baby doesn't like going to bed at night. She becomes restless and starts screaming and crying and refuses to settle down. But we need some peace and quiet, too. So we keep her with us on the couch, or hold and cuddle her, and then she's no trouble at all."
>
> Eve's mom, 8th week

She May Become Shy with Strangers

You may notice that your friendly bundle may not smile so easily at people she does not see often, or she may need more time to warm up to them. Occasionally, some babies will even start crying if other people try to get near them when they are lying contentedly snuggled up to their moms. Some mothers regret this: "She always used to be so cheerful."

Others are secretly pleased: "After all, I'm the one who's there for her all the time."

> "My daughter seems to smile more for me than anyone else. It takes her a little longer to loosen up with other people now."
>
> Ashley's mom, 9th week

She May Lose Her Appetite

At this time, it may seem that if your baby had her way, she'd be on the breast or bottle all day long. But although she is latched onto the nipple, you may notice that she hardly takes any milk at all. Many babies will do this now. As long as they feel a nipple in or against their mouths, they are content. But as soon as they are taken off the breast or the bottle, they start protesting and continue to cry until they feel the nipple again.

This generally occurs only in babies who are allowed to decide for themselves when they want to nurse. Some mothers who breastfeed may begin to think that there is something wrong with their milk supplies, while other mothers question whether the decision to breastfeed was the right one after all. It is not necessary to stop breastfeeding at this point; on the contrary, this would not be a very good time to choose to wean your baby. During this stormy period, the breast is serving as less of a nutritional purpose and more of a comfort to the baby. This explains why some babies will suck their thumbs or fingers more often during this period.

> "Sometimes I feel like a walking milk bottle, on standby 24 hours a day. It really irritates me. I wonder if other mothers who breastfeed go through the same thing."
>
> Matt's mom, 9th week

She May Cling to You More Tightly

Your baby may now hold on to you even tighter the moment she senses that she is about to be set down. Not only will she cling to you with her fingers, she may even cling to you with her toes! This show of devotion often makes it difficult for a mother to put her baby down, both literally and figuratively. You may find it touching and heart-wrenching at the same time.

"When I bend over to put my infant down, she clutches at my hair and clothes as if she's terrified to lose contact. It's really sweet, but I wish she wouldn't do it, because it makes me feel so guilty about setting her down."

Laura's mom, 9th week

She May Sleep Poorly

At a difficult time like this, your baby may not sleep as well as she did before. She may start crying the moment you carry her into her bedroom, which explains why parents sometimes think that their babies are afraid of their cribs. Various sleeping problems may affect your little one. Some babies have difficulty falling asleep, while others are easily disturbed and do not sleep for long periods. Whatever sleeping problems your baby may have, they all have the same result: lack of sleep for everybody in the house. Unfortunately, this also means that your baby is awake for longer periods, giving her more opportunities to cry.

She May Just Cry and Cry

At approximately 8 weeks, it's normal for your baby to have an urgent desire to go "back to mommy." Some infants, of course, will demonstrate this need more than others. Crying and clinging may become part of your everyday life around this age. It is a sign that your baby is making healthy progress, that she is reacting to the changes within her, and that she is taking a leap forward in her development.

Your little one is upset simply because she hasn't yet had time to adjust to these changes and is still confused. This is why she needs to have you around. She wants to return "home," to her safe haven, where she can

My Diary

Signs My Baby Is Growing Again

Between 7 and 9 weeks, you may notice your baby starting to show some of the following behaviors. They are probably signs that he is ready to make the next leap, when the world of patterns will open up to him. Check off the boxes next to the behaviors your baby shows.

❏ Cries more often

❏ Wants you to keep him busy

❏ Loses appetite

❏ Is more shy with strangers

❏ Clings more

❏ Sleeps poorly

❏ Sucks his thumb, or more often than before

OTHER CHANGES YOU NOTICE:

_____

_____

feel secure in familiar surroundings. With you, she will gain enough confidence to explore her new world.

Imagine what it must be like to feel upset with no one around to comfort you. You'd feel the tension mounting and not know what to do. You'd need all your energy just to cope with the stress, and you'd have little strength left to solve your problems. Your baby is no different. To her, every time a big change in her mental development occurs, she feels as if she has woken up in a brand-new world. She will be confronted with more new impressions than she can handle. She cries, and she will continue to cry until she becomes accustomed enough to her new world to feel at ease. If she is not comforted, all her energy will be used just for crying, and she will be wasting valuable time that she could put to much better use discovering her new and puzzling world.

How the Leap May Affect You

These major changes in your baby will have a tremendous impact on you as well. Here are some of the ways they may affect you.

You May Feel Worried

When a baby goes through an inexplicable crying fit, life can unravel for everyone around her. Babies who cry a lot more than they used to can wear down even the most confident of moms. If this is your situation, you may begin to wonder whether you're really fit for the job. But don't despair: Your experience is very normal. The average baby will cry noticeably more than usual and will also be a lot more difficult to comfort. Only a small number of mothers are lucky enough to not have any particular worries about their babies at this age. These mothers have infants who are unusually easygoing or quiet, who won't cry much more than usual, and who are generally easier to comfort.

Temperamental, irritable babies are the most difficult ones to deal with. They will seem to cry 10 times louder and more frequently, and they will thrash around as if they were in boxing rings. Their mothers often worry that the whole family will fall apart.

> "It's a nightmare, the way my baby goes on and on. She cries all of the time and hardly sleeps at all at the moment. Our marriage is going to pieces. My husband comes home in the evening, dragging his feet, because he can't face another night of torment. We're having constant arguments about how to stop her awful crying."
>
> **Jenny's mom, 7th week**

"When my son won't stop crying, I always go to him, although I've reached the stage where I could agree with statements such as 'Children just need to cry sometimes.' I feel so drained. But then I start thinking about how thin these apartments walls are, and so I end up going to him again, hoping I'll be able to get him to settle down this time."

Steven's mom, 9th week

"Sometimes, when my daughter cries and won't stop no matter what I do, I get so upset that I take it out on my poor husband. I often have a good cry myself, which does help to relieve the tension a bit."

Emily's mom, 10th week

"Some days when I'm at a low ebb, I wonder if I'm doing the right thing, if I'm giving my son enough attention or too much. It's so typical that it was on one of those difficult days that I read that babies smile at their mothers when they're 6 weeks old. Mine never did. He only smiled to himself, and that really undermined my confidence. Then suddenly, this evening, he grinned at me. Tears welled up in my eyes, it was so touching. I know this sounds ridiculous, but for a moment I felt like he was trying to tell me it was okay, that he was with me all the way."

Bob's mom, 9th week

At this time, when your baby cries more than usual, you may be desperate to figure out why. You may wonder, "Is my milk supply drying up? Is she ill? Am I doing something wrong? Does she have a wet diaper? When she's on my lap, she's fine—does this mean I'm spoiling her?"

When every other avenue has been explored, some mothers finally decide it has to be colic that's upsetting their babies. Their tiny screamers do seem to be writhing around a lot, after all. Some mothers even have a good cry themselves. It is a particularly hard time for first-time moms, who tend to blame themselves. Occasionally, a mother will go to see her doctor, or she will bring the problem up with the pediatrician.

"Normally my baby never cries. He's so easygoing, as easy as they come. But this week he had terrible problems: stomach cramps, I presume."

John's mom, 9th week

Whatever you do, don't despair—tell yourself it is not your fault! Try to remember that this is your young baby's way of telling you that she is now capable of learning new skills, which means that her mind is developing well. At this age, her crying is normal and only temporary.

You May Be Irritated and Defensive

As soon as you are convinced that your noisy little infant has no valid reason to keep crying and clinging to you, you may feel irritated. You may think that she's ungrateful and spoiled. You still have so much housework to do, and her crying is driving you mad. Plus, you're exhausted. Well, you're not alone. Most mothers have these feelings. Many mothers worry that their babies' fathers, family, friends, or neighbors may regard "mommy's little sweetheart" as a "complete nuisance." They may become defensive when other people tell them to be more stern with their babies.

"Is this what I gave my job up for—8 weeks of crying? I'm at my wit's end. I really don't know what more I can do."

Jenny's mom, 8th week

"It really drives me up the wall when I finally get my baby to sleep after comforting her for an hour, and she starts whimpering again the moment that I set her down. She's only happy when I'm holding her. This irritates me to no end. I don't get a chance to do anything else."

Laura's mom, 8th week

"I had to keep my son occupied all day long. Nothing really helped. I tried walking around, stroking him, and singing. At first I felt completely

 Baby Care

Shaking Can Be Harmful

Having violent feelings about a demanding little screamer is not dangerous, but acting on those feelings is. Whatever you do, don't ever let yourself get into such a state that you might harm him. **Never** shake a baby. Shaking a young child is one of the worst things that you can do. It could easily cause internal bleeding just below the skull, which can result in brain damage that may lead to learning difficulties later on or even death.

helpless and depressed, and then suddenly, I felt really frustrated. I sat down and just started sobbing. So I asked the day care center if they would have him for two afternoons a week, just to give me a few hours to recharge my batteries. His crying sometimes drains me completely. I'm so tired. I'd just like to know how much both of us can take."

Bob's mom, 9th week

You May Really Lose It

Only rarely will a mother admit to having been a bit rougher than necessary when putting her baby down because she was so irritated by the baby's screaming and crying. If this does happen, it is always a disturbing experience, especially because it seemed to be a gut reaction at the time.

"My daughter cried even more this week than she did last week. It drove me crazy. I had more than enough to do as it was. I had her in my arms, and on the spur of the moment, I threw her onto her changing mat on the dresser. Afterward, I was shocked by what I'd done, and at the same time I realized it hadn't helped the situation at all. She screamed even

Cuddle Care: The Best Way to Comfort

A baby of this age loves to be picked up, caressed, and cuddled. You can never give him too much of a good thing.

louder. After it happened, I understood what drives some parents to abuse their children during these 'colic fits,' but I never thought I'd do something like that myself."

Juliette's mom, 9th week

How Your Baby's New Skills Emerge

Because you are concerned about your baby's clinginess, you will automatically keep an extra close eye on her. At the back of your mind, you may have these nagging doubts: "What is the matter with her? Why is she being so troublesome? What can I do? Am I spoiling her? Should she be doing more at this age? Is she bored? Why is she unable to amuse herself?" Soon you'll realize what's really going on—your infant is attempting to master new skills.

At approximately 8 weeks, you will notice that your baby is opening up to her new world: a world of observing and experimenting with simple patterns. She will be ready to acquire several pattern skills at this time, but your baby, with her unique inclinations, preferences, and temperament, will choose which discoveries she wants to make. You can help her do what she is ready to do.

Don't try to push her. While you may think she should be practicing holding a ball (for her future softball career), she may prefer to make her first attempts at talking by babbling to her toys. Let her go at her own pace and respect her preferences. It may be hard on you if you're tone deaf and your baby is keen on sounds. Don't worry. She doesn't need symphonies just yet—talking and humming will do very well.

the Magical Leap Forward

About this age, your baby no longer experiences the world and himself as one universe. He will start to recognize recurring shapes, patterns, and structures. For instance, your baby may now discover that his hands belong to him. At this age, your son will look at them in wonder and wave them around. Once he realizes that they are his, your baby may also try to use his hands by closing them around a toy, for instance. Not only does he begin to see patterns in the world around him, at this time your baby may begin to distinguish patterns in sounds, smells, tastes, and textures, too. In other words, your little tyke now perceives patterns with all of his senses. This new awareness is not just confined to what is going on outside his body—it also includes an enhanced perception of what is happening inside his body. For instance, now your baby may realize that holding his arm in the air feels different than letting it hang down. At the same time, he may also gain more control from within. Your son may be able to maintain certain positions, not only with his head, body, arms and legs, but also with smaller areas of his body. For example, he may start to make all kinds of faces, now that he has more control over his facial muscles. He might make explosive sounds because he can keep his vocal cords in a certain position. He may focus more sharply on an object because he has more control over his eye muscles.

Many of the reflexes that your baby had at birth will start to disap-

Brain Changes

At approximately 7 to 8 weeks, a baby's head circumference dramatically increases. Researchers have recorded changes in the brain waves of babies 6 to 8 weeks old.

(continued on page 69)

 My Diary

How My Baby Explores the New World of Patterns

Check off the boxes below as you notice your baby changing. Stop filling this out once the next stormy period begins, heralding the coming of the next leap.

A new world of possibilities opens up to your baby when he's 8 weeks old. Your baby cannot possibly discover at once everything there is to explore in this new world—although some babies will try to sample everything. Exactly when your baby starts to do what will depend on his preferences and the opportunities offered to him.

Each chapter from now on will list behaviors that your baby may be doing that signal that he has entered his new world. Look for the sections like this one called "How My Baby Explores the New World." Each list is divided up into activity areas, such as "body control" and "looking and seeing." As you move through the book, you may notice a pattern emerging. Each baby has a completely distinctive profile and you should be aware that your baby will not demonstrate at this time many of the skills listed— some will appear later and some will be skipped altogether. Don't forget: All babies have different talents.

BODY CONTROL

❑ Holds his head upright when he is very alert

❑ Consciously turns his head toward something interesting

❑ Consciously rolls from his side onto his stomach

❑ Consciously rolls from his side onto his back

❑ Kicks his legs and waves his arms

❑ Kicks at plaything, with jerking movements

❏ Allows himself to be pulled into a sitting position

❏ Allows himself to be pulled into a standing position

❏ Tries to lift his head and body when lying facedown

❏ Shows an increased desire to sit

❏ Is able to look left and right when lying on his stomach

❏ Makes faces

HAND CONTROL

❏ Swipes at toys

❏ Attempts to grab objects within reach but does not succeed

❏ Closes his hand around objects within easy reach

❏ Holds plaything and moves it jerkily up and down

❏ Touches and feels objects without holding them

LOOKING AND SEEING

❏ Discovers hands

❏ Discovers feet

❏ Discovers knees

❏ Watches people moving or working

❏ Is fascinated by children playing close by

❏ Enjoys watching fast-moving images on TV

❏ Watches pets eating or moving

❏ Is fascinated by waving curtains

❏ Discovers luminous object, such as a flickering candle

(continued)

My Diary (cont.)

❑ Watches treetops outdoors and is particularly fascinated by movements such as rustling leaves

❑ Looks at items on grocery store shelves

❑ Looks at complex shapes and colors, such as abstract art, especially while being rocked

❑ Is fascinated by shiny clothing or jewelry

❑ Enjoys watching people chewing food

❑ Enjoys watching and listening to people talk

❑ Watches facial gestures

LISTENING AND CHATTING

❑ Enjoys listening to voices, singing, and high-pitched sounds

❑ Makes short bursts of sounds, such as *ah, uh, eh, mmm,* and listens to himself

❑ Makes a series of sounds, mumbles, and gurgles, as if he is telling a story

❑ Repeats these sounds if you encourage him

❑ Sings along when you dance and sing with him

❑ "Chats" to and smiles at cuddly toys

❑ Consciously makes *eh* sounds to attract attention

❑ Interrupts while others are talking

OTHER CHANGES YOU NOTICE

_____

_____

_____

pear at this age. They will be replaced by something similar to a voluntary movement. He no longer needs the gripping reflex, for example, because your baby is now able to learn how to close his hand around a toy or other object. Your baby doesn't use the sucking reflex anymore because he is able to latch onto a nipple in one single movement, instead of finding it by what appears to be sheer coincidence after nuzzling for a while. By now, your infant is no longer completely dependent on reflexes. In general, babies will only resort to their old reflexes if they are hungry or upset.

Even so, your baby's first intentional movements are very different from those of an adult. His movements will be quite jerky, rigid, and stiff, like those of a puppet, and they will remain like this until the next big change occurs.

Your Baby's Choices: A Key to His Personality

Why are all babies unique? They have all undergone the same changes and entered the same new world with new discoveries to make and new skills to learn. But every baby decides for himself what he wants to learn, and when, and how. He will choose what he considers the most appealing. Some babies will try to learn a variety of new skills, using one or more of their senses. Some will seem particularly interested in exploring this new world with their eyes. Some will prefer to try out their talking and listening skills. Others will try to become more adept with their bodies. This explains why a friend's baby may be doing something that your baby can't, or doesn't enjoy, and vice versa. A baby's likes and dislikes are determined by his unique makeup—his build, weight, temperament, inclination, and interests.

Babies love anything new. It is so very important that you respond when you notice any new skills or interests. Your baby will enjoy it if you share these new discoveries with him, and his learning will progress more quickly.

The best way to help your baby make this leap is to encourage her to develop the skills that she finds most interesting. When you notice her working on a new skill, show her that you're enthusiastic about every attempt she makes to learn something new. If you praise her, you'll make her feel good, and this will encourage her to continue. Try to find a balance between providing enough challenges and demanding too much of her. Try to discover what she enjoys doing most. Most importantly, stop as soon as you feel she has had enough of a game or toy.

Your baby may want or need to practice some games or activities on her own. As long as you show some enthusiasm, this will be sufficient to reassure her that she is doing well.

Help Her Explore the New World through Sight

If your baby loves to explore her world with her eyes, you can help her by offering her all sorts of visual "patterns," for instance by showing her

How to Tell When He's Had Enough

Practicing a new skill is fun, but it can also be tiring for a baby. When he's had enough for a while, he will usually let you know with some very clear body signals. For example, he may look away, or if he is physically strong enough, he may turn his body away from you.

Stop the game or activity as soon as you notice that your baby has had enough. Sometimes he will only want a short break before resuming a game or activity with renewed enthusiasm, but don't push him. He needs time to let it all sink in. Always let your baby's responses guide you.

brightly colored objects. Make sure you move the object slowly across her line of vision, since this will draw her attention quicker and hold her interest longer. You can also try moving the object slowly backward and then forward, but make sure she is still able to see it move, otherwise she will lose interest.

When your baby is in a playful mood, she may become bored if she always sees, hears, or feels the same objects in the same old surroundings. It's very normal for babies of this age to show boredom, as their new awareness of patterns also means that they understand when things are repetitive. For the first time in her life, your baby may get fed up with the same plaything, the same view, the same sound, the same feel of an object, and the same taste. She will crave variety and learn from it. If she seems bored, keep her stimulated. Carry her around in your arms or provide her with some different objects to look at.

At this time, toys may not be as interesting to your baby as the myriad interesting "real things" in her world. Your home is full of items that may fascinate your baby, such as books, photographs, pets, cooking utensils, and even your eyeglasses. If your baby suddenly prefers the "real thing" to her toys, she will need your help. At this age, she cannot get close enough to objects on her own. She needs you to either take her to the object or pick it up and show it to her. If you notice that she likes looking at "real things," help her do this.

"My baby likes looking at everything: paintings, books on shelves, items in the kitchen cupboard. I have to take her everywhere. I even carry her in my arms when I go outside or when I go shopping."

Hannah's mom, 11th week

At this age, your baby may notice that familiar objects keep waving across her line of vision. If she investigates, she'll discover her hands or feet. She may gaze at them in wonder and begin to study them in detail. Every baby has her own way of investigating this new phenomenon. Some babies will need a lot of time to complete their investigations, while other babies won't. Most babies have a particular fondness for hands. Perhaps this happens because their tiny hands pass by more often.

Help Your Baby Explore the New World through Touch

Hands and arms can be in a myriad of different postures. Each posture is another pattern to be seen and felt. Allow your baby to study her hands as long and as often as she wants. A baby has to learn what her hands are for before she can learn to use them properly. Therefore, it is very important for her to get to know all about these "touching devices."

> "My little darling studies every detail of how his hands move. He plays quite delicately with his fingers. When he's lying down, he holds his hand in the air then spreads his fingers. Sometimes he opens and closes his fingers, one at a time. Or he clasps his hands together or lets them touch. It's one continuous flowing movement."
>
> **Bob's mom, 9th week**

Have you noticed your baby attempting to use her hands by trying to clasp a rattle, for instance? Also, in holding a plaything, a feeling pattern is involved of that hand position plus the object touching the palm of the hand. A baby's first attempts at grasping an object are generally far from successful. Show her that you are enthusiastic about the effort she is making and encourage each serious attempt. Praise from you will encourage her to continue.

> "My son is trying to grab things! His little hand gropes in the direction of his rattle, or he tries to hit it. A moment later he tries to grab the rattle, using a proper clasping motion. He puts a lot of effort into it. When he thinks he's got it, he clenches his fist, but the rattle is still a few inches away. The poor darling realizes his mistake, gets frustrated, and starts to cry."
>
> **Paul's mom, 11th week**

Try to bear in mind that at this age your baby is definitely not yet able to reach out and touch the things that she wants to grab. She is only capable of closing her hands around an object. Make sure that you always place easy-to-grab toys near her waving hands. Your baby will then be able to touch the object and practice closing and opening her hands whenever she wants.

Help Your Baby Explore the New World through Sound

A baby's greatest passion is the latest sounds that she makes herself. This is why you should try to respond to every sound your young infant makes. Your baby's greatest passion might be to make explosive sounds, because from this leap onward she can keep her vocal cords in a certain position. Just like a hand position, a vocal cord position is a feeling pattern. Try to imitate your baby's sounds so that she can hear them from someone else. Respond when she uses sounds to attract your attention. These "conversations" are essential for her learning process, and they will teach her to take turns, listen, and imitate—skills which form the basis of communication. These chats will also teach her that her voice is an important tool, just like her hands are.

"My baby chats away, trying to attract my attention all day long. She listens to my voice as well. It's wonderful."

Hannah's mom, 11th week

Every mother tries to encourage her baby to "chat." Some mothers talk to their babies throughout their waking hours as a matter of course, whereas other mothers do this only at certain times, such as when their babies are on their laps. The disadvantage of planned chat times is that the baby may not always be in the right mood to listen and respond. It appears that babies whose mothers "plan" chat times do not always understand what is expected of them, and their mothers become easily discouraged because they think their babies are not responding properly yet.

Help Your Baby Explore the New World through Body Postures

Your baby may be ready for pull-up games. A little bruiser who is able to lift his head on his own may love being pulled up by his arms from a half-sitting position to an upright position or being pulled from a sitting position to standing. Be careful to support his heavy head. If he is very strong, he may even actively participate. This game teaches the baby how different postures feel and how to maintain them. Each of those postures is another 'pattern' that your baby can perceive inside his body. If he cooperates in the pull-up game, he will jerk rather unsteadily from one position to the next. Once he has jerked into a certain position, he will want to retain it for a moment. Although his movements are still far from supple, he will love being in a certain position for a short while. He may even become very upset when you decide it's time to end the game.

"Suddenly, my son is jerking all over the place when I pull him onto his feet. He also makes jerky, spastic movements when he's lying naked on his changing mat. I don't know if this is normal. It worries me a bit."

Kevin's mom, 11th week

"If my baby had her way, she'd be on her feet all day, listening to me telling her how strong she is. If I don't rush in with compliments, she starts complaining."

Ashley's mom, 10th week

Fathers are usually the first to discover that babies enjoy these pull-up games, then mothers will follow, although they tend to be slightly more enthusiastic with baby boys than with baby girls.

Some Things to Keep in Mind

Your baby will be more eager to learn when he is discovering a new world. He will learn faster, easier, and it will be more fun, if you give him the things that suit his personality.

Very demanding babies will automatically get more attention, as their mothers strive to keep them amused and satisfied. These high-interest babies may become the best students of tomorrow if they are given the right help and encouragement in their early years.

Quiet babies are easily forgotten, because they don't demand as much attention from their mothers. Try to give a quiet baby just that little bit more encouragement and stimulation to get the best out of him.

You may think that your infant should be able to be a little bit more independent now, because you notice the great pleasure he takes in his surroundings, his playthings, his own hands and feet, and because he enjoys lying flat on his back on the floor. You may start using the playpen for the first time at this stage. It's a good place to hang toys within easy reach of your baby's hands, allowing him to swipe at them or watch them swinging backward and forward. You may also try to let your baby amuse himself for as long as possible, presenting him with new playthings when he gets bored. With your help, your baby may be able to amuse himself for about 15 minutes at this age.

A Word of Consolation: A Demanding Baby Could be Gifted

Some babies catch on to new games and toys quickly, soon growing tired of doing the same things, day in and day out. They want new challenges, continual action, complicated games, and lots of variety. It can be extremely exhausting for mothers of these "bubbly" babies, because they run

(continued on page 78)

Top Games for This Wonder Week

These games and activities can be used when your baby enters the world of patterns. Before you start working your way down the list, look back at "How My Baby Explores the New World of Patterns" on page 66 to remind yourself of what your baby likes to do. And remember that the games that don't work for your baby right now may do later on when he's ready.

HANDS OR FEET, A FAVORITE TOY

Give your baby ample opportunity and room to watch his hands and feet. He will need freedom of movement to take in every detail. The best thing to do is to put him on a large towel or blanket. If it is warm enough, let him play without his clothes on, since he will really enjoy the freedom of his naked body. If you want, you can tie a colorful ribbon around his hand or foot as an added attraction. If you do this, however, be sure it is securely attached and watch the baby closely so that he does not accidentally choke on the ribbon should it come loose.

COZY CHATS

When your baby is in a talking mood, sit down and make yourself comfortable. Making sure that you have enough support in your back, draw your knees up, and lie your baby on his back on your thighs. From this position he can see you properly, and you'll be able to follow all of his reactions. Chat to him about anything: his beauty, his soft skin, his eyes, the events of the day, or your plans for later. The most important thing is the rhythm of your voice and your facial expression. Be sure you give him enough time to respond. This means being patient, waiting, smiling, nodding at him so that he realizes it takes two to have a conversation. Watch your baby's reactions to discover what he finds interesting. Remember that a talking mouth, together with a face that shifts from one expression to another, is usually a smash hit!

THE GREAT INDOORS

At this age, an inquisitive baby is still unable to grab objects that catch his eye to take a closer look. Until he is able to do this himself, he will have to rely on you to bring interesting objects to him. Remember, there are many interesting things in the house that will arouse his curiosity. Explain to him what he sees. He will enjoy listening to the intonation in your voice. Let him touch and feel whatever he seems to like.

THE PULL-UP GAME

You can only play this game if your baby is able to lift his head on his own. Sit down and make yourself comfortable. Make sure that you have enough support in your back. Draw your knees up and put your baby on your legs and tummy so that he is virtually in a half-sitting position. He will feel more comfortable like this. Now, hold his arms and pull him up slowly, until he is sitting upright, giving him words of encouragement at the same time, such as telling him what a clever little boy he is. Watch his reactions carefully, and only continue if you're sure he is cooperating and enjoying himself.

TAKING A BATH TOGETHER

Water is a wonderful toy on its own. At this age, "water babies" in particular will enjoy watching water move. Place the baby on your stomach and show him drops and little streams of water running off your body onto his. Babies will also enjoy having small waves washed over their bodies. Lay him on his back on your stomach, and play "row, row, row your boat" together. Move back and forth slowly to the rhythm of the song, and make small waves. He will enjoy the feel of the waves running over his skin. After the freedom of the bath, he is likely to love being wrapped up snugly and securely in a warm towel and given a good cuddle!

out of imagination, and their infants scream if they are not presented with one new challenge after another.

It is a proven fact that many highly gifted children were demanding, discontented babies. They were usually happy only as long as they were offered new and exciting challenges.

A new awareness or new world will offer new opportunities to learn additional skills. Some babies will explore their new world and make discoveries with great enthusiasm, but they demand constant attention and help in doing this. They have an endless thirst for knowledge. Unfortunately, they discover their new world with tremendous speed. They try out and acquire almost every skill the new world has to offer, then experiment a little before growing bored again. For mothers of babies like this, there is little more they can do than to wait for the next big change to occur.

"After every feeding, I put my son in the playpen for a while. I sometimes put him under a musical mobile that he likes to watch, and sometimes I put him under a trapeze with toys dangling from it, which he takes a

Top Toys for This Wonder Week

Here are some toys and things that babies like as they explore the world of patterns.

- Playthings that dangle overhead

- A moving or musical mobile

- A musical box with moving figures

- Playthings to swipe at or to touch

- Cuddly toys to talk to or laugh at

- Mommy—you still top the chart as his favorite toy!

swipe at every now and then. I must say, he's getting rather good at hitting them now."

Frankie's mom, 11th week

Around 10 weeks, another period of comparative ease sets in. Most mothers seem to put the concerns and anxieties of recent weeks quickly behind them. They sing their babies' praises and talk about them as if they had always been easygoing and cheerful babies.

What changes can you see in your baby at this stage? At approximately 10 weeks, your baby may no longer require as much attention as he did in the past. He is more independent. He is interested in his surroundings, in people, animals, and objects. It seems as if he suddenly understands and clearly recognizes a whole range of new things. His need to be with you constantly may also diminish at this time. If you pick him up, he may squirm and wriggle in discomfort and attempt to sit up in your arms as much as possible. The only time he may seem to need you now is when you are willing to show him things of interest. Your baby may have become so cheerful and busy amusing himself that life is much easier for you. You may feel a surge of energy. Lots of mothers regularly put babies of this age in their playpens, as they feel their children are ready for it now.

"My daughter suddenly seems much brighter. She's lost that newborn dependency. I'm not the only who's noticed. Everyone talks properly to her now, instead of making funny cooing noises."

Emily's mom, 10th week

"My baby seems wiser. She's become more friendly, happier, and even roars with laughter once in a while. Thank goodness she's stopped that incessant crying! Life has changed drastically from thinking 'How can I cope with her screaming?' to enjoying having her around now. Even her father looks forward to seeing her in the evening nowadays. He used to come home dragging his feet, dreading the probable torment of her non-stop crying. Now he loves being around her. He feeds and bathes her every evening."

Jenny's mom, 10th week

"My son no longer seems so vulnerable. I see a definite change in him now. He has progressed from just sitting on my lap to gaining a bit of independence and playing."

Steven's mom, 10th week

"I think my baby is really starting to develop into a real little person with a life of her own. At first, all she did was eat and sleep. Now she has a good stretch when I take her out of bed, just like grown-ups do."

Nina's mom, 10th week

"I don't know if there's any connection, but I certainly have noticed that I had a lot more energy this past week, and this coincided with my little boy's newfound independence. I must say I really enjoy watching the progress he's making. It's fascinating the way he laughs, enjoys himself, and plays. We seem to communicate better now. I can let my imagination run wild with his stuffed toys, sing him songs, and invent different games. Now that I'm getting some feedback from him, he's turning into a little friend. I find this age much easier than when he just nursed, cried, and slept."

Bob's mom, 10th week

Place Photo Here

After the Leap

Age: _____

Reflections: _____

chapter 5

Wonder Week 12:
The World of Smooth Transitions

At around 11 or 12 weeks, your baby will enter yet another new world as he undergoes the third major developmental leap since his birth. You may recall that one of the significant physical developments that occurred at 8 weeks was your baby's ability to swipe and kick at objects with his arms and legs. These early flailing movements often looked comically puppetlike. At 12 weeks, this jerky action is about to change. Like Pinocchio, your baby is ready to change from a puppet into a real boy.

Of course, this transformation will not happen overnight, and when it does it will entail more than just physical movement, although that's usually what parents notice most. It will also affect your baby's ability to perceive with his other senses the way things change around him—such as a voice shifting from one register to another, the cat slinking across the floor, and the light in a room becoming dimmer as the sun dips behind the clouds. Your baby's world is becoming a more organized place as he discovers the constant, flowing changes around him.

The realization of these subtleties will enable your baby to enjoy life in new ways. But it's not easy entering a world that's shifting beneath your feet. Overnight, your baby's world has changed. Nothing seems to stand still anymore.

Keep in mind that if your baby is suddenly more fussy, he's probably getting ready to master new skills. Watch him closely during this exciting time.

In this changing world, the one constant is you, his boat on the rolling seas. Is it any wonder he wants to hang on to you for dear life as he enters this next major developmental leap in his life? Fortunately, this fussy period will not last quite as long as the previous one. Some babies will behave normally again after just a day, while others may need a whole week before they feel themselves again.

When a change happens, all babies will cry more often and for longer periods, although some will cry more than others. Some babies will be inconsolable, while others may be fretful, cranky, moody, or listless. One baby may be especially difficult at night, while another may tend to get upset during the day. All babies will usually be a little less tearful if they are carried around or if they are just given extra attention or cuddles. But even under these circumstances, anybody who knows the baby well will suspect that he will cry or fret again at the least opportunity.

How You Know It's Time to Grow

Here are the major signs that your baby is about to make this developmental leap.

He May Demand More Attention

Just when you thought that your baby had learned to amuse himself, he doesn't seem to do so well anymore. He may seem to want you to play with him more and keep him entertained all the time. Just sitting with him may not be enough; he may want you to look at him and talk to him, too. This change in his behavior will be all the more obvious if he had already shown you that he could be independent after the last leap forward. If anything, you may think that he's suffered a setback. You may feel that if your baby previously took three steps forward, here come the two steps back.

> "My son is so terribly dependent on me right now. He is happy only if I hold him close. If he had his way, I think I'd be dancing around with him, too."
>
> Bob's mom, 12th week

He May Become Shy with Strangers

Some babies will be shy with everyone except their moms at this time. If your baby is shy, you will notice that he clings to you whenever you have company. He may start to cry when a stranger talks to him or even looks at him. Sometimes, he may refuse to sit on anyone's lap but yours. If he is safely snuggled up to you, he may give someone else a reluctant smile, but if he is particularly shy, he will quickly bury his head in your shoulder afterward.

He May Cling to You More Tightly

Your baby may cling to you so tightly when you carry him that it seems as if he is afraid of being dropped. Babies who do this may sometimes even pinch their mothers very hard in the process.

He May Lose His Appetite

At this time, your baby may drag out each feeding session. Breastfed babies who are allowed to decide for themselves when they want to nurse behave as if they want to eat all day long. Bottle-fed babies take longer to finish their bottles, if they manage to get that far. These fractious drinkers spend their time chewing and gnawing at the nipples without actually drinking. They do this as a form of comfort and so they hang on for dear life, afraid to let go. Often, they will drift off to sleep with the nipples still in their mouths. Your baby may try to hold on to you or grab your breast during nursing, even if he is being bottle-fed, as if he is afraid of relinquishing his only source of comfort.

> "When I'm bottle-feeding my daughter, she sticks her tiny hand inside my blouse. We call it 'bosoming.'"
>
> Emily's mom, 12th week

He May Sleep Poorly

Your baby will probably sleep less well now. Many babies wake several times a night demanding to be fed. Other babies wake up very early in the morning. Still other babies refuse to take naps during the day. For many families, the normal routine has turned into absolute chaos because the baby's regular feeding and sleeping patterns have changed so drastically.

He May Suck His Thumb More Often

Your infant may now discover his thumb for the first time, or he may suck his thumb longer and more regularly than before. Like sucking at the breast or bottle, this is a comfort and can avert another crying session. Some mothers introduce a pacifier to help soothe the baby at this time.

He May Be Listless

Your baby may be quieter or seem less lively than usual. He may also lie still for quite some time, gazing around or just staring in front of him. This is only a temporary event. His previous sounds and movements will soon be replaced by new ones.

My Diary

Signs My Baby Is Growing Again

Between 11 and 12 weeks, you may notice your baby showing any of the following behaviors. They are probably signs that she is ready to make the next leap, into the world of smooth transitions. Check off the signs your baby shows.

❑ Cries more often

❑ Wants you to keep him busy

❑ Loses appetite

❑ Is more shy with strangers

❑ Clings more

❑ Wants more physical contact during nursing

❑ Sleeps poorly

❑ Sucks his thumb, or does so more often than before

❑ Is less lively

❑ Is quieter, less vocal

OTHER CHANGES YOU NOTICE

_____

_____

_____

"The only thing my baby likes doing right now is cuddling up close to me in her sling. She's very quiet and no trouble at all—she doesn't do much except sleep. To be honest, though, I'd much rather see her full of life."

Nina's mom, 12th week

How This Leap May Affect You

Obviously, your baby will not be the only one affected by the changes occurring within him. His whole family suffers too, especially his mother. Here are some of the feelings you may experience during this turbulent time.

You May Feel Worried

It's normal to feel anxious when you notice that your once-lively infant has become more fussy, is crying more often, is sleeping poorly, or is not nursing well. You may be worried because it seems that your baby has suffered a setback in producing sounds and movements or seems to have lost the independence that he had so recently acquired. Mothers usually expect to see progress, and if this doesn't seem to be happening, even for just a short while, they get concerned. They feel insecure, and they wonder what's the matter. "Is something wrong with the baby? Can he be ill? Could he be abnormal after all?" are the most common worries. Most often, none of these is the case. (When in doubt, always consult your family doctor.) On the contrary, your baby is showing signs of progress. A whole new world is there for him to discover, but when this world reveals itself, the baby will first have to deal with the upheaval it brings. It is not easy for him, and he will need your support. You can do this by showing that you understand that he is going through a difficult time.

> "When my baby is crying incessantly and wants to be carried around all the time, I feel pressured. I can't seem to accomplish even the simplest things. It makes me feel insecure, and it saps all my energy."
>
> Juliette's mom, 12th week

> "I'm trying to find out why my baby cries so much. I want to know what's troubling her so that I can fix it. Then I'll have some peace of mind again."
>
> Laura's mom, 12th week

"There's no way I can cope with my son's crying. I just can't take it anymore. I'd even prefer getting out of bed four times a night to deal with a
baby who is not crying than twice a night to deal with a tiny screamer."

Paul's mom, 11th week

You May Become Irritated

During this period, many mothers grow annoyed with their babies' irreg-
ular eating and sleeping routines. They find it impossible to plan ahead.
Their entire schedule is thrown off balance. They often feel under pressure
from family or friends, too. The mothers' instincts tell them to focus all
their attention on their unhappy infants, but other people often seem to
disapprove of too much babying. Mother may feel trapped in the middle.

"I get irritated every time my son starts fretting, because he can't seem to
amuse himself for even just a short while. He wants me to keep him occupied all day long. Of course, everybody loves giving me advice on
how to deal with him, especially my husband."

Kevin's mom, 12th week

"I seem to cope better with my baby's erratic behavior if I don't make
plans in advance. In the past, when my plans went completely haywire,
I felt irritated. So I've changed my attitude. And would you believe it—I
sometimes find I even have a few hours to spare!"

Laura's mom, 12th week

You May Reach Your Wit's End

Sometimes mothers are unable, or unwilling, to suppress their anger any
longer, and they let their demanding little creatures know they're fed up.

"My boy was so fretful. I kept worrying about what the neighbors would
think of the noise. Sunday afternoon was the last straw. I'd tried every-

 Baby Care

Shaking Can Be Harmful

While it is normal to feel frustrated and angry with your baby at times, **never** shake a baby. Shaking a young child can easily cause internal bleeding just below the skull, which can result in brain damage that may lead to learning difficulties later on—or even death.

thing to make him settle, but nothing helped. At first I felt helpless, but then I became furious because I just couldn't cope, so I left him in his room. I had a good cry myself, which calmed me down a bit."

Bob's mom, 12th week

"We had company, and my son was being terribly trying. Everyone gave me their 2 cents' worth of advice, which always makes me really upset. When I went upstairs to put him to bed, I lost my self-control, grabbed him, and gave him a good shake."

Matt's mom, 11th week

You May Feel Tremendous Pressure

If a mother worries too much about her noisy little grump, and if she is not given enough support from family and friends, she may become exhausted. If she is suffering from lack of sleep as well, she may easily lose control of the situation, both mentally and physically.

Unwelcome advice, on top of panic and exhaustion, could make any mother feel even more irritable and snappish—and her partner often becomes the target. At times, however, her distressed infant will bear the brunt of a mother's pent-up frustration, and she may be a little rougher with him than necessary. When a mother admits to having slapped her baby, this nearly always occurs during one of these fussy periods. It's certainly not because she dislikes the poor infant, but simply because she longs to see him happy, and she feels threatened by other people's criticism. She feels that she has no one to turn to with her problems; she feels alone.

"Every time my baby stopped crying, I felt as if a load had been lifted from my shoulders. I hadn't noticed how tense I was until then."

Emily's mom, 11th week

"After my husband's coworkers told him that he and our son look like two peas in a pod, he stopped criticizing the amount of attention I give his grumpy mirror image. In fact, my husband wouldn't have it any other way now, whereas he used to feel that I was overreacting and spoiling the baby. Things are running a lot smoother now, and I'm not as tense as I used to be when the baby gets upset, and he seems to sense that, too. I feel a lot more comfortable now."

Matt's mom, 12th week

When it all gets to be too much, just remember: It can only get better. At this stage, some mothers fear that these dreadful crying fits may never stop. This is a logical assumption because until now the fussy periods followed each other in rapid succession with only 2 to 3 weeks in between. This barely left enough time for mothers to catch their breath. But don't despair—from now on, the intervals between the fussy periods will be longer. The fussy periods themselves will also seem less intense.

How Your Baby's New Skills Emerge

When your baby is upset, you will usually want to keep an extra close watch on him because you want to know what's wrong. In doing so, you may suddenly notice that your baby has actually mastered new skills or is

Brain Changes

At approximately 10 to 11 weeks, the head circumference of babies dramatically increases.

trying to do so. In fact, you'll discover that your baby is making his next big leap—into the world of smooth transitions.

At approximately 12 weeks, your baby will be able to perceive the many subtle ways that things change around him, not abruptly but smoothly and gradually. He will be ready to experiment with making such smooth transitions himself.

Your baby will make many new discoveries in this new world. He will select the things that appeal to him and that he is ready physically and mentally to attempt. You should, as always, be careful not to push him but help him do what he shows he is ready for. In many ways, however, he will still rely on your help. He will need you to show him things in his world, to put his toys where he can see and reach for them, and to respond to his increasing attempts at communication.

the
**Magical Leap
Forward**

As she enters the world of smooth transitions, for the first time your baby is able to recognize continuous changes in sights, sounds, tastes, smells, and touch. For example, she may now notice how a voice shifts from one tone to the next or how a body shifts from one position to another. Not only can she register these smooth transitions in the outside world, your infant is now able to learn to make them herself. This will enable your baby to work on several important skills.

(continued on page 94)

My Diary

**How My Baby Explores the New World
of Smooth Transitions**

Check off the boxes below as you notice your baby changing.

BODY CONTROL

❏ Barely needs support to keep his head upright

❏ Smooth head movement when turning to one side

❏ Smooth eye movement when following a moving object

❏ Is generally more lively and energetic

❏ Playfully lifts his bottom when his diaper is being changed

❏ Rolls independently from back to stomach or vice versa while
   holding on to your fingers

❏ Sticks his toes in his mouth and twists around

❏ Sits up straight when leaning against you

❏ Pulls himself into sitting position while holding on to your fingers

❏ Is able to move into a standing position when seated on your
   lap, by holding on to two of your fingers

❏ Uses both feet to push off when seated in a bouncing chair
   or lying in a playpen

HAND CONTROL

❏ Grabs and clutches at objects with both hands

❏ Shakes a rattle once or twice

❏ Studies and plays with your hands

❏ Studies and touches your face, eyes, mouth, and hair

❏ Studies and plays with your clothes

❏ Puts everything into his mouth

❏ Strokes his head, from neck to eyes

❏ Rubs a toy along his head or cheek

LISTENING AND TALKING

❏ Discovers shrieking and gurgling; can easily shift between loud and soft tones, low notes and high ones

❏ Produces new sounds that resemble the vowels of real speech: *ee, ooh, ehh, oh, aah, ay*

❏ Uses these sounds to "chat"

❏ Is able to blow saliva bubbles, and laughs as if he finds this very amusing

LOOKING AND SEEING

❏ Turns hands over, studies both sides

❏ Studies his own moving feet

❏ Studies a face, eyes, mouth, and hair

❏ Studies someone's clothing

OTHER SKILLS

❏ Expresses enjoyment by watching, looking, listening, grabbing, or by "talking," then waiting for your response

❏ Uses different behavior with different people

❏ Expresses boredom if he sees, hears, tastes, feels, or does the same things too often; variety suddenly becomes important

OTHER CHANGES YOU NOTICE

_____

_____

You will see that now your baby's movements become much smoother, more flowing, and more like an adult's. This new control applies to her whole body as well as to the parts that she can move consciously—her hands, feet, head, eyes, and even her vocal cords. You will probably notice that when she stretches out toward a toy, the movement is smoother than it was just a few weeks ago. When she bends her knees to sit or pulls herself to stand, the whole exercise looks more deliberate and mature.

Her head movements also become smoother, and she can now vary their speed. She can look around the room in the way that older children do and follow a continuous movement. Her eyes are able to focus more sharply on what they see, and her vision will soon be as good as an adult's.

When your baby was first born, she came ready equipped with a reflex that moved her gaze in the direction of any new sound. This disappeared somewhere between 4 and 8 weeks after birth, but now she can do the same thing consciously, and the response will be quicker. She will be able to follow something or somebody with her eyes in a controlled, well-coordinated manner. She may even begin to do this without turning her head. She will be able to follow people or objects approaching her or moving away. In fact, she will become capable of surveying the whole room. You may feel for the first time that she is really a part of the family as she notices everybody's comings and goings.

This new responsiveness is enhanced by new vocal possibilities as she begins to recognize changes in pitch and in volume of sounds and to experiment with these by gurgling and shrieking. Her improved coordination even helps her to swallow more smoothly.

Although some remarkable developments have occurred in your baby's mind and body, what she cannot do is cope with quick changes in succession. Don't expect her to be able to follow an object that is moving up and down as well as from left to right or a toy that rapidly reverses its direction of movement. And when she moves her own hand, there will be a noticeable pause before any change of direction, almost like a tiny conductor waving a baton.

Parents are generally less concerned if their babies show a reluctance to amuse themselves at this stage. They are too proud of their babies' achievements and efforts in so many directions. There are so many new discoveries to be made and so many new things to be learned and practiced, and for the moment that is what matters the most.

Your Baby's Choices: A Key to Her Personality

If you watch your baby closely, you will be able to determine where her interests lie. As you mark off the things that she is showing you that she can do in this world, be aware of the uniqueness of your child.

Some babies are very aware of the world around them, and they prefer looking, listening, and experiencing sensations to being physically active themselves. Most of the time, professionals, as well as friends and family, assess a baby's development by looking at the physical milestones, such as grasping, rolling over, crawling, sitting, standing, and walking. This can give a one-sided view of progress as it makes the "watch-listen-feel" baby seem slower. These babies usually take longer to begin grasping objects, but once they start, they will examine them very closely. Given a new item, a watch-listen-feel baby will turn it around, look at it, listen to it, rub it, and even smell it. These babies actually are doing something very complicated that will give them a broad base for their later learning skills.

In contrast, babies who are more physically active often become engrossed in the action of grabbing itself, and once they have attained possession of the object, they quickly lose interest and drop it in favor of looking for another challenge. Babies love anything new, and it is important that you respond when you notice any new skills or interests. Your baby will enjoy it if you share these new discoveries, and her learning will progress more quickly.

The more your baby plays or experiments with a new skill, the more adept he will become. Practice makes perfect as far as babies are concerned, too. Your baby may want to try out a new skill over and over again. Although he will play and practice on his own, your participation and encouragement are vital. As well as cheering him on when he does well, you can help when the going gets tough and he feels like giving up. At this point, you can make the task easier for him—usually by rearranging the world so that it is a bit more accommodating. This might mean turning a toy around so that it's easier to grab, propping him up so that he can see the cat through the window, or maybe imitating the sounds he is trying to make.

You can also help to make an activity more complex or vary it a bit so that he stays with it longer and is challenged just a little more. Be careful to watch for signs that your baby has had enough. Remember that he will go at his own pace.

Just as babies are all different, so are their mothers. Some mothers have more imagination than others in certain areas. It may be a particular challenge for you if your baby is the physical type but you prefer talking,

The Gender Gap

Baby boys seem to take up more of their mothers' time than baby girls do during the first months. This probably happens because boys cry more and don't sleep as well as girls.

Also, mothers of baby girls are much quicker to respond to the sounds produced by their daughters than are mothers of baby boys. Mothers also tend to "chat" more to their babies if they are girls.

singing, and storytelling. Gather new ideas from books, your friends, and family members. The baby's father and older siblings can help—most children will be able to go on long after the baby's desire for repetition has exhausted you. But whatever type of baby you have and whatever type of mother you are, your child will always benefit from some help from you.

Help Your Baby Explore the New World through Sound

If your baby has a special love for sound, encourage him to use his voice. He may now begin to shriek, gurgle, or make vowel-like sounds himself. These may range from high- to low-pitched sounds and from soft to loud ones. If he also starts to blow saliva bubbles, don't discourage him. By doing these things, he is playing with 'smooth transitions' and in the process he is exercising the muscles of his vocal cords, lips, tongue, and palate as well. Your baby may often practice when he is alone, sounding like somebody who is chattering away just for fun. He does this because the range of notes with all the high and low vowel sounds and little shrieks in between sound a lot like talking. Sometimes a baby will even chuckle at his own sounds.

Most babies love to have cozy chats with their mommies. Of course, a baby has to be in the mood to do this. The best time to chat is when he attracts your attention with his voice. You will probably find yourself speaking in a slightly higher-pitched tone than usual, which is just right for your baby's ear. It is very important that you stick to the rules of conversation—your baby says something, then you say something back. Make sure you let him finish. Because if you don't give him time to reply, he will feel that you aren't listening to him, and he won't learn the rhythm of conversation. If that happens—if you do not give him enough time to reply—he may become despondent or confused that you are not listening to him. The subjects of your conversation don't matter very much at this age, but it is better to stick to familiar territory and shared experiences. Occasionally, try imitating the sounds he is making. Some babies find this so funny that they will break into laughter. This is all-important groundwork for later language skills.

It is very important to talk to your baby frequently. Voices on the radio or television, or people talking in the same room, are no substitute for a one-on-one conversation. Your baby is prompted to talk because there is someone who listens and responds to him. Your enthusiasm will play an important role here.

"I always talk back whenever my son makes sounds. Then he waits a little, realizes it's his turn, and replies with a smile or by wriggling around. If he's in the right mood, he'll gurgle back at me again. If I reply once more, he gets so excited that he waves his arms and legs all over the place and sometimes shrieks with laughter as well. When he's had enough, he turns away and looks at something else."

John's mom, 13th week

Your baby may use one of his latest sounds when he wants something. This is often a special "attention!" shriek. If he does this, always answer him. This is important since it will give him the sense that you understand what he is trying to communicate, even if you don't have time to stop and

When Your Baby Laughs, She's on Top of the World

When you make your baby laugh, you have struck the right chord with her. You have stimulated her in exactly the right way. Don't overdo it because you may intimidate her. On the other hand, half-hearted attempts on your part could lead to boredom on hers. You must find the comfortable middle ground for your baby.

play with him at that moment. He will begin to use his voice to attract your attention. That's a significant step toward language.

When he's happy, a baby will often use a special "cry for joy" sound. He will use it when he notices something he finds amusing. It's natural to respond to these cries for joy with a kiss, a cuddle, or words of encouragement. The more you are able to do this, the better. It shows your baby that you share his pleasure and that you understand him.

"When my son saw that I was about to feed him, he shrieked with excitement and grabbed my breast, while my blouse was still only half undone."

Matt's mom, 13th week

Help Your Baby Explore the New World through Touch

As your baby now lives in the world of 'smooth transitions', you may notice that he stretches out toward a toy more smoothly. Help him. He just entered this new world and reaching is still very difficult. Hold a toy within easy reach of your baby's hands and watch him to see if he is able to reach out for it. Hold the object right in front of him, keeping in mind that at this age he is only able to make a controlled movement with his arm in one direction at a time. Now pay close attention to what he does. If he is only just starting to master this skill, he will probably react something like this baby.

"My son is really starting to reach out to grab things! He reached for a toy dangling in front of him with both hands. He put out his right hand on one side of the toy and his left hand on the other side of the toy. Then, when both hands were just in front of the toy, he clasped them together . . . and missed! He'd tried really hard, so it wasn't at all surprising that he got very upset when he found himself empty-handed."

Paul's mom, 12th week
(continued on page 102)

Top Games for This Wonder Week

Here are some games and activities that work for babies at this point in their development. At this age, your baby will particularly enjoy games where you move her whole body around. Try to do this gently, with slow and even movements, remembering that these are the only kind that your baby can properly understand. It is better to play several different games in a row, rather than continue the same game for too long.

THE AIRPLANE

Lift your baby up slowly, while making a sound that increases in volume or changes from a low-pitched to a high-pitched sound. She will stretch out her body automatically as you raise her above your head. Then start the descent, making the appropriate airplane sounds. When she is in line with your face, welcome her by burying your face in her neck and giving her a nibble with your lips. You will soon notice that your baby expects you to do this and will open her mouth and nibble back. You will also see your baby opening her mouth again, as if anticipating the nibble, when she wants you to repeat this flying game.

THE SLIDE

Sit down on the floor or a sofa, lean back, and make your body as straight as possible. Place your baby as high up on your chest as you can and let her slide gently down to the floor, while you make the appropriate sliding sound.

THE PENDULUM

Place the baby on your knees so that she is facing you and slowly sway her from side to side. Try to make all kinds of clock sounds, such as a high-pitched, fast tick-tock, or a low-pitched, slow bong-bong. Try to make sounds that range from high to low and from fast to slow, or whatever clock sound you notice that your baby enjoys the most. Make sure that you hold her firmly and that her head and neck muscles are strong enough to move with the rhythm.

THE ROCKING HORSE
Place the baby on your knees so that she is facing you and make stepping movements with your legs, so your baby sways up and down as if she were sitting on a horse. You can also make the accompanying clip-clop noises or "schlupping" sounds that babies love at this age.

THE NIBBLING GAME
Sit in front of your baby and make sure that she is looking at you. Move your face slowly toward her tummy or nose. Meanwhile, make a drawn-out sound, increasing in volume, or changing in tone, for instance "chooooomp" or "aaaaaah-boom" or sounds similar to those the baby makes herself.

FEELING FABRICS
Here's a way to play and get chores done! Fold your laundry with your baby nearby, and let her feel different types of fabrics, such as wool, cotton, terry cloth, or nylon. Run her hand over the fabrics to allow her to feel the different textures, too. Babies like touching materials with their fingers and mouths. Try something unusual such as chamois, leather, or felt.

JUMPING AND BOUNCING
A physically active baby loves repeating the same flowing movements over and over again when she is on your lap. Let her stand up and sit down again at her own pace. She will want to repeat this "stand up, sit down, stand up, sit down" game endlessly. It will probably make her laugh, too, but, again, hold her tightly and watch her head.

If your child reaches for objects and misses, encourage him to try again, or make the game a little easier for him so that he gets a taste of success. At this age, he is not yet able to make an accurate estimate of the distance between his hands and the plaything he is trying to grab. He will not be able to learn this properly until he is between 23 and 26 weeks old.

As your baby becomes more adept at grabbing objects, he will want to play the "grabbing game" more often. Because he can turn his head smoothly and look around the room, he can choose what he wants from the entire world of things that is now waiting for him to grab, feel, and touch. After the last developmental leap, most babies spent about one-third of their waking hours playing and experimenting with their hands. After about 12 weeks, this suddenly doubles to two-thirds of their waking hours.

If you notice that your baby enjoys stroking things with his hands, encourage this activity as much as you can. Not only the stroking movement involves a "smooth transition," but also the feeling in his hand caused by the moving contact with the object. Carry your baby around the house and garden, letting him feel all kinds of objects and experience their properties—hard, soft, rough, smooth, sticky, firm, flexible, prickly, cold, wet, and warm. Tell him what the items are, and describe the sensations. Help to get your meaning across by using your tone of voice to express the feeling an object or surface arouses. He really will be able to understand more than he is able to tell you.

> "I washed my baby's hands under running water, which made her laugh out loud. She couldn't seem to get enough of it."
>
> Jenny's mom, 15th week

Many babies like to examine their mothers' faces. As your little one runs his hands over your face, he may linger slightly longer by your eyes, nose, and mouth. He might tug on your hair or pull at your nose, simply because they are easy to grasp. Items of clothing are interesting as well.

Babies like to stroke and feel fabrics. Watch out for your earrings, too!

Some babies are interested in their mothers' hands. They will study, touch, and stroke them. If your baby enjoys playing with your hands, help him to do this. Slowly turn your hand over, and show him the palm and back of your hand. Let him watch while you move your hand or pick up a toy. Try not to make your movements too fast or to change direction too quickly, or you will lose his attention. Simple movements are all he can cope with in this world. Your baby won't be able to deal with more complicated movements until after another big change in his nervous system, which is the start of the next developmental leap.

Help Your Baby Explore the New World through Body Movement

At this age, all babies are getting livelier. They are playing with 'smooth transitions' felt inside their bodies, while they kick and wave their arms about. Some babies perform acrobatics; for example, they might stuff their toes in their mouths and almost spin around on their backs in the process. Obviously, some babies are much livelier and stronger than others. Some babies are not really interested in gymnastic feats, while others will be frustrated if their physical strengths are not yet up to the task.

> "My son moves his body, arms, and legs around like mad, grunting and groaning in the process. He's obviously trying to do something, but whatever it is he's not succeeding because he usually ends up having an angry screaming fit."
>
> Frankie's mom, 14th week

Whatever your baby's temperament, he will benefit from a little time spent without his clothes in a warm environment. You may already have noticed that he is lively when you are changing him, enjoying the opportunity to move freely without being hampered by diaper and clothes. It's

Top Toys for This Wonder Week

Here are some toys and things that babies like best as they explore the world of smooth transitions:

- Wobbly toys that bounce back when the baby swipes them

- The clapper inside a bell

- A rocking chair

- Toys that emit a slow squeak, chime, or other simple sound

- Rattles

- Dolls with realistic faces

easier to bend the little limbs, to wave, kick, and roll over naked. Success comes more easily, and the baby will get to know his body better and control it more precisely.

Some babies attempt to roll over at this age, but nearly all of them will need a bit of help in doing so. If your little squirmer tries to roll over, let him hold on to one of your fingers as he practices. A very persistent baby who is also physically strong may manage to roll from tummy to back. Some can do it the other way around and go from back to tummy. However persistent the infant, he won't manage it unless his physical development is far enough along. So give help and support, but also be ready to help your baby deal with his frustration if he just can't manage something that he would clearly like to do.

Many babies love pushing themselves up with their legs. If your baby enjoys doing this, he will practice pushing off in his playpen, in his bouncing chair, on his changing table (watch out for this one!), or while sitting on your lap. You need to hold on tight to an active squirmer. If your baby is able to do these push-ups unaided, give him lots of opportunities to practice.

If your baby is physically strong, he may also try to pull himself up into a sitting position when he is on your lap. If he likes to do this, you can help him by making a game out of it.

After the Leap

Between 12 and 13 weeks, another period of comparative calm settles in. Parents, family, and friends will notice what a cheerful little person your baby has become and admire the wonderful progress she has made. You may find your baby much smarter now. When she is carried around or sits on your lap, she acts like a little person. She turns her head immediately in the direction of something she wants to see or hear. She laughs at everyone, and answers them when she is talked to. She shifts her position to get a better look at something she wants to see, and she keeps an eye on everything going on around her. She is cheerful and active. It may strike you that other family members show a lot more interest in her as a person now. It appears that she has gained her own place in the family. She belongs!

"My daughter is developing an interest in a whole variety of things now. She talks or shrieks at different objects, and when we watch her more closely, we think, 'My goodness, can you do that already?' Or 'Aren't you clever noticing all of those things?'"

Jenny's mom, 13th week

"My little one is definitely wiser. She's all eyes these days. She responds to everything and immediately turns her little head in response to sounds. She's suddenly gained her own little place in the family."

Hannah's mom, 14th week

"It's wonderful watching my baby enjoying herself so much and chatting affectionately to her cuddly toys and to people."

Juliette's mom, 14th week

"We have a lot more interaction with my child now because she responds to everything. After I've played a game with her, I can tell when she's waiting for me to play again. She also 'replies' a lot more now."

Ashley's mom, 13th week

"My daughter used to be so easygoing and quiet, but she's turned into a real little chatterbox now. She laughs and gurgles a lot more often. I really enjoy getting her out of bed to see what she'll do next."

Eve's mom, 14th week

"My son is much more interesting to watch now because the progress he's made is so obvious. He responds immediately with a smile or a gurgle, and he can turn his head in the right direction, too. I love giving him a good cuddle because he's so soft and chubby now."

Frankie's mom, 14th week

Place Photo Here

After the Leap

Age: _____

Reflections: _____

chapter 6

Wonder Week 19: The World of Events

The realization that our experience is split up into familiar events is something that we as adults take for granted. For example, if we see someone drop a rubber ball, we know that it will bounce back up and will probably continue to bounce several times. If someone jumps up into the air, we know that she is bound to come down. We recognize the initial movements of a golf swing and a tennis serve, and we know what follows. But to your baby, everything is new, and nothing is predictable.

After the last leap forward, your baby was able to perceive smooth transitions in sound, movement, light, taste, smell, and texture. But all of these transitions had to be simple. As soon as they became more complicated, he was no longer able to follow them.

At around 19 weeks (or between 18 and 20 weeks), his ability to understand the world around him becomes far more developed and a little more like our own. He will begin to experiment with events. The word "event" has a special meaning here and has nothing to do with special occasions. In fact, here it means a short, familiar sequence of smooth transitions from one pattern to the next. Sound like a mouthful? Let's try to explain what it means.

While at 12 weeks it may have taken all your baby's cross-eyed concentration simply to grasp an object with both hands that you held in front of him, he'll now begin to understand that he can reach out to a toy, grab it with one hand, shake it, turn it around to inspect it, and put it in his mouth. This kind of physical activity is much more complicated than it seems and far more than just the physical mastery of his arms and hands. It actually depends upon a high degree of neurological development. This change will enable your baby to develop a whole new set of skills.

Although the subtleties of these skills may escape you at first, they will gradually become more obvious. The sounds your infant emits may still just seem like baby babble to you for a while, but they are actually becoming much more complicated. No doubt you'll notice when he strings his consonants and vowels together to say "mommy" and "dada." You also will be very aware of his attempts to roll over and his first attempts to crawl. In all of these activities, he is now capable of learning how single patterns and transitions string together like beads to become what we as adults recognize as events.

This process is also vital for your baby to understand something that adults take completely for granted—that the world is made up of objects that continue to exist, whether or not we can completely see them at the time. You can see just how hard your baby is working in this first year of life to make sense of his world.

Your baby's awareness of the new changes that accompany this leap in his development actually begins at approximately 15 weeks (or between 14 and 17 weeks). These changes affect the way he sees, hears, smells, tastes, and feels. He needs time to come to terms with all of these new impressions, preferably in a place where he feels safe and secure. He will once again show a pronounced need to be with his mommy, cling to her for comfort, and grow into his new world at his own pace. From this age on, the fussy periods will last longer than before. This particular one will often last 5 weeks, although it may be as short as 1 week or as long as 6. If your baby is fussy, watch him closely to see if he is attempting to master new skills.

Because your baby is upset by what is happening to her, she will be much quicker to cry at this time. A very demanding little one, in particular, will cry, whine, and grumble noticeably more often than she did in the past. She will make no bones about the fact that she wants to be with her mommy.

Your baby will generally cry less when she is with you, although she may insist that you give her your undivided attention. She may not only want to be carried around constantly but also expect to be amused all through her waking hours. If she is not kept busy, she may continue to be extra cranky even when sitting on your lap.

How You Know It's Time to Grow

Watch for these sometimes subtle, sometimes not so, clues that your baby is changing and about to leap into the world of events.

She May Have Trouble Sleeping

Your baby may not settle down well at night now. It may be more difficult to get her to go to bed in the evenings, or she may lie awake at night. She may want a night feeding again, or she may even demand to be fed several times a night. She may also wake up much earlier in the morning.

She May Become Shy with Strangers

Your baby may refuse to sit on anyone else's lap but yours, or she may get upset if a stranger looks at or talks to her. She may even seem frightened of her own father if he is not around her for much of the day. Generally, her shyness will be more apparent with people who look very different from you.

> "When my daughter sees my sister, she gets extremely upset and starts screaming at the top of her lungs and buries her face in my clothes, as if she's afraid to even look at my sister. My sister has dark eyes and wears black eye makeup, which tends to give her a rather hard look. I'm blonde and wear hardly any makeup at all. Perhaps that has something to do with it."
>
> Nina's mom, 16th week

> "My son won't smile at people who wear glasses anymore. He just stares at them with a stern look on his face and refuses to smile until they have taken their glasses off."
>
> John's mom, 16th week

She May Demand More Attention

Your baby may want you to amuse her by doing things together, or at the very least, she may want you to look at her all the time. She may even start to cry the moment you walk away.

> "I have to give my son extra attention between feedings. In the past, he'd lie quietly on his own. Now he wants to be entertained."
>
> John's mom, 17th week

Her Head May Need More Support

When you carry your fussy baby around, you may notice you have to support her head and body more often. She may slump down a little in your arms when you hold her, particularly during crying fits. When you carry her, it may strike you that she feels more like the tiny newborn she used to be.

She May Always Want to Be with You

Your baby may refuse to be set down, although she may agree to sit in her bouncing chair as long as you stay near by and touch her frequently.

> "My little one wants to be closer to me, which is unusual for her. If I let go of her for even a second, she starts to cry, but as soon as either my husband or I pick her up, everything's fine again."
>
> Eve's mom, 17th week

She May Lose Her Appetite

Both breastfed and bottle-fed babies can temporarily have smaller appetites as they approach this leap. Don't worry if your little one is more easily distracted by the things she sees or hears around her than she used to be, or if she is quick to start playing with the nipple. Occasionally, babies may even turn away from the bottle or breast and refuse to drink completely. Sometimes, a fussy eater may eat her fruit but refuse her milk, for example. Nearly all mothers who breastfeed see this refusal as a sign that they should switch to other nourishments. Some mothers feel as if their babies are rejecting them personally. This is not at all the case. Your baby is simply upset. It is not necessary to stop breastfeeding at this point; on the contrary, it would be a bad time to choose to wean your baby.

> "Around 15 weeks, my daughter suddenly started nursing less. After 5 minutes, she would start playing around with my nipple. After that had gone on for 2 weeks, I decided to start supplementing my milk with formula, but she wouldn't have any of that either. This phase lasted 4 weeks. During that time, I worried she would suffer from some kind of nutrition deficiency, especially when I saw my milk supply starting to diminish. But now she is drinking like she used to again, and my milk supply is as plentiful as ever. In fact, I seem to have more."
>
> Hannah's mom, 19th week

My Diary

Signs My Baby Is Growing Again

Between 14 and 17 weeks, you may notice your baby starting to show any of the following behaviors, signs that he is ready to make the next leap into the world of events. Cross off the signs your baby shows on the list below.

❏ Cries more often; is often bad-tempered, cranky, or fretful

❏ Wants you to keep him busy

❏ Needs more support for his head

❏ Wants more physical contact

❏ Sleeps poorly

❏ Loses his appetite

❏ Is shier with strangers than he was before

❏ Is quieter, less vocal

❏ Is less lively

❏ Has pronounced mood swings

❏ Wants more physical contact during nursing

❏ Sucks his thumb, or sucks more often than before

OTHER CHANGES YOU NOTICE

_____

_____

She May Be Moody

Some babies' moods swing wildly at this time. One day they are all smiles, but the next they do nothing but cry. These mood swings may even occur from one moment to the next. One minute they're shrieking with laughter, and the next they burst into tears. Sometimes, they even start to cry in the middle of laughing. Some mothers say that both the laughter and the tears seem to be dramatic and exaggerated, almost unreal.

She May Be Listless

Your baby may stop making his familiar sounds for a brief period or may occasionally lie motionless, staring into thin air or fidgeting with her ears, for example. It's very common for babies at this age to seem listless and preoccupied. Many mothers find their infants' behavior peculiar and alarming. But actually, this apathy is just a lull before the storm. This interlude is a sign that your baby is on the brink of making many discoveries in a new world where she will learn to acquire many new skills.

How This Leap May Affect You

On one hand, you may find it hard to believe your baby is 19 weeks old, but on the other, you may have felt every hour of those 19 weeks, having been up for so many of them, comforting a wailing baby. Here are some ways this latest leap may be affecting you.

You May (Still) Be Exhausted

During a fussy period, most mothers complain increasingly of fatigue, headaches, nausea, backaches, or emotional problems. Some less fortunate mothers contend with more than one of these problems at the same time. They blame their symptoms on lack of sleep, having to constantly carry their little screamers, or worrying about their unhappy infants. The real cause of these symptoms, though, is the stress of constantly coping with a cranky baby. Some mothers visit their family doctor and are prescribed an iron supplement, or go to a physiotherapist for their back troubles, but the real problem is that they are nearing the end of their tether. Especially now, make time for yourself, and give yourself a treat now and then. But remember that your baby will eventually come to your aid by learning the skills that she needs to deal with her new world, and then the sun will shine again.

> "If my daughter won't settle down for a few nights in a row and wants to be walked around all the time, I get a terrible backache. At times like these, I wish she was gone for just one night. I'm a total wreck."
>
> Emily's mom, 17th week

You May Feel Trapped

Toward the end of a fussy period, a mother sometimes feels so confined by her baby's demands that she almost feels she's in prison. It seems as if the baby is calling all the shots, and the mother feels irritated by her "selfishness." It's no wonder that mothers sometimes wish their babies would just disappear for a while. Some even daydream about how wonderful it would be if they could put them out of their minds for just one night.

> "This week, there were moments when I would have liked to forget that I had a son altogether. Aren't human beings weird creatures? At times, I felt so closed in. I just had to get away from it all, and so that's what I did."
>
> Bob's mom, 18th week

> "When I'm at the store with my baby and he wakes up and starts crying, everybody stares at me. I get all hot and bothered. Sometimes I think, 'Why don't you shut up, you stupid kid!'"
>
> Steven's mom, 18th week

You May Feel Resentful

After a few weeks of living with a fussy baby, you may be shocked to find that you are beginning to resent this demanding little person who disrupts your life so much. Don't blame yourself. This is an understandable and surprisingly common reaction. Many mothers grow more irritated toward the end of a fussy period. They are convinced their baby has no valid reason for making such a fuss, and they are inclined to let their babies cry a little longer than they used to. Some begin to wonder what "spoiling" actually means, and think they may be giving in to his whims too much. They may also begin to wonder if they should be teaching their little ones to consider that mothers have feelings, too.

Now and then, a mother may feel a surge of aggression toward her persistent little screamer, especially when the baby won't stop crying, and the mother is at her wit's end. Having these feelings is not abnormal or dangerous, but acting on them is. Get help long before you lose control. Shaking, especially, can be harmful. Remember, while it is normal to feel frustrated and angry with your baby at times, *never* shake a baby. Shaking a young child can easily cause internal bleeding of the spine just below the skull which can result in brain damage that may lead to learning difficulties later on or even death.

"My son refused to continue with his feeding and started having an incredible crying tantrum, while I just kept trying to get his milk down his throat. When the same thing happened with the next bottle, I felt myself becoming terribly angry because none of my little distraction tricks were working. I felt as if I were going around in circles. So I put him on the floor where he would be safe and let him scream his lungs out. When he finally stopped, I went back into the room, and he finished his bottle."

Bob's mom, 19th week

"I started to feel my temper rise every time my daughter launched into one of her crying fits because I'd left her on her own for just a second. So I let her get on with it and ignored her."

Ashley's mom, 17th week

"The last four evenings, my son started screaming at 8:00 P.M. After consoling him for 2 nights in a row, I'd had enough. So I let him cry until 10:30 P.M. He's certainly persistent, I'll give him that!"

Kevin's mom, 16th week

How Your Baby's New Skills Emerge

Because this fussy phase lasts longer than the previous ones, most mothers immediately sense that this period is different. They are concerned about their babies' seemingly slower progress and the fact that the babies seem to have a sudden aversion to the things they liked in the past. But don't worry. From this age on, the new skills are much more complicated to learn. Your little one needs more time.

"My baby seems to be making such slow progress. Before he was 15 weeks old, he developed much faster. It's almost as if he's come to a standstill these past few weeks. At times, I find this to be very upsetting."

Matt's mom, 17th week

"It's almost as if my son is on the verge of making new discoveries, but something seems to be holding him back. When I play with him, I can sense there's something missing, but I don't know what it is. So I'm playing the waiting game, too."

Steven's mom, 17th week

"My daughter has been trying to do lots of new things this week. All of a sudden, it hit me how much she can do at just 4 months, and to tell you the truth, I feel very proud of her."

Jenny's mom, 18th week

At approximately 19 weeks, you will notice that your baby is trying again to learn new skills, because this is the age when babies will generally begin to explore the world of events. This world offers her a huge repertoire of event-skills. Your baby will choose the skills best suited to her—the ones that she wants to explore. You can help her do what she really is ready to do, rather than trying to push her in any and every direction.

After the last leap forward, your baby was able to see, hear, smell, taste, and feel smooth and continuous transitions. But all these transitions had to be relatively simple, such as a toy moved steadily across the floor in front of him. As soon as they became more complicated, he was no longer able to follow them. In the new world that babies begin to explore at approximately 19 weeks, most babies will start to perceive and experiment with short, familiar sequences. This new ability will affect a baby's entire behavior.

As soon as a baby is able to make several flowing movements in sequence, this will give him more opportunities with objects within his grasp. He may, for instance, be able to repeat the same flowing movement several times in succession. You may now see him trying to shake playthings from side to side or up and down. He may also attempt to press, push, bang, or beat a toy repeatedly. Besides repeating the same movement, he may now learn to perform a short sequence of different movements smoothly. For instance, he may grab an object with one hand, then try to pass it to the other hand. Or he may grab a plaything and immediately attempt to put it in his mouth. He may now even learn to use a toy such as a telephone, putting a finger in a hole and spinning the dial. He is capable of turning a plaything around and looking at it from every pos-

Brain Changes

Recordings of babies' brain waves show that dramatic changes occur at approximately 4 months. Also, babies' head circumferences suddenly increase between 15 and 18 weeks.

sible angle. From now on, he is able to carry out a thorough examination of any object within reach.

In addition, your baby may now learn how to adjust the movements of his body, especially his upper arm, lower arm, hand, and fingers, to reach the exact spot where the plaything lies, and he can learn to correct his movements as he goes along. For instance, if a toy is farther to the left, his arm will move to the left in one flowing movement. If it is more to the right, his arm will immediately move to the correct spot. The same applies to an object near at hand, one that is farther away, or a toy hanging higher or lower. He will see it, reach for it, grab it, and pull it toward him, all in one smooth movement. As long as an object is within arm's length, your little one will now actually be able to reach out and grasp the object of his choice.

When your baby is toying with these movements, you may see him twist and turn. He may now learn to roll over or spin on his back more easily. He may also make his first crawling attempts, because he is now capable of pulling his knees up, pushing off, and stretching.

He may also learn to make a short series of sounds now. If he does, he will develop his chatter, which started after the previous leap, to include alternating vowel and consonant sounds. He will gradually use all of these sounds to speak in "sentences." This *abba baba tata* is what adults fondly call "baby talk." You could say he is now able to become just as flexible with his voice as he is with the rest of his body.

All over the world, babies start making these short sentences when they reach this age. For example, Russian, Chinese, and American babies

(continued on page 124)

 My Diary

How My Baby Explores the New World of Events

Check off the boxes below as you notice your baby changing. Stop filling this out once the next stormy period begins, heralding the coming of the next leap.

The big change that allows your baby eventually to make sense of the world of events begins at around 15 weeks. The leap into this world is a pretty big one, and the skills that come with it only start to take wing around 19 weeks. Even then, it may be a while before you see any of the skills listed here. It's most likely he will not acquire many of these skills until months later.

BODY CONTROL

❑ Starts moving virtually every part of his body as soon as he is put on the floor

❑ Rolls over from his back onto his tummy

❑ Rolls over from his tummy onto his back

❑ Is able to fully stretch his arms when lying on his tummy

❑ Lifts his bottom and attempts to push off; does not succeed

❑ Raises himself onto his hands and feet when lying on his tummy, then tries to move forward; does not succeed

❑ Attempts to crawl; manages to slide forward or backward

❑ Supports himself with forearms, and raises upper half of his body

❑ Sits up straight (all by himself) when leaning against you

❑ Attempts to sit up straight when he's by himself and briefly succeeds by leaning on his forearms and bringing his head forward

❑ Remains upright in high chair with cushions for support

❑ Enjoys moving his mouth—puckers his lips in a variety of ways, sticks his tongue out

GRABBING, TOUCHING, AND FEELING

❑ Succeeds in grabbing objects

❑ Grabs things with either hand

❑ Is able to grab an object with either hand if it comes into contact with the object, even if he is not looking at it

❑ Is able to pass objects between hands

❑ Sticks your hand in his mouth

❑ Touches or sticks his hands in your mouth as you talk

❑ Sticks objects in his mouth to feel and bite them

❑ Is able to pull a cloth from his face by himself, slowly at first

❑ Recognizes a toy or other familiar object, even if it is partially covered by something; will soon give up unsuccessful attempts to retrieve the toy

❑ Tries shaking a plaything

❑ Tries banging a plaything on a tabletop

❑ Deliberately throws a plaything on the floor

❑ Tries grabbing things just out of reach

❑ Tries to play with an activity center

❑ Understands the purpose of a particular toy; for example, he will dial his toy telephone

❑ Studies objects closely; he is especially interested in minute details of toys, hands, and mouths

(continued)

My Diary (cont.)

WATCHING

❑ Stares in fascination at repetitive activities, such as jumping up and down, slicing bread, or brushing hair

❑ Stares in fascination at the movements of your lips and tongue when you are talking

❑ Searches for you and is able to turn around to do this

❑ Looks for a plaything that is partially hidden

❑ Reacts to his own reflection in mirror; he is either scared or laughs

❑ Holds a book in his hands and stares at pictures

LISTENING

❑ Listens intently to sounds coming from your lips

❑ Responds to his own name

❑ Is now able to distinguish one particular sound in a medley of different sounds, so responds to his own name even if there are background noises

❑ Genuinely understands one or more words; for example, he looks at his teddy bear if asked "Where's your teddy bear?" (Won't respond correctly if the toy is not in its usual place.)

❑ Will respond appropriately to an approving or scolding voice

❑ Recognizes the opening bars of a song

TALKING

❑ Makes new sounds, using his lips and tongue: *ffft-ffft-ffft, vvv-vvv, zzz, sss, brrr, arrr, rrr, grrr, prrr*. This *rrr* is known as the "lip r." Your baby may particularly like to do this with food in his mouth!

❏ Uses consonants: d, b, l, m

❏ Babbles. Utters first "words": *mommom, dada, abba, hada-hada, baba, tata*

❏ Makes noises when yawning and is aware of these noises

BODY LANGUAGE

❏ Stretches his arms out to be picked up

❏ Smacks his lips when hungry; waves arms and legs

❏ Opens his mouth and moves his face toward food and drink

❏ "Spits" when he's had enough to eat

❏ Pushes the bottle or breast away when he has had enough

❏ Turns away from the feeding of his own accord when full

OTHER SKILLS

❏ May exaggerate his actions; for example, when you respond to his coughing, he will cough again, then laugh

❏ Gets grumpy when becoming impatient

❏ Screams if he fails to do what he seems to be trying to do

❏ Has one special cuddly toy, such as a blanket

OTHER CHANGES YOU NOTICE

_____

_____

_____

all babble the same language initially. Eventually, the babies will start to develop their babble-sounds into proper words of their native language, and they will stop using the universal babble sounds. Each baby will become more proficient at imitating the language he hears being spoken around him because he will get the most response and praise when he produces something close to home.

Apparently, everyone's ancestors must have felt as if they were being addressed personally when they heard their offspring say "dada" or "mommom," because the words for mommy and daddy are very similar in many different languages. The truth, though, is that the little babbler is carrying out a number of technical experiments with short, familiar sequences of the same sound element: "da" or "mom."

Your baby may now begin to recognize a short series of flowing sounds. He may be fascinated by a series of notes running smoothly up and down a musical scale. He may now respond to all voices that express approval, and he may be startled by voices that scold. It doesn't matter what language is used to express these feelings, since he will be able to perceive the differences in tones of voice. For the first time, he is now able to pick out one specific voice in the middle of a commotion.

Your baby may also start to recognize short, familiar tunes. At 19 weeks, babies are even capable of hearing whether interruptions in a piece of music being played are genuine or do not belong to that particular piece of music, even if they have never heard the music before. In an unusual experiment, researchers found that if a part of a minuet by Mozart was played to babies, they showed a definite response if the music was interrupted by random pauses. Babies may also start recognizing words for the very first time.

Your baby may now learn to see a short, familiar sequence of images. For instance, he may be fascinated by the up-and-down motion of a bouncing ball. There are endless examples to be seen, all disguised as normal, everyday activities or events, such as someone shaking his bottle up and down, stirring a saucepan, hammering a nail, opening and closing a door, slicing bread, filing nails, brushing hair, the dog scratching itself, somebody pacing back and forth in the room, and a whole range of other events and activities.

Two more basic characteristics of the world of events should be mentioned here. First, as adults, we usually experience an event as an inseparable whole. We do not see a falling-rising-falling ball—we see a bouncing ball. Even when the event has only just begun, we already know it is a bouncing ball. As long as it continues, this remains one and the same event—an event for which we have a name. Second, most events are defined by the observer. For instance, when we speak, we don't separate the words clearly, but run one into the next without a pause. The listener creates the boundaries between words, giving the impression that they are heard one at a time. It is exactly this special power of perception that will begin to be available to your baby between 14 and 17 weeks.

Your Baby's Choices: A Key to His Personality

The world of events offers a wide range of new skills to your baby. From the opportunities available to him, your little one will make his own selections, based on his own inclinations, interests, and physical characteristics. Some babies may want to concentrate on feeling skills, while others may choose the watching skills, and yet another group will specialize in physical activities. Obviously, there are also babies who like to learn a variety of different skills without specializing in any one of them. Every baby makes his own choice, because every baby is unique.

Watch your baby closely to determine his particular interests. If you respect his choices, you will discover the special pattern that makes your baby unique. All babies love anything new. It's important that you respond when you notice any new skills or interests. Your baby will enjoy it if you share these new discoveries, and his learning will progress more quickly.

The more your baby comes in contact with events and the more she plays with them, the greater her understanding of them will be and the more proficient she will become. It doesn't matter which discoveries she chooses to make in this new world. She may pay close attention to music, sounds, and words. Or she may choose looking and observing, or physical activities. Later on, it will be easy for her to put the knowledge and experience she has gained learning one skill to good use when learning another.

Besides wanting to experiment with the discoveries she makes in this world of events, your baby will also become tremendously interested in everything going on around her. This may now occupy most of her waking hours, because she will want to look at and listen to everything she possibly can. Even better (or worse!), every toy, household item, and gardening or kitchen utensil within a small arm's length is hers for the taking. You are no longer her only toy. She may try to become involved in the world around her by pushing herself forward with her hands and feet, toward something new, and away from her mom. She may now have less time to spare for her old cuddling games. Some parents feel a little rejected by this.

Even so, she still needs your help just as much as ever. Your baby's fascination with the whole world around her is typical at this age. You probably have begun to sense these new needs, and your main contribution can be supplying your baby with enough playthings and waiting to see how she responds. Only if you notice that she has real difficulties in fully understanding a toy should you give her a hand. You'll also want to keep an eye on your baby to make sure she uses her hands, feet, limbs, and body properly when reaching out to grab objects. If you see that she has a particular problem, you can help her to practice activities like rolling over, turning, and sometimes even crawling, sitting, or standing up.

Help Your Baby Explore the New World through Body Movement

Perhaps you have seen your baby spin on her back and squirm in an attempt to roll over from her tummy onto her back. If you did, you saw your little one toying with a short series of flowing movements of several body parts. She can now make these because she is living in the world of events. However, being able to make several flowing movements in succession does not automatically mean that she is successful in rolling over or crawling, for that matter. It usually takes quite some trial and error to get there.

"My little one is trying to roll over from her back onto her tummy. She's not having much success yet, and it's making her awfully upset. She really gets exasperated."

Ashley's mom, 20th week

"My son is practicing like crazy to learn to roll over properly. But when he's lying facedown, he pulls both arms and legs up at the same time, straining and moaning like mad, and that's as far as he gets."

John's mom, 21st week

"My daughter manages to roll over only when she gets really angry. To her own surprise, I might add."

Laura's mom, 20th week

Here's a playful way to help your baby practice rolling from her back onto her tummy. Lay your baby on her back, and hold a colorful plaything next to her. To reach it, she will be forced to stretch her body and turn so that she can't help but roll over. Of course, you have to encourage her in her efforts and praise her for trying.

You can also make a game out of helping her to roll from her tummy onto her back. One way is to lay your baby on her stomach and hold a colorful toy behind her, either to her left or to her right. When she turns to reach for it, move the plaything farther behind her back. At a certain point, she will roll over, simply from turning a little too much when reaching for the toy. Her heavy head will automatically help her in the process.

At about this age, babies often try to crawl. The problem with crawling is the moving forward part. Most babies would love to move forward, and they do try. Some babies get into the right starting position—they tuck their knees under their bodies, stick their bottoms in the air, and push off—but they're not successful. Other babies get into the crawling position but bounce up and down without moving forward. There are also little squirmers who slide backward, because they push off with their hands. Others push off with one foot, thus going around in circles. Some lucky babies fumble around for a while and hit on forward motion seemingly by accident. This is the exception rather than the rule at this age.

"I think my baby may want to crawl, but I have the feeling he doesn't know how yet. He squirms and wriggles, but he doesn't move an inch. He gets really upset then."

Frankie's mom, 20th week

Many mothers try to help their babies crawl. They carefully push their wriggling infants' bottoms forward, or they put all kinds of attractive ob-

Let Him Wriggle Around Naked

Your baby has to practice if he wants to learn how to roll over, turn, and crawl properly. It will be a lot more fun, and much easier for him, if he is not wearing his clothes and diaper. Lots of physical exercise will give him the opportunity to get to know his body and help him to increase his control over it.

jects just out of their reach in an attempt to coax them forward. Sometimes these maneuvers will do the trick, and the baby somehow manages to move a little. Some babies do this by throwing themselves forward with a thud. Others lie on their tummies and push themselves forward with their legs, while using their arms to steer themselves in the right direction.

If you imitate your baby's attempts, she may find it absolutely hilarious. She may also really enjoy watching you show her how to crawl properly. Nearly every child who is having crawling problems will be fascinated by your attempts. Just try it and see!

Help Your Baby Explore the New World through Manipulation and Examination

In the world of events, your baby's arms, hands, and fingers are just like the rest of her body—able to make several flowing movements in succession. As a result, she is able to practice reaching for, grabbing, and pulling a toy toward herself in one smooth movement and manipulate it in all sorts of ways such as shaking, banging, or poking. Thus she can examine the objects she can lay her hands on. And that is just what she wants to do at this age, though again she needs a lot of practice to become perfect.

Let her explore as many objects as she wants. She may turn them around, shake them, bang them, slide them up and down, and stick an interesting part in her mouth to feel and taste it. An activity center offers a variety of these hand and finger exercises all on one board. It usually has an old-fashioned telephone dial, which produces the appropriate clicking sounds when the baby turns it. It may have a knob that also makes a noise when pressed. There could be animals to slide up and down and revolving cylinders and balls to turn, and so on. Each separate activity will emit a different sound when your baby handles it. Lots of babies love their activity centers. But don't expect your little one to understand and use all these features properly at first. She's just a beginner!

When you see that your baby is trying to do something without much success, you can help her by holding her hand to show her how to do it properly. Or if your baby has a preference for observing how things are done, let her watch how your hand does it. Either way, you will encourage her to be playful and clever with her little hands.

"We had an activity center hanging in the playpen for weeks. My son looked at it from time to time, but he wouldn't do anything with it. But this week, he suddenly started grabbing it. Now he just loves touching and turning all those knobs. You can tell he's really exploring the whole board. He does get tired quickly, though, because he has to push himself up with one hand all the time."

Paul's mom, 18th week

If your baby gets tired because she has to push herself up with one hand all the time, support her so she can use her hands freely. For instance, put her on your lap and examine a toy together. She will love being able to play while sitting comfortably. Besides, when she is sitting, she will be able to look at playthings from a completely different angle. Just watch her to see if she does different things with toys when she is sitting comfortably. Perhaps you may even see new activities.

"I put my baby in his high chair for the first time and propped him up with a cushion. He immediately discovered that you can do certain things with toys while sitting up that you can't do on the floor. When I gave him his plastic key ring, he first started banging it on the tabletop, and then he kept throwing it on the floor. He did that about 20 times in a row. He thought it was great fun and couldn't stop laughing."

Paul's mom, 19th week

If your baby is a keen explorer, you can enrich her environment by offering her playthings and other objects of different shapes, such as round or square things, or made of different materials, such as wood and plastic. Give her fabrics with different textures or soft, rough, and smooth paper to play with. Many babies love empty, crisp bags, because they slowly change shape and make wonderful crackling sounds when crumpled. Give your baby objects with rough edges or dents. Most babies have a weakness for weird shapes. The shape of a plastic key, for instance, will challenge her to make a closer inspection. Many babies find the jagged edge particularly intriguing and will want to touch it, look at it, and taste it.

Some babies are drawn to the smallest details. If you have such a tiny researcher, she will probably look at an object from all sides, examining it

 Baby Care

Make Your Home Baby-Proof

You probably began this process a long time ago, but since your baby is now becoming increasingly mobile, it's time to do a quick safety check to make sure he is safe.

- Never leave small objects, such as buttons, pins, or coins, near your baby.

- When your baby is on your lap during feeding, make sure he can't suddenly grab a cup or mug containing a hot drink.

- Never leave hot drinks on a table within your baby's reach. Don't even leave them on a high table. If the baby tries to reach it by pulling at the leg of the table—or, even worse, the tablecloth—he could spill the drink over himself.

- Use a guard or fence around stoves and fireplaces.

- Keep poisonous substances such as turpentine, bleach, and medicine out of your baby's reach and in childproof containers when possible.

- Make sure electrical outlets are secured with socket covers and that there are no trailing wires anywhere.

very carefully. She will really take her time and carry out a close inspection of the object. She will fuss with the smallest of protrusions. It may take ages before she's finished stroking, feeling, and rubbing textures and examining shapes and colors. Nothing seems to escape her inquisitive eyes and probing mind. If she decides to examine you, she will do this meticulously, too. If she studies your hand, she will usually begin with one finger, stroke the nail, and then look and feel how it moves, before she proceeds to the next finger. If she's examining your mouth, she will usually inspect every single tooth. Stimulate her eye for detail by giving her toys and objects that will interest her.

> "My daughter is definitely going to be a dentist. I almost choke every time she inspects my mouth. She probes around and practically shoves her whole fist inside my mouth. She makes it very clear she doesn't appreciate being interrupted while she's working when I try to close my mouth to give her a kiss on the hand."
>
> Emily's mom, 21st week

Does your baby want to grab everything you are eating or drinking? Most babies do. So, take care not to drink hot tea or coffee with a wriggly baby on your lap. In an unguarded moment, she may suddenly decide to grab your cup and tip the hot contents all over her hands and face.

> "My son will try to grab my sandwich with his mouth already open in anticipation. Whatever he manages to grab, he swallows immediately. The funny thing is, he seems to enjoy everything."
>
> Kevin's mom, 19th week

Help Your Baby Explore the New World through Sight

Is your baby a real observer? The daily routine in every household is full of events that your baby may enjoy watching. Many babies love to watch their mothers preparing food, setting the table, getting dressed, or working in the garden. They are now capable of understanding the different actions or events involved in various activities, such as putting plates on the table, slicing bread, making sandwiches, brushing hair, filing nails, and mowing the lawn. If your baby enjoys observing things, let her watch your daily activities. All you have to do is to make sure she is in a perfect position to observe them. It really is no extra trouble for you, but it will be an enjoyable learning experience for her.

> "My little one smacks her lips, kicks her legs, and reaches out with her hands as soon as she sees me making sandwiches. She's obviously aware of what I'm doing, and she's asking to be fed."
>
> Hannah's mom, 20th week

Some babies at this age already enjoy looking at picture books in which events are shown. If your baby enjoys this, she may want to hold the book herself, using both hands, and gaze at the illustration in wonder. She may make a real effort to hold the book and concentrate on the pictures, but after a while the book will usually end up in her mouth.

You can start to play the first peek-a-boo and hide-and-seek games at this age. As soon as your baby becomes familiar with the world of events, she may recognize a plaything, even when she can see only part of it. If you see her looking quizzically at a partially hidden toy, or if you want to turn her attempts to retrieve a toy into a game of hide-and-seek, move the object about a little to make it easier for her to recognize. At this age, she is still quick to give up. The idea that an object continues to exist all the time, wherever it is, is not yet within her mental grasp.

Help Your Baby Explore the New World through Language and Music

Does your baby make "babbling sentences"? Sometimes it may sound as if your little one is really telling you a story. This is because in the world of events your baby becomes just as flexible with her voice as with the rest

(continued on page 136)

Top Games for This Wonder Week

Here are games and activities that most babies like best now. Remember, all babies are different. See what your baby responds to best.

HAPPY TALK

Talk as often as possible to your baby about the things he sees, hears, tastes, and feels. Talk about the things he does. Keep your sentences short and simple. Emphasize the important words. For instance: "feel this—*grass*," "*daddy's* coming," "listen—the *doorbell*," or "open your *mouth*."

WHAT HAPPENS NEXT?

First you say, "I'm going to (dramatic pause) pinch your *nose*." Then grab his nose and gently wiggle it about. You can do the same with his ears, hands, and feet. Find out what he enjoys most. If you play this game regularly, he will know exactly what you are going to do next. Then he will watch your hands with increasing excitement and shriek with laughter when you grab his nose. This game will familiarize him with both his body and the words for its parts as you play together.

LOOKING AT PICTURES

Show your baby a brightly colored picture in a book. He may even want to look at several pictures. Make sure the pictures are bright, clear, and include things he recognizes. Talk about the pictures together, and point out the real object if it's in the room.

SING SONGS

Many babies really love songs, particularly when they are accompanied by movements, such as "*Pat a cake, pat a cake, baker's man.*" But they also enjoy being rocked to the rhythm of a song or nursery rhyme. Babies recognize songs by their melody, rhythm, and intonation.

TICKLING GAME

This familiar song encourages tickling, which your baby may love.

This little piggy went to market . . .
And this little piggy stayed at home . . .
This little piggy ate roast beef . . .
And this little piggy had none . . .
This little piggy went . . .
Weeweeweewee all the way home.

While saying this, wiggle each of your baby's toes in turn, before finally running your fingers up his body and tickling him in the neck.

PEEK-A-BOO

Cover your baby's face with a blanket, and ask: "Where's. . . . ?" Watch him to see if he can remove the blanket from his face on his own. If he can't do this yet, help him by holding his hand and slowly pulling the flannel away with him. When he can see you again each time, say "boo"—this helps to mark the event for him. Keep the game simple at this age; otherwise, it will be too difficult for him.

MIRROR GAME

Look in a mirror together. Usually a baby will prefer looking and smiling at his own reflection first. But then, he will look at your reflection, and then back to the real you. This normally bewilders him, and he will usually look back and forth at you and your reflection, as if he can't make up his mind which one is his real mother. If you start talking to him, he will be even more amazed, because no one but his real mother talks like that. This may reassure him that he's with the right person, so he may start laughing before he snuggles up to you.

of her body. She starts to repeat whatever syllables she already knows and string them together to form a "sentence," such as *dadadada* and *babababababa*. She may also experiment with intonation and volume. When she hears herself making a new sound, she may stop for a while and laugh before resuming the conversation.

It's still important to talk to your baby as often as possible. Try to respond to what she says, imitate her new sounds, and reply when she "asks" or "tells" you something. Your reactions encourage her to practice using her voice.

You may notice that your baby understands a word or short sentence, although she cannot say the word or words herself. Try asking in familiar surroundings "Where's your teddy?" and you may see her actually look at her teddy bear.

In the world of events, babies are able to understand a short, familiar series of sounds such as "Want to go for a ride?" This doesn't mean that they understand a sentence in the same way that an older child or an adult does. Your baby is hearing a familiar pattern of syllables along with the intonation of your voice as a single sound event. This is just the kind of simple string of patterns and changes that makes up an event for her in this world.

Being able to recognize the teddy-bear-sentence event doesn't mean that your baby can recognize sound events under all circumstances. If you were looking in a toy store window with your baby and saw a teddy identical to her own, for example, you might try "Where's your teddy?" with absolutely no success, since she really won't be able to understand meaning in a context so far removed from her own familiar surroundings.

Because mothers naturally repeat the same or similar sentences over and over again as they go through their daily routines, babies gradually come to recognize them. This is the only way they can begin to learn about speech, and all babies understand words and phrases long before they can say them.

Top Toys for This Wonder Week

Here are toys and other objects that most babies like best as they explore the world of events. Nearly all everyday household items will appeal to your baby. Try to find out what your baby likes best. Be careful, though, to screen out any that may be harmful to him.

- Bath toys. Your baby will enjoy playing with a variety of household items in the bath, such as a measuring cup, plastic colander, plant spray bottle, watering can, soap dish, and plastic shampoo bottles.

- Activity center

- Ball with gripping notches, preferably with a bell inside

- Plastic or inflatable rattle

- A screw-top container with some rice in it

- Crackly paper

- Mirror

- Photographs or pictures of other babies

- Photographs or pictures of objects or animals he recognizes by name

- CD with children's songs

- Wheels that really turn, such as those on a toy car

"In our living room, there's a painting of flowers on one wall and a photo of my son on another. When I ask him 'Where are the flowers?' or 'Where's Paul?' he always looks at the correct picture. I'm not imagining it, because the pictures are on opposite sides of the room."

Paul's mom, 23rd week

You will be really enthusiastic and proud when you discover that your baby understands her first short sentence. Initially, you may not believe what happened. You may keep repeating the sentence until you are convinced it wasn't just a coincidence. Next, you may create a new situation to practice the little sentence your baby already recognizes. For instance, you may put the teddy bear in every conceivable spot in a room to test if your baby knows where it is. You may even show her photographs of her teddy bear to see if she recognizes it. Many mothers change the way they talk to their babies at this age. They will say sentences more slowly to their babies, and often they will use just single words instead of whole sentences.

Is your baby a budding music lover? In the world of events she may be fascinated by a series of notes running smoothly up and down the musical scale, and she is able to recognize a short, familiar sequence such as the opening tune of a commercial on TV. Help her with her musical talents. Let her hear the music she likes best. Your music lover may also appreciate all kinds of sounds. If so, it is worth stimulating and encouraging this interest. Some babies grab toys and objects primarily to find out if they will make a noise of any kind. They turn around sound-producing objects, not for inspection, but to see if the sound changes when the object is turned quickly or slowly. These babies will squeeze a toy in a variety of ways to see if it produces different sounds. Give her sound-producing objects to play with and help her to use them properly.

The Virtue of Patience

When your baby is learning new skills, she may sometimes try your patience. Both you and your baby have to adjust to her progress and rene-

gotiate the rules to restore peace and harmony. Remember, from now on
your baby will no longer be completely dependent on you for her enjoyment, since she is now in touch with the world around her. She can do and
understand a lot more than she did in the past, and, of course, she thinks
she knows it all. You may think *she* is a handful. She thinks *you* are! If you
recognize this behavior, you could say you are having the first independence struggle with your infant.

"Every time my daughter sits with me on my favorite chair, she tries to
grab the tassels on the lamp shade. I don't like her doing that, so I pull
her away and say 'no.'"

Jenny's mom, 20th week

What irritates many mothers more than anything else is a baby's ob-
session for grabbing everything within reach or anything she sees in
passing—especially when she seems to prefer doing this over playing with
her mother. Some see it as antisocial—sometimes even slightly selfish—on
the part of their little ones. Others feel that the baby is still too young to
be touching everything in sight—plants, coffee cups, books, stereo equipment, eyeglasses—nothing is safe from her exploring hands. Most mothers
try to curb this urge for independence by stopping their babies in every
way possible when they again push away from them and toward the things
that take their fancy now. A mother may often try to distract her infant
with cuddling games or a tight embrace as she wriggles and squirms in her
arms to get at something. But both methods will nearly always have the
opposite effect. The baby will squirm and wriggle with even more determination as she struggles to free herself from her long-suffering mother.
Other mothers try to discourage this grabbing mania by firmly saying
"no." Sometimes this works.

Impatience can be a nuisance. Most mothers think their babies should
learn a little patience at this age. They don't always respond to their babies as quickly as they used to. When the baby wants something, or wants
to do something, a mother may now make her wait for a few brief mo-

ments. She may insist on sitting up straight, on being where the action is, and staying somewhere as long as she likes. The same goes for eating and sleeping. Grabbing food impatiently is particularly irritating to most mothers. Some put an immediate stop to it.

> "My daughter went berserk as soon as she saw her bowl of food. She couldn't seem to gobble it up fast enough. I found it terribly annoying, so I taught her to wait until we all sat down at the table. Now she's no longer impatient. She really waits and watches us serve dinner."
>
> Nina's mom, 22nd week

Hurting someone is not funny. Now that the baby is stronger and understands the world of events, she is also capable of causing physical pain. She may bite, chew, and pull at your face, arms, ears, and hair. She may pinch and twist your skin. Sometimes she will do this hard enough that it really hurts. Most mothers feel that their babies could easily show a little more consideration and respect for others. They are no longer amused by biting, pulling, and pinching.

Some mothers rebuke their babies if they get too excited. They do this by letting them know immediately that they have gone too far. Usually they do this verbally by saying "ouch," loudly and sternly. If they notice that a baby is preparing to launch a new attack, they warn her with

♡ Baby Care

Don't Lose Control

Now and again, a mother may feel a surge of aggression toward her little troublemaker. Remember that having these feelings is not abnormal or dangerous, but acting on them is. Try to calm yourself, and if you can't, be sure to get help long before you lose control.

"careful." At this age, babies are perfectly capable of understanding a cautioning voice. Occasionally, a mother will really lose her temper.

"When my baby bites my nipple really hard, I really have to work to keep my cool. My immediate reaction is a furious desire to slap him. Before I had a baby, I couldn't understand how people could hit their children. Now I can."

Matt's mom, 20th week

Between 20 and 22 weeks, another period of comparative calm begins. Many mothers praise their babies' initiative and love of enterprise. Babies seem to have boundless energy now.

You are no longer your baby's only toy. He explores his surroundings with great determination and enjoyment. He grows increasingly impatient with only mother to play with. He wants action. He may try to wriggle off of your lap at the least opportunity if he spots anything of interest. He is obviously a lot more independent now.

"I put away my son's first baby clothes today and felt a pang of regret. Doesn't time fly? Letting go isn't easy. It's a very painful experience. He suddenly seems so grown up. I have a different kind of relationship with him now. He has become more of his own little person."

Bob's mom, 23rd week

"My baby drinks her bottle with her back toward me now, sitting up straight, not wanting to miss any of the world around her. She even wants to hold the bottle herself."

Laura's mom, 22nd week

"When my son is on my lap, he tries to lie almost flat so he doesn't miss anything going on behind him."

Frankie's mom, 23rd week

"I hardly ever put my baby in the playpen now. I think that he's too restricted in such a small space."

Bob's mom, 22nd week

"My son is starting to resent being carried around in the sling. At first, I thought he wanted more room because he's so active. But then I put him facing forward, and he's happy now that he's able to see everything."

Steven's mom, 21st week

Babies who like to be physically active no longer need to be handed the objects they want, because they will twist and turn in every direction to get them themselves.

"My daughter rolls from her tummy onto her back and wriggles and squirms all over the place to get to a plaything, or she'll crawl over to it. She's as busy as a bee all day long. She doesn't even have time to cry. I must say she seems happier than ever, and so are we."

Jenny's mom, 21st week

"My baby crawls and rolls in every direction. I can't stop her. She tries getting out of her bouncing chair, and she wants to crawl up onto the sofa. The other day we found her halfway into the dog basket. She's also very busy in the bath. There's hardly any water left in it once she's practically kicked it all out."

Emily's mom, 22nd week

During this time, the calm before the next storm, most babies are more cheerful. Even demanding, trying babies are happier at this stage. Perhaps this is because they are able to do more now and are less bored. Parents delight in this less-troubled, well-deserved time.

"My little one is in such a cheerful mood now. She laughs and 'tells stories.' It's wonderful to watch her."

Juliette's mom, 23rd week

"I'm enjoying every minute I spend with my daughter again. She's such a cutie, really easygoing."

Ashley's mom, 22nd week

"My son is suddenly easier. He's back in a regular routine, and he's sleeping better."

Frankie's mom, 23rd week

"My son is surprisingly sweet and cheerful. He goes to sleep without any complaining, which is an achievement in itself. He sleeps much longer now in the afternoons, compared to these past weeks. He's so different from how he was several months ago when he cried all day. Apart from a few ups and downs now and again, things are steadily improving."

Paul's mom, 22nd week

Place Photo Here

After the Leap

Age: _____

Reflections: _____

chapter 7

Wonder Week 26: The World of Relationships

At about 26 weeks, your baby will start to show the signs of yet another significant leap in his development. If you watch closely, you will see him doing or attempting to do many new things. Whether or not he is crawling at this stage, he will have become significantly more mobile as he learns to coordinate the action of his arms and legs and the rest of his body. Building on his knowledge of events, he his now able to begin to understand the many kinds of relationships among the things that make up his world.

One of the most significant relationships that your baby can now perceive is the distance between one thing and another. We take this for granted as adults, but for a baby it is an alarming discovery, a very radical change in his world. The world is suddenly a very big place in which he is but a tiny, if very vocal, speck. Something he wants can be on a high shelf or outside the range of his crib, and he has no way of getting to it. His mother can walk away, even if only into the next room, and she might as well have gone to China if he can't get to her because he's stuck in his crib or hasn't yet mastered crawling. Even if he is adept at crawling, he realizes that she moves much faster than he does and can get away from him.

This discovery can be very frightening for a baby, and it may make these few weeks quite taxing for his parents. But when you understand the source of this fear and uneasiness, there are many things you will be able to do to help. Naturally, once your baby learns to negotiate the space around him and control the distance between himself and the things he wants, he will be able to do much more on his own than he used to. But there will be a period during which he will need a lot of support.

Entering the world of relationships will affect everything your baby perceives and does. He senses these changes taking place at around 23 weeks, and that's when the disturbances begin. Caught up in a tangle of new impressions, he needs to touch base, return to his mommy, and cling to her for comfort. The familiar feeling of security and warmth she provides will help him to relax, let the newness sink in, and grow into the new world at his own pace. This fussy period often lasts about 4 weeks, although it may be as short as 1 week or as long as 5. Since one of the important skills he has to learn during this leap is how to handle the distance between his mom and himself, your baby may actually become fussy again for a while around 29 weeks, after his new skills have started to take wing. Do remember that if your baby is fussy, watch him closely to see if he is attempting to master new skills.

This Week's Fussy Signs

When your baby becomes aware that her world is changing, she will usually cry more easily. Many mothers may now call their babies cranky, bad-tempered, whiny, or discontented. If your baby is already strong willed, she may come across as being even more restless, impatient, or trouble-some. Almost all babies will cry less when they are picked up and cud-dled, nestled up against mommy, or at least kept company while they're playing.

> "My baby is starting to stand up for herself more and more. She makes demands, angrily ordering me to come to her or stay with her. In this way, she makes sure I am there to help reach her toys."
>
> Hannah's mom, 25th week

How You Know It's Time to Grow

Here are some of the signals that your baby may give you to let you know he's approaching this leap into the world of relationships.

She May Sleep Poorly

Your baby may sleep less than you are used to. Most babies have difficulty falling asleep or wake up sooner. Some don't want to nap during the day, and others don't want to go to bed at night. There are even those who refuse to do either.

> "Bedtime and naptime are accompanied by terrible screaming fits. My son yells furiously and practically climbs the walls. He'll shout at the top of his voice and practically wind himself. I just can't handle it. It seems as if I never see him lying peacefully in his crib anymore. I just pray it doesn't last forever."
>
> Bob's mom, 26th week

> "My baby's rhythm is totally off because he keeps waking up a little earlier each day. But apart from that, his sleep is normal."
>
> Frankie's mom, 25th week

She May Have "Nightmares"

Your baby may sleep uneasily at this time. Sometimes, babies can toss and turn and thrash about so much during their sleep that it looks as if they're having nightmares.

> "My daughter is a very restless sleeper. Sometimes, she'll let out a scream with her eyes closed, as if she's having a nightmare. So I'll lift her up for a minute to comfort her. These days, I usually let her play in the bathtub in the evening. I'm hoping it will calm her down and make her sleepier."
>
> Emily's mom, 23rd week

She May Become Shier

Your baby may not want other people to look at him, talk to him, or touch him, and he certainly won't want to sit on their laps. He may even start to want you in plain sight more often from this age on, even when there aren't any strangers around. Almost every mother will notice this now. At this age, shyness is especially obvious, for a very good reason—your baby is now able to understand that you can walk away and leave him behind.

> "My baby gets shier every day now. I need to be where he can see me at all times, and it has to be close to him. If I walk away, he'll try to crawl right after me."
>
> Matt's mom, 26th week

> "Even when I sit, I can hardly move without my daughter crying out in fear."
>
> Ashley's mom, 23rd week

She May Demand More Attention

Your baby may want you to stay with her longer, play with her more, or just look at her and her alone.

"My daughter is easily discontented and has to be kept busy. When she wakes up in her crib, for instance, she's really eager to see one of us right away. Also, she's quick to react. She doesn't just cry; she gets really mad. She's developing a will of her own."

Hannah's mom, 26th week

"All my baby wants is to get out of his playpen. I really have to keep him occupied on my lap or walk around with him."

Frankie's mom, 27th week

"My daughter was up to mischief all the time, behaving badly and acting cranky when she wanted attention. I had to play with her or find some way to occupy her all day long. As long as I did that, everything was okay."

Jenny's mom, 25th week

She May Always Want to Be with You

Your baby may insist on remaining in your arms. Many babies don't want to be put down very much. But some are not completely satisfied with the peaceful rest on mommy's lap that they cried for. As soon as they reach their goal, they start to push off and reach out for interesting things in the world around them.

"My son keeps on bothering me to sit on my lap. But as soon as I take him, there's almost no controlling him. He crawls all over me and gropes around like a monkey for anything he can get his hands on. It bothers me. I try playing games, but it's a waste of time. So he doesn't feel like playing with me, okay, but at least he could stop being so difficult. To be honest, I feel rejected when he refuses to play my game, so I put him back in his playpen. But as soon as I do, he'll immediately start wailing for me again."

Matt's mom, 27th week

The Gender Gap

Girls who want physical contact usually agree to play with their mothers, but boys who want physical contact insist on exploring the world around them at the same time.

She May Lose Her Appetite

Both babies who are breastfed and those who are bottle-fed sometimes drink less milk or refuse to drink at all. Other food and drink may be rejected, too. Often, babies also take longer to finish their meals. Somehow they seem to prefer the comfort of sucking or playing with the nipple over the contents of the bottle or breast.

"My baby always refuses to nurse in the morning and at night. He just pushes my breast away, and it really hurts. Then, when he's in bed and can't get to sleep, he does want to nurse. He'll drink a little and doze off in the middle of it."

                                            Matt's mom, 26th week

She May Be Listless

Your baby may stop making her familiar sounds. Or she may lie motionless, gazing around or staring in front of her. Mothers always find this behavior odd and alarming.

"Sometimes, all of a sudden, my little one will stare or gaze around silently. On days when she does it more than once, it makes me feel insecure. I start to wonder whether perhaps there's something wrong. I'm not accustomed to seeing her that way. So lifeless. As if she's sick or mentally challenged."

                                            Juliette's mom, 24th week

She May Refuse to Have Her Diaper Changed

Your baby may cry, kick, toss, and turn when she is set down to be changed or dressed. Many babies do. They just don't want their mothers to fiddle with their clothes.

> "When I put my baby on her back for a clean diaper, she'll cry every time. Usually not for very long, but it's always the same old story. Sometimes I wonder if there could be something wrong with her back."
>
> **Juliette's mom, 23rd week**

> "Almost every time I dress or change my baby, he'll scream bloody murder. When I have to pull a sweater over his head, we really have a field day. It drives me crazy."
>
> **Bob's mom, 24th week**

She May Reach for a Cuddly Object More Often

Some babies reach for a teddy, slipper, blanket, or towel more often. For most babies, anything soft will do, but some babies will accept only that one special thing. Sometimes, they'll cuddle it while sucking a thumb or twiddling an ear. It seems that a cuddly object spells safety, especially when mommy is busy.

> "When my daughter realizes whining and complaining aren't going to get her out of her playpen, she gives up. She sits and sucks her thumb with her blanket in her hand. It's adorable."
>
> **Ashley's mom, 24th week**

> "Thumb sucking is the big thing now. A lot of the time when my son starts to grow tired, he'll stick his thumb in his mouth, put his head on his teddy bear, and fall asleep. It's so touching."
>
> **Steven's mom, 23rd week**

My Diary

Signs My Baby Is Growing Again

Between 22 and 26 weeks, you may notice your baby starting to show any of these behaviors. They are probably signs that he is ready to make the next leap into the world of relationships. Check off the signs you see on the list below.

❏ Cries more and is bad-tempered, cranky, or whiny more often

❏ Wants you to keep him busy

❏ Wants more physical contact

❏ Sleeps poorly

❏ Loses appetite

❏ Doesn't want to be changed

❏ Is shier with strangers than he used to be

❏ Is quieter, less vocal

❏ Is less lively

❏ Sucks his thumb, or sucks more often than before

❏ Reaches for a cuddly toy, or does so more often than before

OTHER CHANGES YOU NOTICE

_____

_____

How This Leap May Affect You

Your baby certainly lets you know how these changes make her feel. This is bound to affect you. Here are some emotions you may feel this time around.

You May Be (Even More) Exhausted

Fussy periods can be nerve-racking. Mothers of especially demanding babies may feel like complete wrecks toward the end. They complain of stomachaches, backaches, headaches, and tension.

> "My son's crying gets on my nerves so much that I'm totally obsessed with keeping myself from crying. The tension it creates swallows up all of my energy."
>
> **Steven's mom, 25th week**

> "One night, I had to keep walking back and forth to put the pacifier in my daughter's mouth. Suddenly, at 12:30 A.M., she was wide awake. She stayed awake until 2:30 A.M. I'd already had a busy day, with a lot of headaches and backaches from walking her up and down. I just collapsed."
>
> **Emily's mom, 27th week**

You May Be Concerned

It's natural that you may feel troubled or nervous every time something seems to be the matter, and you can't figure out what it is. When very young babies are involved, mothers generally rationalize that they must be suffering from colic because nothing else seems to be wrong. At this age, however, mothers are quick to put two and two together and embrace the thought that their babies are fussy because they're teething. After all, most babies start cutting their teeth around this age. Still, there is no connection between clinginess due to a big change in the baby's mental development and teething. Just as many babies start teething during a fussy period as in between them. Of course, if your baby starts teething at the same time as she undergoes a big change in her mental development, she can become super-troublesome.

> "My daughter right now is extremely bad-tempered, only wanting to sit on my lap. Perhaps it's her teeth. They've been bothering her for 3 weeks

now. She seems pretty uncomfortable, but they still haven't come through."

Jenny's mom, 25th week

"My little guy became very weepy. According to the doctor, he has a whole bunch of teeth waiting to come through."

Paul's mom, 27th week

(His first tooth was not cut until 7 weeks later.)

You May Become Annoyed

Many mothers get angry as soon as they feel sure their babies have no good reason for being so troublesome and fussy. This feeling tends to get stronger toward the end of the fussy period. Some mothers, especially those with very demanding babies, just can't take it anymore.

Being Fussy Doesn't Necessarily Mean Teething

Despite detailed descriptions in baby books of the order in which teeth are generally cut, babies are not machines. Your baby will cut his first tooth whenever he is ready. How quickly teeth are cut in succession also has nothing to do with the state of health or mental or physical development of the baby. All babies can cut their teeth early or late, fast or slow.

Generally speaking, the lower front teeth are cut when the baby reaches 6 months. By his first birthday, a baby generally has six teeth. At about age 2 ½, the last molars come through, completing the full set of baby teeth. The toddler then has 20 teeth.

Despite the old wives' tale, a high temperature or diarrhea has nothing to do with teething. If your baby shows one of these symptoms, call his pediatrician.

"It was a terribly trying week. My son would cry over anything. He demanded attention constantly. He was up until 10:00 P.M., and agitated. I carried him around an awful lot in the infant carrier. This he liked. But I felt tired, tired, tired from all that schlepping and the continuous crying. Whenever he'd start to throw one of his temper tantrums in bed at night, it was as if I'd crossed a line. I could feel myself getting really angry. This happened often this past week."

Bob's mom, 25th week

Don't lose control. Remember that having feelings of anger and frustration at times is not abnormal or dangerous, but acting on them is. Try to get help long before you lose control.

You May Start to Argue

Arguments may develop around mealtimes. Most mothers hate it when their babies won't eat and continue to feed them. They try doing it playfully, or they try to pressure them into eating. Whatever the approach, it's usually to no avail.

At this age, strong-willed babies can be extremely stubborn about their refusal. This sometimes makes mothers, who are also being stubborn (but out of concern!) very angry. And so mealtimes can mean war.

When it happens to you, try to stay calm. Don't fight about it. You can't force her to eat, anyway. During this fussy phase, many babies are poor eaters. It's a temporary thing. If you make an issue out of it, chances are your baby will continue to refuse food even after the fussy period is over. She will have made a habit of it.

At the end of the fussy phase, you may correctly sense that your baby is capable of a lot more than you thought possible. Many mothers do. That is why an increasing number of mothers now get fed up with the annoying clinginess and decide that it's time to put a stop to it.

"My little girl keeps whining for attention or to be picked up. It's really aggravating and, what's worse, she has no excuse whatsoever! I have enough to do as it is. So when I'm fed up now, it's off to bed with her."

Juliette's mom, 26th week

How Your Baby's New Skills Emerge

At about 26 weeks, you'll discover that your baby is again trying to learn one or more new skills. This is the age at which babies will generally begin to explore the world of relationships. This world offers her many opportunities to develop skills that depend upon understanding the relationships among objects, people, sounds, and feelings. Your baby, depending on her own temperament, inclinations, preferences, and physical makeup, will focus on the sorts of relationships that appeal to her the most. She will use this understanding to develop the skills best suited to her personally. You can help her best by encouraging her to do what she is ready to do, rather than trying to push her in directions that don't interest her. This will be increasingly hard to do, anyway, as her personality begins to emerge and her own ideas start to dominate.

"I keep seeing this pattern of a difficult, sometimes extremely trying period that peaks at the end, and is then followed by a peaceful stage. Every time I think I can't take it anymore, my little boy changes course and suddenly does all these new things."

Bob's mom, 26th week

For the first time, your baby can perceive all kinds of relationships and act on them. He can now discover that there is always a physical distance between two objects or two people. And of course, his distance from you is one of the first things he will notice and react to. While observing this phenomenon, he discovers that you can increase the distance too much for his liking, and it dawns on him that he cannot do anything about it. Now he knows that he has lost control over that distance, and he gets frightened. So he will start to cry.

> "We have a problem. My girl doesn't want to be put in her playpen anymore. Her lips start to tremble if I even hover her anywhere above it. If I put her in it, she starts screaming. It's fine, though, if I put her on the floor, just outside of the 'cage.' Immediately, she rolls, swivels, and squirms in my direction."
>
> Nina's mom, 25th week

The juxtaposition of objects comes as a real revelation to your baby when the idea first dawns. He begins to understand that something can be *inside, outside, on top, above, next to, underneath* or *in between* something else. He will love to toy with these notions.

> "All day long, my son takes toys out of his toy box and puts them back in again. Sometimes, he'll toss everything over the side of the playpen. Another time, he'll carefully fit each item through the bars. He clears cupboards and shelves and is thrilled by pouring water from bottles and containers into the tub. But the best thing yet was while I was feeding him. He let go of my nipple, studied it with a serious look on his face, shook my breast up and down, sucked once, took another look, and continued this way for a while. He's never done this before. It's as if he was trying to figure out how anything could come from there."
>
> Matt's mom, 30th week

Next, your baby can begin to understand that he can cause certain things to happen. For example, he can flip a switch that causes music to play or a light to come on. He becomes attracted to objects such as stereo
(continued on page 162)

 My Diary

How My Baby Explores the New World of Relationships

The world of relationships opens up so many possibilities that your baby could not explore them all, even if she wanted to. What aspects of this world she will explore depend entirely on what sort of child she is growing up to be and what her talents are. A very physical baby will use the distance perception to improve balance and to crawl after you if she is able. The watching-listening baby will find plenty to occupy her as she tries to figure out just how this world works. As you read the following list of possibilities, check off the ones that apply to your baby just now. You might want to do this two or three times before the next leap happens, since not all of the skills your baby will develop are going to appear at once. In fact, some won't appear at all until much later.

BALANCE

❏ Sits up by herself from lying down

❏ Stands up by herself; pulls herself up

❏ Sits down again by herself after standing

❏ Stands without support

❏ Walks with support

❏ Makes a jumping movement without leaving the ground

❏ Grabs a toy from an overhead shelf or table

BODY CONTROL

❏ Walks around the edge of the crib, table, or playpen while holding on

❏ Walks around, pushing a box in front of her

❏ Lunges from one piece of furniture to another

❑ Crawls inside or under things, such as chairs and boxes

❑ Crawls back and forth over small steps

❑ Crawls in and out of rooms

❑ Crawls around the table

❑ Bends over or lies flat on her stomach to get something from under the couch or chair

GRABBING, TOUCHING, AND FEELING

❑ Opposes her thumb and index finger to grasp small objects

❑ Can play with something using both hands

❑ Lifts a rug to look under it

❑ Holds a toy upside down to hear sound inside

❑ Rolls a ball across the floor

❑ Invariably grabs a ball rolled toward her

❑ Knocks over wastepaper basket to empty out its contents

❑ Throws things away

❑ Puts toys in and next to a basket, in and out of a box, or under and on a chair, or pushes them out of the playpen

❑ Tries to fit one toy inside another

❑ Tries prying something out of a toy, like a bell's clapper

❑ Pulls own socks off

❑ Pries your shoelaces loose

❑ Empties cupboards and shelves

❑ Drops objects from high chair to test how something falls

❑ Puts food in the mouth of the dog, mommy, or daddy

❑ Pushes doors closed

(continued)

My Diary (cont.) --

WATCHING

❑ Observes adult activities, such as putting things into, on, or through something

❑ Looks from one animal to another in different picture books

❑ Looks from one person to another in different photographs

❑ Looks from one toy, object, or food to another in her hands

❑ Observes the movements of an animal, particularly when it's unusual, such as a dog pattering across a wooden floor

❑ Observes the movements of a person behaving unusually, such as daddy standing on his head

❑ Explores own body—particularly the penis or vagina

❑ Pays a lot of attention to smaller details or parts of toys and other objects, such as labels on towels

❑ Selects a book to look at

❑ Selects a toy to play with

LISTENING

❑ Makes connections between actions and words; comprehends short commands, such as "no, don't do that" and "come on, let's go"

❑ Listens to explanations intently and seems to understand

❑ Likes to hear animal sounds when looking at animal pictures

❑ Listens intently to voices on the telephone

❑ Pays attention to sounds that are related to a certain activity, such as chopping vegetables. Listens to sounds she makes herself, such as splashing bathwater

TALKING

❏ Understands the link between actions and words. Says her first words in the correct context. For instance, says *oo* (for "oops") when she falls and *a-choo* when you sneeze

❏ Puffs and blows

MOTHER-BABY DISTANCE

❏ Protests when her mommy walks away

❏ Crawls after her mommy

❏ Repeatedly makes contact with her mommy although busy playing on her own

MIMICKING GESTURES

❏ Imitates waving good-bye

❏ Claps her hands on request

❏ Mimics clicking with her tongue

❏ Mimics shaking and nodding her head, although often only nods with her eyes

MISCELLANEOUS

❏ Dances to the sound of music (sways her tummy)

OTHER CHANGES YOU NOTICE

_____

_____

_____

equipment, television sets, remote controls, light switches, and toy pianos.

He can now start to comprehend that people, objects, sounds, or situations can be related to each other. Or that a sound is related to an object or a particular situation. He knows, for example, that bustling in the kitchen means that someone is preparing his dinner, the key in the front door means "daddy's home," the dog has its own food and toys, and mommy and daddy and he belong together. Your baby's understanding of "family" won't be anywhere near as sophisticated as your own, but he does have his own understanding of what it means to belong together.

Next, your baby can begin to understand that animals and people coordinate their movements. Even if two people are walking separately, he still notices that they are taking each other's movements into consideration. That is a "relationship" as well. He can also tell when something goes wrong. If you drop something, let out a yell, and bend down quickly to catch it, if two people accidentally bump into each other, or if the dog falls off the couch, he understands that it is out of the ordinary. Some babies find this highly amusing; others are scared out of their wits. And still others become curious or take it very seriously. After all, it is something that is not meant to happen. Each brand-new observation or skill can, for that matter, make your baby feel wary until these things prove themselves harmless.

> "I've noticed my son is scared of the slicing machine at the bakery. As soon as the bread goes into it, he glances at me as if to ask, 'Are you sure that it's okay?' Then he looks frightened, then he looks at me, then frightened again, then at me again. After a while, he calms down."
>
> **Paul's mom, 29th week**

Your baby may also begin to discover that he can coordinate the movements of his body, limbs, and hands and that they work together as one. Once he understands this, he can learn to crawl more efficiently. Or he may try to sit up by himself or pull himself up to stand and sit down again. Some babies now take their first steps with a little help. And the exceptional baby will even do it without help, just before the next leap begins. All this physical exercise can also be frightening to a baby. He fully realizes that he could be losing control over his body. He still needs to learn how to keep his balance. And keeping one's balance has a lot to do with being familiar with the idea of distances.

When your baby starts to be active in the world of relationships, he will do it in his unique way. He will use the skills and concepts that he has acquired from previous leaps in his mental development. So he will only be able to perceive and experiment with relationships that involve things he already understands—things he has learned from the worlds of patterns, smooth transitions, and events.

Your Baby's Choices: A Key to His Personality

Between 26 and 34 weeks, you can discover what your baby likes best in the world of relationships. Take a good look at what your baby is doing. Use the "My Diary" list to help you determine where his interests lie, and respect your baby's choices. It's only natural to make comparisons with other mothers' observations of their babies, but don't expect all babies to be the same. The only thing you can be certain of is that they won't be!

Keep in mind that babies love anything new. Whenever you notice your baby showing any new skills or interests, be sure to respond. Your baby will enjoy it if you share these new discoveries. Your interest will help his learning progress more quickly. That's just how babies are.

What You Can Do to Help

Every baby needs time, support, and lots of opportunities to practice and experiment with new skills. You can help her by encouraging her when she succeeds and comforting her when she fails (by her own baby standards). If she persists too long in trying something she's not able to master yet, you may be able to distract her by coming up with something she can do.

Most of your activities as an adult are firmly rooted in the world of relationships—loading the car, getting dressed, putting cards in envelopes, holding a conversation, following an exercise video, to name a few. Let your baby watch these and join in where she can. Let her share your experience of sights, sounds, sensations, smells, and tastes whenever she wants to. You are still her guide in this complex world.

Always keep in mind that she will almost certainly be specializing in some kinds of activities at the expense of others. It really doesn't matter whether your baby learns about relationships from the watching or listening areas only. Later on, she will quickly and easily be able to put this understanding to use in other areas.

Show Her That You Are Not Deserting Her

In the world of relationships, almost every baby begins to realize at this time that her mommy can increase the distance between them and can walk away and leave her. Previously, her eyes could see it, but she didn't grasp the full meaning of leaving. Now that she does, it poses a problem. She gets frightened when it hits her that her mommy is unpredictable and beyond her control—she can leave her behind at any time! Even if she's already crawling, Mommy can easily outdistance her. She feels she has no control over the distance between herself and her mother, and this makes her feel helpless. It's hard to accept at first that this state of affairs is progress, but it is a clear sign of a mental leap forward. Your baby has to learn how to deal with this development and make it a part of her new world so that it is no longer frightening. Your task is to help her achieve this. It takes understanding, compassion, practice, and above all, time.

If your baby shows fear, accept that fear. She will soon realize that there is nothing to be afraid of, since her mother is not deserting him. Generally, babies panic the most around 29 weeks. Then it improves somewhat, until the next leap begins.

"My son has his moods when he screams until he's picked up. When I do, he'll laugh, utterly pleased with himself."

Frankie's mom, 31st week

"Everything's fine as long as my daughter can see me. If not, she starts crying out in fear."

Eve's mom, 29th week

"My little girl had been with the babysitter, as is usual. She wouldn't eat, wouldn't sleep, wouldn't do anything. Just cried and cried. I've never seen anything like it with her. I feel guilty leaving her behind like that. I'm considering working shorter hours, but I don't know how to arrange it."

Laura's mom, 28th week

"If my daughter even suspects I'll be setting her down on the floor to play, she starts to whine and cling with intense passion. So now, I carry her around on my hip all day long. She has also stopped smiling the way she used to. Just last week, she had a smile for everyone. Now it's definitely less. She's been through this once before, but in the past she'd always end up with a tiny grin on her face. Now, it's out of the question."

Nina's mom, 29th week

"This was a week of torment. So many tears. Five minutes on his own was already too much for my guy. If I so much as stepped out of the room, there'd be a crying fit. I've had him in the infant carrier a lot. But at bedtime, all hell would break loose. After 3 days, I was beat. It was too much. I started feeling extremely angry. It looked like it was starting to become a vicious circle. I was really pushing myself, feeling lonely and completely exhausted. I kept breaking things, too—they would just drop from my hands. That's when I took him to the day care center for the first time. Just so I could catch my breath. But it didn't work out, so I quickly went to get him. I felt really bad about dumping him somewhere, while at the same time, I had given it a lot of thought and felt it was the best solution. I push myself too far too often, and it only makes me feel lonely, aggressive, and confined. I also keep wondering whether it's me, whether I'm to blame for being inconsistent or for spoiling him too much."

Bob's mom, 29th week

To ease your baby's anxiety, make sure she feels you near her in case she really needs you. Give her the opportunity to grow accustomed to the new situation at her own pace. You can help her by carrying her more often or staying a bit closer to her. Give her some warning before you walk away, and keep talking to her while you walk away and when you're in the other room. This way, she will learn that you are still there, even if she can't see you anymore. You can also practice "leaving" by playing peek-a-boo games. For example, you can hide behind a newspaper while sitting next to your baby, then you can hide behind the couch close to your baby, then behind the cupboard a little farther away, and finally behind the door.

If your baby is already a little mobile, you can reassure her on the question of desertion by helping her to follow you. Try first telling her you are leaving—this way, your baby will learn that she does not have to keep an eye on you, that she can continue to play at ease. Then slowly walk away, so that she can follow you. Always adjust your pace to your baby's. Soon, your baby will learn that she can control the distance between the two of you. She will also come to trust you not to disappear when you have to get something from another room, and she won't bother you as much.

"At first, my son used to cling to my leg like a monkey and ride on my shoe when I walked. I had to drag this 'ball and chain' around everywhere. After a few days, he started keeping a slight distance. I could take a few steps to the side before he'd crawl up to me. Now, I can go into the kitchen while he's crawling around. He won't actually come looking for me unless I stay there for a while."

Bob's mom, 31st week

Often, the desire to be near you is so strong that even the inexperienced crawler is willing to put in some extra effort and ends up improving her crawling. The desire to keep up with mommy, along with the coordination she's able to utilize at this point, might provide just the extra incentive she needs.

If your baby was already a little mobile after the last leap, you will see a big difference now. Her effortful journeys used to take her farther away from you, and she would stay away longer than she does now. Suddenly, she's circling you and making short dashes backward and forward, making contact with you each time.

"My baby keeps crawling back and forth. Then he'll sit under my chair for a while. He also stays nearer to me than he used to."

John's mom, 31st week

Offer your baby the chance to experiment with coming and going, with you as the center point. If you sit on the floor, you'll notice she will interrupt her excursions to crawl over you.

Over the weeks, parents grow more and more irritated if they don't get the opportunity to continue their everyday activities. Once their baby has reached 29 weeks, most mothers call it a day. They start to gradually break the old habit ("I am always here for you to cling to") and lay down a new rule ("I need some time and space to move as well"). They do so most times by distracting the babies, sometimes by ignoring their whines for a while, or by putting the babies to bed if they are really fed up with their behavior.

Whatever you decide to do, take into consideration how much your baby can handle before she gets really afraid. Knowing that you can leave

The Gender Gap

Are boys different from girls after all?

Mothers of boys sometimes seem to have a harder time with their babies than mothers of girls. They often don't understand their sons. Does he or doesn't he want to play with his mom?

"My son often whines for contact and attention. I always respond. But when I pick him up to play a game, it's obviously not what he had in mind. Then he'll spot something, and all of a sudden that's what he wants, and he reaches and whines to get at it. He seems to want two things—me and exploring. But he always makes a mess of these adventures. He'll grab something pretty roughly and hurl it aside. He likes to go through the entire house this way. I would have liked him to be a bit more cuddly. We could talk, play games—just do nice things together and have some fun. Whereas now, I'm constantly trying to prevent accidents from happening. Sometimes I feel dissatisfied myself."

Matt's mom, 32nd week

Mothers with both boys and girls usually find that they can do more with their girls. They feel they can better sense what a girl wants. They share more of the same interests, which they call sociable and fun.

"I'm able to play mother with my daughter more. We do all kinds of things together. When I talk, she really listens. She enjoys my games and asks for more. Her brother was much more his own man."

Eve's mom, 33rd week

her whenever you choose can be very frightening for her and very difficult to deal with.

> "It's so annoying the way he keeps clinging to my legs when I'm trying to do the cooking. It's almost as if he chooses to be extra difficult because I am busy. So I put him to bed."
>
> Kevin's mom, 30th week

Help Your Baby Explore the New World through Roaming His Surroundings

If your baby loves to crawl, allow him to roam around freely in a room where he can do no harm. Watch him to see just what he does. When he enters the world of relationships, an early crawler begins to understand that he can crawl *into, out of, under, over, in between, on top of,* and *through* something. He will love to toy with these various relationships between himself and the objects in his surroundings.

> "I like to watch my son play in the living room. He crawls up to the couch, looks under it, sits down, quickly crawls over to the closet, crawls into it, rushes off again, crawls to the rug, lifts it up, looks under it, heads toward a chair that he crawls under, whoosh, he's off to another cupboard, crawls into that one, gets stuck, cries a little, figures out how to get out and closes the door."
>
> Steven's mom, 30th week

If your baby takes pleasure in doing these things, leave some objects around that will encourage him to continue his explorations. For instance, you can make hills for him to crawl over out of blankets, quilts, or pillows. Of course, you should adjust this soft play circuit to suit what your baby can do.

You can also build a tunnel from boxes or chairs that he can crawl through. You can make a tent out of a sheet, which he can crawl into, out of, and under. Many babies enjoy opening and closing doors. If your baby likes this, too, you can include a door or two. Just watch out for his fingers. If you crawl along with him, it will double the fun. Try adding some variety with peek-a-boo and hide-and-seek games, too.

If your baby enjoys moving his toys around, make this into a game. Give him the opportunity to put playthings *inside, on top of, next to*, or *under* objects. Allow him to throw his toys—it's important in getting to understand how the world works. Let him pull toys *through* something, such as the legs of a chair or a box made into a tunnel. To the outsider, it may seem as if he is flying like a whirlwind from one object to the next, but this frenzied activity is providing exactly the input his brain needs to understand this new world of relationships.

"My baby will lay her blocks, her pacifier, and her bear in a basket. When she's standing, she'll pick up toys from the floor and toss them on the chair. She also pushes things into her playpen through the bars. If she's actually in the playpen, she'll throw everything out over the top. She likes to watch what she's done. She's a real little rascal."

Jenny's mom, 30th week

Give your baby a shelf or cupboard of his own, which he can empty *out* and you can easily tidy up again. Give him a box he can put his things *in*. Turn a box upside down, so he can put things *on top of* it. Allow him to push things *out of* the playpen *through* the bars, or throw them out *over* the top. This is an ideal way for babies who aren't yet interested in crawling to explore relationships like *inside, outside, underneath*, and *on top of*.

Another way your baby can toy with relationships is by throwing, dropping and overturning objects. He may do so to see and hear what happens. Maybe he wants to find out just how a particular object breaks into several pieces. You can watch him enjoy knocking over towers of blocks, which you have to keep building up again. But he will gain just as much pleasure from tipping over the wastepaper basket, overturning the cat's water bowl, dropping a glass of milk or a bowl of cereal from his high chair, or any other activity that is bound to make a mess.

"My daughter loves experimenting with the way things fall. She's been trying it with all kinds of things—her pacifier, her blocks, and her cup. Then, I gave her a feather from Big Bird, the parakeet. This took her by surprise. She prefers things that make a lot of noise!"

Nina's mom, 28th week

"Boy, did my son laugh when I dropped a plate, and it shattered into a million pieces. I've never seen him laugh so hard."

John's mom, 30th week

In the world of relationships your baby may discover that things can be *taken apart*. Give him some things that are designed for exactly that purpose—nesting cups and bright laces tied into bows. He will tug and pull at things that are attached to objects or toys, such as labels, stickers, eyes and noses of cuddly toys, and wheels, latches, and doors of toy cars.

 Baby Care

Make Your Home Baby-Proof

Remember that your baby can be fascinated by things that are harmful to him. He can stick a finger or tongue into anything with holes or slots, including things such as electrical outlets, electronic equipment, drains, and the dog's mouth. Or he can pick up and eat little things he finds on the floor. Always stay near your baby whenever you let him explore the house freely.

But take care: Buttons on clothing, switches and wires trailing from electrical equipment, and bottle caps are equally attractive and just as liable to be taken apart whenever possible. To your baby, there is no such thing as off limits in this new and exciting world.

"My son keeps pulling his socks off."

Frankie's mom, 31st week

If your baby dearly loves watching things disappear *into* something else, invite him to watch your activities. You may think cooking is ordinary, but to him it is magic to watch all the ingredients disappear *into* the same pot. But keep an eye on him, too, because he may look for disappearing acts of his own.

"My daughter likes to watch the dog emptying his bowl. The closer she can get, the better. It seems pretty dangerous to me, because with all that attention, the dog gulps it down faster and faster. On the other hand, the dog suddenly seems to be paying more attention to my daughter as well when she's eating. She'll be sitting at the table in her high chair, with the dog right next to her. So what do you know? It turned out she was dropping little pieces of bread and watching him wolf them down."

Laura's mom, 31st week

Sometimes babies like putting one thing *inside* another. But this happens only by coincidence. He can't yet distinguish between different shapes and sizes.

"My girl tries fitting all kinds of things together. A lot of the time, the size is right, but the shape never is. Also, she isn't accurate enough. But if it doesn't work, she gets mad."

Jenny's mom, 29th week

"My son discovered his nostrils. He stuck an inquisitive finger in one. I hope he doesn't try the same with a bead!"

John's mom, 32nd week

Is your baby intrigued by a toy with a squeak in it when he pushes, or a toy piano that produces a musical tone when he hits a key? Let him explore these things. They concern relationships between an action and an effect. But beware, he can also turn over a bottle filled with nail polish or perfume or some other dangerous substance.

"I held a toy bear upside down so that it growled. Then I put the bear on the floor, and my son crawled right over and rolled it around, until it made that sound. He was so fascinated that he kept turning the bear over and over, faster and faster."

Paul's mom, 33rd week

Help Your Baby Explore the New World through Using His Body

In your baby's body, relationships abound between the various body parts. Without the efforts of all the muscles the relationships between the various parts of the skeleton would be lost and we would collapse like a sack with bones. About this time, your baby may start to try to sit up by himself, depending on his balance skills.

"My son's learned to sit up now. He started out by balancing on one buttock with both hands flat on the floor in front of him. Then he lifted one hand. Now he can sit without using his hands at all."

Matt's mom, 25th week

"Now my baby sits alone without any fear of losing her balance. She couldn't do that last week. She sometimes takes things, holds them over her head with both hands, and then throws them away."

Jenny's mom, 28th week

"When my little one sits up, he often rolls over. He also topples forward or backward. Whenever that happens, I'm quick to laugh. Then he'll often start laughing, too."

                                        Bob's mom, 26th week

If your baby is not sitting steadily enough to feel confident on his own, help him. Try to find out if you can make him more confident by playing balancing games in which he has to regain his balance every time the wobble sets in. Look for favorite balancing games under "Top Games for This Wonder Week" on page 185.

Some babies try to stand up. If your baby does, how is his balance? Help your baby when he's not standing firmly, or if he's afraid of tumbling down. Play balancing games with him—these will make him familiar with his vertical position. But never try to hurry your baby toward sitting or standing. If you try too early for his liking, he may get afraid and you may even slow his development.

"We tried to put my son on his feet by the table. He stood there, very unstable, swaying like a puppet on a string, looking as if he was about to topple over. It's too soon for him."

                                        Steven's mom, 31st week

"My daughter is beginning to stand up, but she doesn't know how to sit back down. It's tiring. Today, I found her standing in her crib for the first time, wailing. That irritates me. She's supposed to go to sleep when she's in bed. I just hope it doesn't take too long and that she works out how to sit back down sometime soon."

                                        Juliette's mom, 31st week

"My baby insists on me sitting her back down after she's stood up. Her sister isn't allowed to help her, even though there are many things she

First Steps

Once your baby has acquired the knack of perceiving and experimenting with relationships, she can understand what walking is, but understanding doesn't mean she will actually do it. To really start walking, she must choose to. And even if she does, she might not succeed because her body is not ready. Your baby won't learn how to walk at this age unless the proportions between the weight of her bones, her muscles, and the length of her limbs compared to her torso meet certain specifications. If your baby is occupied with something else—for instance, speech, sounds, and music—there may simply be no time left to spend on walking. She can't do everything at once.

will let her do. She's obviously scared that she won't be able to do it well enough."

Ashley's mom, 32nd week

"My baby kept trying to pull herself up this week, and at a certain point she succeeded. She had pulled herself up in bed, stood up right away, and stayed standing up, too. Now she can really do it. She pulls herself up using the bed, playpen, table, chair, or someone's legs. She also stands by the playpen and takes toys from it with one hand."

Jenny's mom, 28th week

If and only if you notice that your baby has great fun walking, give him a hand. Hold on to him tightly, because his balance is usually unstable. Play games with him that will familiarize him with keeping his balance, especially when he shifts his weight from one leg to the other. Never go on hour-long walks with him. He really won't learn any faster that way. Your baby won't start walking until he is ready to.

"When I hold both of my baby's hands, she walks in perfect balance. She crosses the small gap between the chair and the television when she's standing. She walks alongside the table, around the bends. She'll walk through the room pushing a Pampers box. Yesterday, the box slid away, and she took three steps by herself."

Jenny's mom, 34th week

"I'm irritated by my son's slow coordination. He doesn't crawl, he won't pull himself up. He just sits there and fiddles with his playthings."

Frankie's mom, 29th week

Remember that your baby has no motive for learning to walk or crawl just yet. Plenty of other activities will teach him things worth knowing. For him, these things are more important right now.

Babies who have entered the world of relationships can also begin to understand the connection between what their two hands are doing, and they can get better control over them. This way, they can cope with two things at once. If you see your baby trying to use both hands at the same time, encourage him to go on. Let him hold a toy in either hand and clash them together. Or let him make this clashing movement without toys, so that he claps his hands. Let him knock toys against the floor or the wall. Encourage him to pass toys from one hand to the other. And let him put two toys down at the same time, and pick them up again.

"My daughter has the hitting syndrome. She beats anything she can lay her hands on."

Jenny's mom, 29th week

If your baby tries to master the concerted action between two fingers—for instance his thumb and forefinger—again he is toying with relationships between the two. In the process he is also busy inventing a new tool, the pincer grip, that he can put to use immediately. He can learn how to pluck extremely small objects, such as threads, from the carpet. He can learn to pick blades of grass, or he may take pleasure in touching and stroking all kinds of surfaces with his finger. And he may have great fun examining every detail of very small objects.

"My baby goes through the entire room and spots the smallest irregularities or crumbs on the floor, picks them up between her thumb and her index finger, and sticks them in her mouth. I really have to pay attention so she doesn't eat anything peculiar. I let her eat small pieces of bread by herself now. At first, she kept sticking her thumb in her mouth instead of the bread she was holding between her fingers. But she's starting to improve now."

Hannah's mom, 32nd week

Help Your Baby Explore the New World through Language and Music

Babies who were extra sensitive to sounds and gestures in the past may start to grasp the connection between short sentences and their meaning or particular gestures and their meaning as soon as they have entered the world of relationships. In fact, they may even make the connection between words and gestures that go with them. But you will still find that these babies can understand these things only in their own surroundings and as a part of a familiar routine. If you were to play the same sentences from a tape recorder in a strange place, they wouldn't have a clue. That skill doesn't develop until much later.

If your baby likes playing with words and gestures, use this to his advantage. There are several things you can do to help your baby to understand what you're saying. Use short sentences with clear and obvious gestures. Explain the things you are doing. Let him see, feel, smell, and taste the things you are talking about. He understands more than you think.

"Once, I told my son to watch the rabbit, and he understood what I meant. He listens very closely."

Paul's mom, 26th week

"I get the feeling that my son knows what I mean when I explain something or make a suggestion, such as, 'Shall we go for a nice little walk?' or 'I think it's bedtime!' It's so cute—he doesn't like hearing the word 'bed'!"

Bob's mom, 30th week

"When we say, 'Clap your hands,' my daughter does. And when we say, 'Jump up and down,' she bends her knees and bounces up and down, but her feet don't leave the ground."

Jenny's mom, 32nd week

"When I say 'bye, say bye, bye' while waving at daddy who is leaving, my daughter waves while keeping a steady eye on my waving hand."

Nina's mom, 32nd week

If your baby attempts to say or ask something with a sound or gestures, make sure you let him know that you are thrilled with his potential. Talk and signal back to him. The best way to teach your baby to talk is by talking to him a lot yourself. Call everyday items by their names. Ask questions, such as, "Would you like a sandwich?" when you put his plate down. Let him hear nursery rhymes, and play singing games with him. In short, make speech attractive.

"Whenever my son wants to do something, he'll put his hand on it and look at me. It's as if he's trying to ask, 'May I?' He also understands, 'no.' Of course, it doesn't stop him from trying, but he knows what it means."

Bob's mom, 32nd week

"Last week, my daughter said 'oo' (oops) for the first time when she fell. We also noticed that she was starting to copy sounds from us, so we've started teaching her to talk."

Jenny's mom, 29th week

"My daughter is a real chatterbox. She's especially talkative while crawling, when she recognizes someone or something. She talks to her stuffed toys and to us when she's on our laps. It's as if she's telling entire stories. She uses all kinds of vowels and consonants. The variations seem endless."

Hannah's mom, 29th week

"My son nods his head and makes a certain sound. If I imitate him, he starts giggling uncontrollably."

Paul's mom, 28th week

If your baby loves music, make sure you do a lot of singing, dancing, and clapping songs with him. This way, your baby can practice using words and gestures. If you don't know many children's songs, you can buy a music CD. Some public libraries lend these out, too.

Her First Word

Once your baby has gained the ability to perceive and experiment with relationships, she may discover her first word. It doesn't mean that she will start to talk, though. The age at which babies begin to use words differs greatly. So don't worry if she puts it off for a few more months. Most babies produce their first real word during the 10th or 11th month.

If your baby is obsessed with something else, such as crawling and standing, there may simply be no time left to spend on words. She can't do everything at once.

"When we were singing at the baby swimming class, my baby suddenly started singing along."

Nina's mom, 30th week

"Whenever my daughter hears music or I start to sing, she immediately starts wiggling her tummy."

Eve's mom, 32nd week

Promoting Progress by Raising Expectations

Whatever new things your baby comprehends, you can demand from him nothing more, but also nothing less. Breaking old habits and setting new rules are also part of developing new skills. When your baby is busy learning new skills, he can be very irritating in the process. This is because old ways of doing things and established rules of behavior may no longer suit the baby's current progress. Both mother and baby have to renegotiate new rules to restore peace and harmony.

At first parents worry when their baby enters a new fussy phase. They get annoyed when they discover that nothing is wrong with their baby and, to the contrary, he is in fact ready to be more independent. It is then that they start demanding that their baby do the things they feel he is able to do. As a consequence, they promote progress.

"I've always rocked him to sleep while breastfeeding. But now it irritates me. I feel he's old enough to just go straight to bed. My husband likes putting him to bed, too, but that's out of the question now. And you never know, someday it might have to be done by someone else. I've started getting him used to going straight to bed once a day. But he's certainly putting up a fight."

Matt's mom, 31st week

Just like mothers get annoyed when their babies keep insisting on being rocked to sleep, so there are at least three other situations where you may feel the urge to make demands: mealtime aggravations, having to forbid things, and impatience.

At this age, many babies get fussy over food, while before they enjoyed whatever they grabbed from your mouth. In the world of relationships many babies come to realize that certain foods taste better than others. So why not pick the tastier one? Many mothers think it's funny at first. Soon, however, almost every mother becomes irritated when her baby gets fussy. She wonders whether the baby is getting enough nutrition. She tries to distract the fussy eater so she can stick the spoon in her mouth at an unsuspected moment. Or she runs after her the whole day with food.

Don't do it. Strong-willed babies will resist something that is being forced upon them even more. And a worried mother will in turn react to that. This way, meals become a battleground. Stop arguing. You cannot force a baby to swallow, so don't even try it. If you do, you might only increase his dislike of anything that has to do with food. Resort to different tactics and make use of other new skills your baby can learn now. He can try holding something between his thumb and forefinger now, but he still needs a lot of practice, so it's good for his coordination to feed himself. A baby this age also loves to make his own decisions, and the freedom to eat by himself will make eating more enjoyable. Use these new skills to his advantage. While he finger-feeds himself, he could be in a better mood to allow you to feed him as well. It can be messy, but encourage him anyway. Keep putting two pieces of food on his plate, so that he will keep himself occupied. Usually, it will be easy to feed him in between.

You can also make eating more pleasurable for your baby by feeding him in front of a mirror. This way, he can watch as you put a spoonful of food in his mouth or in your own. Don't worry if it doesn't work the first time. Many babies go through eating problems, and they also get over them.

(continued on page 188)

Top Games for This Wonder Week

Here are some games and activities that work best for babies exploring the world of relationships. Whatever kind of game you choose, language can now begin to play a big part in your games.

PEEK-A-BOO AND HIDE-AND-SEEK GAMES
These are very popular games at this age. The variations are endless.

PEEK-A-BOO WITH A HANDKERCHIEF
Put a handkerchief over your head and see if your baby will pull it away. Ask "Where's mommy?" Your baby will know you're still there, because he can hear you. If he doesn't make any attempts to pull away the handkerchief, take his hand and pull it away together. Say "peek-a-boo" when you reappear.

VARIATIONS WITH PEEK-A-BOO
Cover your face with your hands and take them away, or pop up from behind a newspaper or book held between you and the baby. Babies also like it when you appear from behind a plant or under a table. After all, they can still see parts of you.

Or hide in a conspicuous place, such as behind a curtain. This way, she can follow the movements of the curtain. Make sure your baby sees you disappear. For example, announce that you're going to hide (for non-crawlers), or that she has to come look for you (for crawlers). If she didn't watch you or was distracted for a moment by something else, call her name. Try it sometime in the door opening too. This will teach her that leaving is followed by returning. Reward her every time she manages to find you. Lift her up high or cuddle her—whatever she likes best.

WHERE'S THE BABY?
A lot of babies discover they can hide themselves behind or under something. They usually start with a cloth or an item of clothing while being changed. Take advantage of any opportunity to develop a game that the baby has started. This way, he'll learn that he can take the lead.

HIDING TOYS
Try hiding toys under a blanket. Make sure you use something your baby likes or that she's attached to. Show her how and where you hide it. Make it easy for her the first time around. Make sure she can still see a tiny part of the toy.

HIDING TOYS IN THE BATHTUB
Use bath foam in the bathtub and allow your baby to play with it. Try hiding toys under the foam some time and invite him to look for them. If he can blow, try blowing at the foam. Or give him a straw and encourage him to blow through it.

TALKING GAMES
You can make talking attractive by talking to your baby frequently, by listening to him, by reading books together, and by playing whispering, singing, and word games.

LOOK AT PICTURE BOOKS TOGETHER
Take your baby on your lap—he usually likes that best. Let him choose a book to look at together. Call by name whatever your baby looks at. If it's a book with animals in it, mimic the sounds the animals make. Babies generally love hearing and making sounds like bark, moo, and quack. Let him turn the pages by himself, if he wants to.

(continued)

Top Games for This Wonder Week (cont.) -------------------

WHISPERING GAME
Most babies love it when sounds or words are whispered in their ears. Making little puffs of air that tickle his ear is interesting, too, perhaps because a baby can now understand what blowing is.

SONG AND MOVEMENT GAMES
These games can be used to encourage both singing and talking. They also exercise the baby's sense of balance.

GIDDY-UP, GIDDY-UP, LITTLE ROCKING HORSE
Take your baby on your knee, upright and facing you. Support him under his arms and jog him up and down gently, singing:

Giddy-up, giddy-up, little rocking horse
Giddy-up, giddy-up, little rocking horse
Giddy-up, giddy-up, little rocking horse
Ride away, away to Candy Land.

THIS IS THE WAY THE LADY RIDES
Take your baby on your knee, upright and facing you. Support her under her arms, and sing the following song:

This is the way the lady rides,
The lady rides,
The lady rides,
This is the way the lady rides,
So early in the morning.
(Sing slowly and solemnly, and jog her neatly up and down on your knee.)
This is the way the gentleman rides,
The gentleman rides,
The gentleman rides,

This is the way the gentleman rides,
So early in the morning.
(Sing faster, and jog her faster.)
This is the way the farmer rides,
The farmer rides,
The farmer rides,
This is the way the farmer rides,
So early in the morning.
(Sing wearily and jog her up, down, and sideways.)
CLIP CLOP CLIP CLOP
AND DOWN INTO THE DITCH!
("DOWN" comes as a surprise. Pull your knees apart and let her "fall" between your knees.)

BALANCING GAMES
A lot of singing games, like those above, are also balancing games. Here are some others.

SITTING GAME
Sit down comfortably. Take your baby on your knee. Hold his hands, and move him gently from left to right, so that he shifts his weight from buttock to buttock. Also try letting him lean forward or backward carefully. Babies find the latter the most exciting. You can also move him in small or large circles, to the left, backward, to the right, and forward. Adjust yourself to your baby. The movement has to challenge him just enough to make him want to find his balance himself. You can also let him swing like a pendulum of a clock while you sing: *tick tock, tick tock* in time with the movement.

(continued)

STANDING GAME

Kneel comfortably on the floor and let him stand in front of you while you hold his hips or hands and move him gently from left to right, so that he transfers his weight from one leg to the other. Do the same thing in a different plane so that his body weight shifts from back to front. Adjust yourself to your baby. It has to challenge him just enough to make him want to find his balance himself.

FLYING GAME

Grasp your baby firmly, lift her, and let her "fly" through the room. Let her rise and descend. Turn left and right. Fly in small circles, in a straight line, and backward. Vary the movement and speed as much as possible. If your baby enjoys this, then try letting her land carefully upside down, head first. Naturally, you'll accompany the entire flight with different zooming, humming, or screeching sounds. The more alert you can be to her reactions, the more easily you will be able to adjust this game so it's just right for her.

STANDING HIM ON HIS HEAD

Most physically active babies love horsing around and being stood on their heads. However, others find standing on their heads frightening or over-exciting. Play this game only if your baby likes playing rough. It's a healthy exercise for him. Remember to support his body completely as you hold him upside down.

GAMES WITH TOYS

For now, the best "toys" are all the things babies can find to get into around the house. The best games are emptying cupboards and shelves, dropping things, and throwing things away.

BABY'S OWN CUPBOARD GAME

Organize a cupboard for the baby and fill it with things that she finds super attractive. Usually this will include empty boxes, empty egg cartons, empty toilet paper rolls, plastic plates, and plastic bottles with lids and filled with something rattly. But also include things she can make a lot of noise with, such as a pan, wooden spoons, and an old set of keys.

FALLING GAME

Some babies like hearing a lot of noise when they drop something. If your baby does, you could make a game of it by putting him in his high chair and placing a metal serving tray on the floor. Hand him blocks, and show him how to let them go so that they fall on the tray and make a big bang.

OUTDOOR GAMES

Babies love riding in a baby seat on a bicycle, in a baby jogger, or in a baby backpack. Stop frequently to point out things along the way and talk to your baby about what she is seeing.

SWIMMING FOR BABIES

Many babies love playing in the water. Some swimming pools have specially heated pools for small children and special hours when a group of babies can play games with parents in the water.

CHILDREN'S FARMS

A visit to a children's farm or duck pond can be extremely exciting for your baby. She can see the animals from her picture book. She'll enjoy looking at their wobbly, pattering, or leaping motions. And she'll particularly like feeding the animals and watching them eat.

Finally, certain eating habits are perceived as irritating by some mothers, while others find them perfectly normal.

"What really gets to me is that she wants to stick her thumb in her mouth after every bite. I won't allow it! Minor disagreement!"

Ashley's mom, 29th week

Now that the baby is in the middle of learning new skills, many mothers constantly find themselves having to forbid things. A crawling baby especially is liable to inspect all your possessions. After all, her pleasures are by no means the same as yours. So anything you can do to make life easier for both of you will be worthwhile. Try to prevent what you cannot allow and help her with the activities she is interested in. Above all, remember that you are not the only mother with this problem.

"I constantly have to forbid things. My daughter rampages from one thing to the next. Her favorite targets are the wine rack, the video, my needlepoint kit, cupboards, and shoes. Another one of her hobbies is knocking down plants, digging up plants, and eating cat food. I can't warn her enough. So sometimes, I slap her hand when I feel it's gone far enough."

Jenny's mom, 31st week

After this leap, babies can be very impatient. This may have several reasons. They don't want to wait for their food. They get mad if a toy refuses to behave as they wish it would. Or if something is not allowed. Or if mommy doesn't pay attention to them quickly enough. Unfortunately, babies do have an idea of what it is they want to have or achieve, but they don't understand why their mommies don't allow it or why they can't have it in a flash. This frustrates them, so be understanding but see what you can do to stop the "I want it now" problem.

Top Toys for This Wonder Week

These are toys and things to play with that suit the new skills your baby is developing as he explores the world of relationships.

- His very own cupboard or shelf
- Doors (watch his fingers)
- Cardboard boxes in different sizes; also empty egg cartons
- Wooden spoons
- Round nesting or stacking cups
- Wooden blocks
- Balls (light enough to roll)
- Picture books
- Photo books
- CDs with children's songs
- Bath toys: things to fill and empty out, such as plastic bottles, plastic cups, a plastic colander, a funnel, a watering can
- Toy cars with rotating wheels and doors that can be opened
- Cuddly toys that make noise when turned upside down
- Squeaky toys
- Drums
- Toy pianos
- Toy telephones

It's important to put away or take precautions with electrical outlets, plugs, wires, keys, drains, stairs, bottles (such as perfume and nail polish and remover), tubes (such as toothpaste and antiseptics), stereo equipment, remote controls, television sets, plants, wastepaper baskets, trash cans, alarm clocks, and watches.

"My daughter's becoming very impatient. She wants to have it all, and she gets furious if she can't reach something and I tell her 'no.' Then she'll really start screaming. It irritates me and makes me think she's only doing it because I work. She's much sweeter with the baby-sitter."

                                    Laura's mom, 31st week

"I put my baby to bed this past week because she was carrying on something awful and screaming during supper. She feels it isn't going fast enough, so she starts yelling, twisting, and wriggling after every bite. Once I got over my anger, about 5 minutes later, we continued. Both of us had calmed down by then."

                                    Ashley's mom, 28th week

Between 30 and 35 weeks, another comparatively easy period begins. For anywhere from 1 to 3 weeks, the baby is admired for her cheerfulness, independence, and progress.

"My girl is becoming less and less shy. She laughs a lot. And she's good at keeping herself occupied. She has become very agile and active again. Actually, I started to see this change last week, but it seems to be progressing."

                                    Nina's mom, 33rd week

"Because she was so sweet, my baby seemed like a totally different child. She used to cry and whine a lot. The way she tells stories is also delightful. She's actually already like a little toddler, the way she trots through the room."

Jenny's mom, 35th week

"My son was extremely cheerful, so it wasn't hard to have fun with him. It also pleases me to see him a little more active and lively in the physical sense. But he's at his best when he can observe people. He's very talkative, too, a great kid."

Frankie's mom, 30th week

"My daughter's obviously gotten bigger and older. She reacts to everything we do. She watches everything. And she wants to have whatever we have. I'd almost say that she wants to be a part of it."

Ashley's mom, 34th week

"Finally, some rest after a long period of constant changes. A wonderful week. He's gone through another change. He cries less, sleeps more. I can see a certain pattern starting to develop again, for the umpteenth time. I talk to him much more. I've noticed myself explaining everything I do. When I go to prepare his bottle, I tell him. When it's time for him to go to bed, I tell him. I explain why he has to take a nap. And these talks seem to do me good. The day care center is going well now, too."

Bob's mom, 30th week

"We seem to have a different kind of contact now. It's as if the umbilical cord has finally been cut. The feeling of complete dependency is also gone. I'm quicker to rely on a babysitter. I also notice that I've been giving my son a lot more freedom. I don't have to be on top of him all the time."

Bob's mom, 31st week

"This was a really nice week. My baby is cheerful, and he can occupy himself pretty well on his own with his toys. Everything's still going fine at day care. He reacts in a friendly way to other children. He is a cute little guy, and he's much more his own little person."

Bob's mom, 32nd week

Place Photo Here

After the Leap

Age: _____

Reflections: _____

chapter 8

Wonder Week 37: The World of Categories

At about 37 (or between 36 and 40) weeks, you may notice your baby attempting to do new things. At this age, a baby's explorations can often seem very methodical. For example, you may notice your little tyke picking up specks from the floor and examining them studiously between his thumb and forefinger. Or a budding little chef may rearrange the food on his plate by testing the way a banana squashes or spinach squishes through tiny fingers. He will assume the most serious, absorbed expression while carrying out these investigations. In fact, that is just what they are—investigations that will help the little researcher begin to categorize his world.

Your baby is now able to recognize that certain objects, sensations, animals, and people belong together in groups or categories. For example, a banana looks, feels, and tastes different than spinach, but they are both food. These are important distinctions and similarities to sort out. The leap into the world of categories will affect every sense—sight, hearing, smell, taste, and touch. Your baby will learn more about other people and his own emotions, too. Language skills will be developing. Your baby may not yet use words himself, but he will understand much more.

Like all of the previous worlds, the arrival of these new perceptions begins by turning your baby's world inside out. Babies' brain waves show drastic changes again around this time. These changes will begin to alter the way your baby perceives his world, which will be disturbing to him at first. You can expect a fussy period to begin around 34 weeks, or between 32 and 37 weeks. This fussy period will often last for 4 weeks, but it may last anywhere from 3 to 6 weeks. As your baby enters this fussy phase, play close attention to see if he is attempting to master new skills.

this
Week's Fussy Signs

As they prepare to leap into the world of categories, all babies will cry more easily than they did during the past few weeks. To their mothers, they may seem cranky, whiny, fidgety, grumpy, bad-tempered, discontented, unmanageable, restless, or impatient. All of this is very understandable.

Your little one is now under extra pressure because from her last leap she knows that you can go away from her whenever you please and leave her behind. At first, most babies were temporarily distressed by this discovery, but over the past few weeks they have learned to deal with it in their own ways. It all seemed to be going much more smoothly—and then the next big change came along and ruined everything. Now the little worrier wants to stay with her mommy again, while at the same time she realizes perfectly well that her mother can walk away whenever she chooses. This makes the baby feel even more insecure and increases her tension.

"These past few days, my daughter insists on sitting on my lap constantly. For no apparent reason, I might add. When I don't carry her around, she screams. When I take her for walks in her stroller, the moment she even thinks I've stopped, she demands to be lifted out."

Ashley's mom, 34th week

"My baby acts cranky and seems to be bored. She picks up everything and just tosses it away again."

Laura's mom, 35th week

"Everything's fine, as long as my little girl can sit on someone's lap. Otherwise, she whimpers and wails. I'm not used to this behavior from her. She seems to grow bored quickly wherever she is—in the playpen, in her high chair, or on the floor."

Eve's mom, 34th week

A fussy baby will usually cry less when she is with her mother, especially when she has her mother all to herself.

"My son kept screaming and grumping and acting horribly. Everything was fine as long as I stayed with him or took him on my lap. I put him to bed several times when I got fed up with his demands."

Frankie's mom, 36th week

How You Know It's Time to Grow

Here are some giveaways that your little one is about to make another developmental leap.

She May Cling to Your Clothes

Your baby may become anxious when you walk around. Non-crawlers can do nothing but cry. For some, every step her mommy takes is reason for genuine panic. Crawling babies are able to follow their mothers, and sometimes they cling to them so tightly that they can hardly move.

"It was another difficult week with a lot of crying. My son literally clings to my skirt. When I leave the room, he starts crying and crawling after me. When I'm cooking, he'll crawl behind me, grab hold of my legs, and hold on in such a way that I can't move. He'll only play if I play with him. A few times, it just got to be too much. Putting him to bed is a struggle all over again. He falls asleep very late."

Bob's mom, 38th week

"At the moment, my daughter is a real little mommy's girl. As long as she can see me, everything's okay. Otherwise she howls."

Jenny's mom, 38th week

"I call my baby my little leech. She persists in holding on to my trousers. Once again, she wants to be around, with, and on me constantly."

Emily's mom, 36th week

She May Be Shy

Your baby may want to keep other people at a greater distance now than she usually does. The desire to be close to you may become even more apparent in the presence of other people—sometimes even when that other person is the father or a brother or sister. Often, mother is the only one allowed to look at her and talk to her. And she is almost always the only one allowed to touch her.

"My daughter is shier with strangers again."

Hannah's mom, 34th week

"When strangers talk to my son or pick him up, he starts yelling, immediately."

Paul's mom, 34th week

"When visitors arrive, my son will race to me, climb on my lap, tummy-to-tummy, cling to me, and only then look to see who's here."

> Kevin's mom, 34th week

"My girl's shy around strangers again. She becomes very frightened when someone wants to touch her or lift her up."

> Emily's mom, 36th week

She May Tightly Hold On to You

When she is sitting on your lap or being carried, your baby may hold on to you as tightly as she can. She may even react furiously if you dare to put her down unexpectedly.

"My baby gets mad if I put her down even for a second. Then, when I lift her up again, she always pinches me. When our poor old dog happens to be within the reach of her hand, she'll pinch him even before I can lift her up."

> Emily's mom, 35th week

"My son wants to be carried all of the time, and he clings to my neck or hair really tightly in the process."

> Matt's mom, 36th week

"It's almost as if there's something about my baby's bed. I'll take her upstairs, sound asleep, and as soon as she feels the mattress, her eyes pop open. And boy, does she start screaming!"

> Laura's mom, 33rd week

She May Demand Attention

Most babies start asking for more attention, and even easy ones are not always content at being left alone. Some demanding little persons are not satisfied until their mothers' attention is completely focused on them. Some may become super troublesome as soon as their mothers dare to shift their attention to someone or something else, as if they are jealous.

"When I'm talking to other people, my son always starts screaming really loudly for attention."

> Paul's mom, 36th week

"My baby is having more difficulty staying in the playpen on his own. He's clearly starting to demand attention. He likes having us close."

> Frankie's mom, 34th week

She May Sleep Poorly

Your baby may start sleeping less well. Most babies do. She may refuse to go to bed, fall asleep less easily, and wake up sooner. Some are especially hard to get to sleep during the day. Others at night. And some stay up longer both during the day and at night.

"My son keeps waking up at night. Sometimes, he'll be up playing in his crib for an hour and a half at 3:00 A.M."

> Matt's mom, 33rd week

"My daughter stays up late in the evenings and doesn't want to go to bed. She doesn't sleep much."

> Hannah's mom, 35th week

"My baby cries herself to sleep."

> Juliette's mom, 33rd week

She May Have "Nightmares"

A fussy baby can also be a very restless sleeper. Sometimes, she may yell, toss, and turn so much that you think she is having a nightmare.

"My son wakes up often during the night. One time, he seemed to be dreaming."

Paul's mom, 37th week

"My daughter keeps waking up in the middle of the night screaming. When I lift her from her crib, she quiets down again. Then, I put her back, and she'll go back to sleep."

Emily's mom, 35th week

She May Act Unusually Sweet

At this age, your baby may employ entirely new tactics to stay close to you. Instead of whining and complaining, she may opt for something entirely different and kiss and cuddle up to you. Often, she will switch back and forth between troublesome and sweet behavior, trying out what works best to get the most attention. A mother of an independent baby is often pleasantly surprised when her baby finally starts cuddling up to her!

"Sometimes, my baby didn't want anything. At other times, she became very cuddly."

Ashley's mom, 36th week

"My son is more affectionate than he's ever been. Whenever I get near him, he grabs and hugs me tightly. My neck is full of red blotches from nuzzling and snuggling. He's also not as quick to push me away anymore. Sometimes, he'll sit still so I can read a book with him. I love it! He finally wants to play with me, too."

Matt's mom, 35th week

"My baby expresses his clinginess by acting sweeter and more affectionate, coming to lie down with me and snuggling up against me. I enjoy being with him."

Steven's mom, 36th week

She May Be Listless

Your baby may become altogether more quiet. You may hear her babbling less often, or you may see her moving around and playing less. At other times, she might briefly stop doing anything and just lie there, gazing into the distance. Don't worry, it is only temporary.

"My son's quieter and often lies there staring into nothingness. I wonder if something's bothering him or he's starting to get sick."

Steven's mom, 36th week

She May Refuse to Have Her Diaper Changed

When you set your baby down to be dressed, undressed, or changed, she may protest, scream, wriggle, act impatient, and be unmanageable. Most babies do now.

"Dressing, undressing, and changing diapers is a nightmare. My baby screams the moment I put her down. It drives me crazy."

Juliette's mom, 35th week

"My daughter has started to hate getting dressed and undressed. She usually carries on like there's no tomorrow."

Emily's mom, 36th week

She May Seem More Babyish

For the first time, some mothers will notice the recurrence of infantile behavior that they thought had been left behind. Setbacks have probably been experienced before, but the older the baby gets, the more obvious they become. Mothers dislike seeing setbacks. It makes them feel insecure, but they really are perfectly normal. They promise you that something new is on the verge of breaking through. Try to find out what it is. Brief setbacks may happen during every fussy phase. Be happy with them; your baby is doing well.

My Diary

Signs My Baby Is Growing Again

Between 32 and 37 weeks, you may notice your baby starting to show any of these behaviors. They may be signs that he is ready to make the next leap. Check off the signs that your baby shows below.

❑ Cries more often and is frequently bad-tempered or cranky

❑ Is cheerful one moment and cries the next

❑ Wants you to keep him busy, or does so more often than before

❑ Clings to your clothes, or clings more often than before

❑ Acts unusually sweet

❑ Throws temper tantrums, or does so more often than before

❑ Is more shy

❑ Wants physical contact to be tighter or closer

❑ Sleeps poorly

❑ Seems to have nightmares, or does so more often than before

❑ Loses appetite

❑ Babbles less

❑ Is less lively

❑ Sometimes just sits there, quietly daydreaming

❑ Refuses to have diaper changed

❑ Sucks his thumb, or does so more often than before

❑ Reaches for a cuddly toy, or does so more often than before

❑ Is more babyish

OTHER CHANGES YOU NOTICE

_____

_____

"My baby has difficulty falling asleep. She starts crying the same sort of cries as she did when she'd just been born."

> Juliette's mom, 32nd week

"I have to rock and sing my son to sleep again every night, just like I used to."

> Steven's mom, 35th week

She May Lose Her Appetite

Many babies seem less interested in food and drink at this time. Some seem to have no appetite and may dig in their heels and refuse some meals altogether. Others will only eat what they put into their mouths themselves. Others still are picky, spill things, and spit things out. Because of this, mealtimes may take longer than they used to.

If you have a fussy eater, she may also be unmanageable during meals, not wanting to eat when her food is there and wanting it as soon as it has been taken away. Or she may demand a lot of food one day and refuse to eat the next. Every variety is possible.

"My son refused my breast for 3 days. It was terrible. I felt like I was going to explode. Then, just when I decided it might be time to start cutting down on breastfeeding because it was getting to be that T-shirt time of year again, he decided he wanted to nurse all day long. So then I was afraid I might not have enough because he wasn't eating anything else anymore. But it seems to be working out okay. So far, I haven't heard him complain."

> Matt's mom, 34th week

How This Leap May Affect You

Like the leaps that preceded it, the changes that your baby is going through will inevitably affect you. Here are some emotions you may encounter.

You May Feel Insecure

A fussy baby usually makes a mother worry. She wants to understand what is making her behave this way, and when she believes she has found a good explanation, it puts her mind at ease. At this age, most mothers decide it must be teething pain, but this may not be the case.

> "My daughter's top teeth are bothering her. She keeps wanting me to do things with her, such as go for walks or play with her."
>
> **Eve's mom, 34th week**
> (She did not cut her next tooth until the 42nd week.)

You May Be Exhausted

If you have a demanding little tyke who needs little sleep, you may feel extremely tired, especially toward the end of the fussy phase. Most mothers of demanding babies get very exhausted. They may think that they can't go on much longer. Some also complain of headaches, backaches, and nausea.

> "It makes me feel so discouraged at times when my little one stays up until midnight, even if she keeps playing happily. When she's finally asleep, I completely collapse. I feel drained and unable to think straight. My husband gives me no support whatsoever. He's even angry that I pay so much attention to her. His philosophy is 'just let her cry.'"
>
> **Nina's mom, 37th week**

> "The days seem to linger on forever when my son's cranky, cries, and sulks a lot."
>
> **Bob's mom, 35th week**

You May Become Aggravated

Almost all mothers become increasingly irritated by their babies' behavior during fussy periods. They become more and more annoyed by bad tempers, impatience, crying, whining, and constant demands for physical contact or attention. They are aggravated by constant clinging, the trouble they have to go through to change or dress their babies, and finicky eating habits.

"When my baby was having another one of her moods, not wanting anything and being terribly restless, I put her to bed. I am dog tired of it and terribly annoyed."

Jenny's mom, 37th week

"While I was getting my daughter dressed, her whining really got to me, and I put her down very roughly. I just couldn't stand her whining and wriggling anymore. She'd been whimpering all day."

Juliette's mom, 35th week

"When my son became so unmanageable during changing, I put him on the floor in his room and left him there. That made him stop immediately. A few moments later, he came to get me, with a howl. Then he was willing to be a bit more cooperative."

Kevin's mom, 37th week

"This week, I got angry with my baby once. He'd been screaming so relentlessly that I suddenly shouted out angrily, 'Now shut up!' That frightened him out of his wits. First he looked at me with big, round eyes, then his head drooped, as if he was genuinely ashamed of his behavior. It was such a touching sight. After that, he became a lot calmer."

Paul's mom, 37th week

"I've decided to let my son breastfeed only twice a day. I'm fed up with his fickleness. One day, he wants it all, the next he wants nothing. At home, I don't lull him to sleep at my breast anymore either. That seems to be working out fine. But when we're at someone else's house, I still do it."

Matt's mom, 37th week

You May Quarrel

Toward the end of every fussy period, most mothers who breastfeed consider stopping. The baby's fickle behavior, sometimes wanting to nurse, sometimes not, irritates them. And the demanding fashion in which a little one continuously tries to get his way is another reason mothers think seriously about giving up breastfeeding.

> "My son wants my breast whenever it suits him. And he wants it immediately. If it happens to be in some way inconvenient for me, he'll throw a raging temper tantrum. I'm afraid those tantrums are starting to turn into a habit and that pretty soon he'll try getting his way every single time by kicking and screaming. So I'm stopping right now, I think."
>
> Steven's mom, 36th week

Quarrels can also develop when mothers and babies fail to negotiate the amount of physical contact and attention the little person wants and her mommy is willing to give.

> "I keep getting more and more annoyed by my baby's clinging and whining. When we go to visit friends, he'll hardly let go of me. It makes me feel like just pushing him away from me, and sometimes I do. But that only makes him angrier at me."
>
> Kevin's mom, 37th week

It's just part of life. Having feelings of anger and frustration at times is not abnormal or dangerous, but acting on them is. It's critical that you get help long before you lose control.

How Your Baby's New Skills Emerge

When your baby is approximately 37 weeks, you will notice her becoming calmer. If you watch closely, you may see her trying or doing new things.

For example, you may see her handling her toys in a different way, enjoying new things, or behaving in a more concentrated and inquisitive way. Congratulations! Your baby is making another leap. She is beginning to explore the world of categories.

> *"I noticed a big change. My son's toys are lying somewhere in a corner. They have been for some weeks now. I think that I need to supply him with more stimulating toys that will challenge him. But outside, he's very lively because there's plenty to see."*
>
> Bob's mom, 36th week

After the last leap, your baby started to understand relationships between different things he came across, both in the outside world and as they relate to his own body. He became more familiar with every aspect of his world. He discovered that he is the same kind of being as his mommy and that he could move in exactly the same way she does. He learned that other things can move as well, but that they move in very different ways from human beings, and that still other things cannot move at all on their own.

Once your baby acquires the ability to perceive and experiment with categories, he begins to understand that he can classify his world into groups. It will dawn on him that certain things are very much alike, that they look similar, or they make a similar sound, or they taste, smell, or feel the same. In short, he discovers that different things can share the same traits.

For instance, he can now discover the meaning of the word "horse." He can learn that every horse falls into this category, whether it is brown, white, or spotted; whether the horse is out in a field, in a stable, in a pho-

---

More Like One of Us

The use of different categories in our speech is indicative of our way of thinking. Now your baby will be able to start understanding and using this way of thinking as well. This will make it easier for you and your baby to understand one another from now on.

---

tograph, in a painting, or in a picture book; whether it is a clay horse or a live horse. It is still a horse.

Naturally, this new understanding will not happen overnight. He must first get to know people, animals, and objects well. He has to realize that things must possess certain similarities in order to belong to a certain category. Therefore, he has to be able to spot these similarities, and this takes practice and time. When your baby acquires the ability to perceive categories, he will start experimenting with them. He will start to study people, animals, and objects in a particular way. He will observe, compare, and arrange them according to similarities, and then place them in specific categories. Your baby's comprehension of a category is the result of a lot of research that he conducts much as a real researcher would. He observes, listens to, feels, tastes, and experiments with both similarities and differences. Your baby works hard at his investigations.

Later on, when your child starts talking, you will see that he has already discovered many of the categories we use and sometimes will have made up his own names for them. For instance: he may call a garage a "car house," an apartment building a "block house," or a fern a "feather plant." The names he uses refer directly to whatever trait he found most characteristic.

As soon as your baby acquires the ability to divide his world into categories, he can start doing just that. He not only examines what makes something a *horse, dog,* or *bear,* but also what makes something *big, small, heavy, light, round, soft,* or *sticky,* as well as what makes something *sad, happy, sweet,* or *naughty.*

Games played during research with babies clearly show that from this age on, babies' reactions take on a different quality. Some researchers believe that intelligence makes its first appearance at this age. At first look, it might seem that way, but it does not follow that babies never had any thoughts prior to this age. In fact, they have had their own way of thinking that perfectly suited each stage of their development. Unfortunately, these ways are lost to adults, and we can only imagine what they might be like. When the baby begins to classify the world in groups as we do, though, his way of thinking becomes more like an adult's. Because he starts to think in the same way we do, we are able to understand him better.

This ability to perceive and experiment with categories affects everything a baby does. His way of experiencing things has changed, and it is now time to make sense of it.

Your Baby's Choices: A Key to His Personality

A new world, full of possibilities, is open to your baby in the world of categories. Between the ages of 37 and 42 weeks, your baby will make his own selection from the wide array of things available for him to experiment with. He will choose whatever suits him best at this stage in his development and his interests. You may find him building on certain strong inclinations he showed previously, or he may launch out into new terri-

Brain Changes

Your baby's brain waves will show dramatic changes again at approximately 8 months. In addition, the baby's head circumference increases, and the glucose metabolism in the brain changes at this age.

(continued on page 212)

 My Diary

How My Baby Explores the New World of Categories

Don't be alarmed if many of these activities don't show up until much later. What your baby is really learning in this world is the concept of categories, and once she has got a grasp of this through learning one skill, it will sooner or later be carried forward into other skills. The golden rule is "help, don't push."

RECOGNIZING ANIMALS AND OBJECTS

❏ Shows that she can recognize a category, such as animals, in pictures, toys, and real life

❏ Shows that she distinguishes shapes

❏ Shows that she thinks something is dirty, for instance by wrinkling her nose

❏ Shows that she thinks something is fun or good by making a characteristic sound or movement

❏ Understands names of animals or objects, such as toothbrush, sock, bread stick, cat, lamb, or duck. When you ask, "Where's . . . ?" she will look for it. When you say, "Get your . . . " she will sometimes get it

❏ Repeats words after you now and then

❏ Compares things seen directly and through a screen, for instance through a sieve, the mesh of a screen door, or glass

RECOGNIZING PEOPLE AS PEOPLE

❏ Relates more to other people with sounds and gestures

❏ Imitates other people more often; mimics what they do

❏ Clearly wants to play games with other people more often

❏ Calls family members. Each has his or her own sound

RECOGNIZING PEOPLE IN DIFFERENT CIRCUMSTANCES

❏ Recognizes people, even in unrelated situations

❏ Makes silly faces at his mirror image and laughs

❏ Looks at a thing or person in the room and then tries to find the same thing or person in the mirror

RECOGNIZING EMOTIONS

❏ Becomes jealous for the first time when another child is receiving mother's attention

❏ Comforts a cuddly toy when dropped or thrown

❏ Acts extra sweet when she wants something

❏ Exaggerates her mood to let everyone know how she is feeling

❏ Starts to cry when another child is crying

SWITCHING ROLES

❏ Can initiate a game by himself

❏ Plays peek-a-boo with a younger baby

❏ Uses the bottle to feed mother

❏ Asks mother to sing a song, then starts clapping his hands

❏ Asks to play hide-and-seek by crawling behind something

❏ Asks you to build blocks by handing you his blocks

OTHER CHANGES YOU NOTICE

_____

_____

point. There's a very big world out there for him to explore,
important not to compare your baby too closely to other babies.
by is unique.

watch your baby closely as you check off the skills he selects from the
list "How My Baby Explores the New World of Categories" on page 210.
You will learn where his interests lie and what makes him unique. Respect
his choices, and help him explore the things that interest him.

Babies love anything new and it is important that you respond when
you notice any new skills or interests. He will enjoy it if you share these
new discoveries, and his learning will progress more quickly.

what
You Can Do to
Help

Your baby needs time and help to come to understand why something
does or does not fall into a certain category. You can help her with this by
giving her the opportunity and the time to experiment and play in such a
way that she will learn why something belongs to a certain category. You
can encourage and console her when necessary and present her with new
ideas.

Give your baby the opportunity to expand her understanding of categories. It makes no difference which categories she explores first. Once
she gets the idea about one or two categories, it will become easier for her
to apply this understanding to other categories later on. Some little ones
will prefer to start out with recognizing objects, while others will begin
with recognizing people. Let your baby be your guide. After all, it is impossible for her to learn everything at once.

Help Your Baby Explore the New World through Investigation

When your baby starts experimenting with categories, you will notice that
she is actually busy examining an entire range of characteristics and com-

paring them. She is using relationships to work out what categories are about. By doing this, she will learn the most important characteristics of whatever she is examining. She will find out whether or not something *bounces* back, whether it is *heavy* or *light*, how it feels to the touch, and so on. She will examine something from all sides, hold it upside down or hold her head sideways, move it around quickly and slowly. This is the only way for her to find out: "This is a *ball*, that isn't" or "This block is *round*, the other one isn't."

Some babies are particularly interested in different shapes, such as *round, square,* and *notched* shapes. They look at the shape and trace its perimeter with one little finger. Then they do the same with a different shape. They are comparing shapes, so to speak. With blocks, they usually pick out round ones first, which shows they are able to recognize them. If your baby seems fascinated by shapes, give her a set of blocks with all sorts of different shapes.

You may also see that your baby will find plenty of things in the house that have shapes that interest her. Have you ever noticed how your baby looks at things that are at a distance and attract her attention? She usually does this while moving her head from left to right. She does this to learn that even when she moves around, things stay the same size and shape. Find out what your baby likes to explore and how she wants to do it. Offer her the opportunities she needs.

"My son tries to catch the running water in the tub when the tap is on. Apparently he thinks it's something he can grab. He'll close his hand around the water, and then when he opens it there's nothing in it. He finds this most peculiar. But he can keep it up for some time."

— Paul's mom, 43rd week

Many babies like to examine the different components of things. By exploring an object this way, she will eventually find out how that object is assembled and to what category it belongs. If your baby is such a scientist, she may suck successively on different sides of an object, for instance, or press on the top, in the middle, and on the bottom of something. But her explorations can have surprising side-effects.

> "My baby's crazy about knobs. This week, he explored every nook and cranny on the vacuum cleaner. He touched the knobs as well. Accidentally, he pushed the right button and whoosh, the vacuum switched on. It scared the living daylights out of him."
>
> Bob's mom, 38th week

Some babies love touching things with their hands to find out how they feel. This way they test for categories such as *firmness, stickiness, roughness, warmth, slipperiness,* and so on. Allow your baby to explore.

The Advantages of Demolishing

If your baby is examining the different components of things, he often ends up by taking something apart bit by bit. If your baby starts to demolish, give him playthings he can explore in this way. Stack some blocks for him so that he can remove them one by one. Show him how to do it. You can do the same with doughnut rings of different sizes that stack on a rod. Also try giving him a pile of magazines, which he can move one by one. See what other games your baby invents by himself and support him if it is not dangerous or too costly. You may also show how you take things apart yourself. This experience is very important, because after the next leap he can use this knowledge to his advantage when he starts to assemble instead of demolish.

> "My son likes to fiddle with locks on cabinets and doors. Even if the key's been turned a quarter of the way, he still manages to get it out."
>
> John's mom, 37th week

"My son's playing is much more concentrated now. Sometimes, he'll even examine two things at the same time. For instance, he will take his time to mash a piece of banana with one hand, and crush a piece of apple with the other. Meanwhile, he'll look from one hand to the other."

Frankie's mom, 42nd week

"My baby examines sand, water, pebbles, and sugar by putting some in his fist and feeling it for a very long time. Then he'll put it in his mouth."

Bob's mom, 40th week

Sometimes, a baby loves rubbing other parts of her body against objects, or she will pick something up and run it past her body. This way, the baby will become even more familiar with whatever she is examining, so give her this opportunity.

"I put a swing up for my son in a doorway. There's a knot under the seat, and that's his favorite part. He'll sit under the swing and hold on to the doorpost, so that he can raise himself a little when the knot swings past his head and touches his hair. He'll just sit there, experiencing the feeling of it."

Bob's mom, 39th week

In the world of categories some babies like to experiment with handling people, animals, and objects *roughly* and *carefully*. If you see yours doing this, let her know that certain things hurt and objects can break. If she experiments like this, she knows perfectly well what she is doing.

"My son often bites me and sometimes handles his toys and other things very roughly. And yet, at times he can also be careful in an exaggerated way. He'll stroke flowers and ants with one little finger, only to squash them seconds later. Then, when I say 'shh, careful' he'll start touching with one little finger again."

Bob's mom, 40th week

"When we were in the bath, my son started to examine my nipple very carefully, with one little finger, only to continue pushing, pulling, and poking it around. His own penis was next. He was a bit more careful with that!"

Matt's mom, 41st week

"First, my baby examines my eyes, ears, and nose with her little index finger. Then she tickles them. Then, as she gets more and more excited, she gets rougher, pushing and poking at my eyes, pulling at my ears and nose, and sticking a finger up my nostril."

Nina's mom, 39th week

Some babies compare the weights of playthings and other objects. If yours is discovering the categories *heavy* and *light*, give her the opportunity to experiment.

"My baby lifts everything she walks past up for a moment."

Jenny's mom, 41st week

Usually, your baby studies the concepts *high* and *low*, *little* and *large* through crawling, climbing, standing, or walking. She will climb onto, over, and under everything. She will do this sedately, in a controlled manner, almost as if she is planning out how to do things.

"My son tries to crawl under and through everything. He looks for a while, then off he goes. Yesterday, he got stuck under the bottom step of the stairs. We all panicked!"

John's mom, 40th week

Give an Active Baby Room to Investigate

From this age on, it usually becomes more and more important to give a mobile baby enough room in order to give him ample opportunity to investigate all sorts of categories. An already physically active baby may now become more dexterous and stable while sitting, standing, crawling, and walking. As a result, he will be able to do much more with his body. He can choose to squat, crawl, or climb up onto furniture or stand on his toes when he wants to reach something. Allow him to crawl through your home, climb onto things, and hoist himself up on the most impossible ledges. Secure the safety gates by the stairs on the second or third step, and allow him to practice going up and down stairs. Place a mattress at the bottom of the stairs, so that he can not hurt himself.

"My son clambers up everything. He even tried to scale the smooth surface of a wall."

John's mom, 42nd week

"My little girl was sitting in her high chair at the table, and before I knew it, she had climbed onto the table. I guess I need eyes in the back of my head now."

Emily's mom, 42nd week

Your little crawler can learn a lot outside as well. Give him room there, too. For instance, walk with him in the woods, at the beach, at a lake, in the sandbox, and in the park. Just as long as you do not lose sight of him.

 Baby Care

Make His Surroundings Baby-Proof

Make sure that the space your baby is exploring is safe. But nevertheless, do not take your eyes off him for a single second. He will always manage to find something that can be dangerous that you might not have thought of.

Top Games for This Wonder Week

Here are games and activities that most babies like best now and that will help them practice their newly developing skills.

EXPLORING

Some things will seem absolutely fascinating to your baby, but venturing out on his own voyage of discovery may be dangerous or impossible. So help him. You can help him handle breakable picture frames or heavy figurines, for instance, so that he won't break them or hurt himself but will satisfy his curiosity.

Bells and Switches

Allow your baby to ring a doorbell. He will be able to hear right away what he is doing. You could let him press a button in the elevator as well. This way, he will feel he's doing something grown-up. Allow him to turn on the light when it is very dark, so that he can see what the effect is. Let him push the button in the bus sometimes, or at a pedestrian crossing, and explain to him what is happening that he should look for. This will teach him something about the relationship between what he is doing and what happens next.

Outdoor Exploration

At this age, most babies can not get enough of being outdoors. Taking your baby outdoors will teach him a lot as well. He will see new things. Whether you're bike riding, walking, stroller jogging, or backpacking, be sure to stop now and then to allow your baby to look closer at, listen to, and touch things.

Dressing

Many babies seem to have no time for dressing and grooming. They are far too busy with other things. But they love to look at themselves and are even more interested when something is being done to them. Use this to its advantage. Towel your baby off, dress, and undress him in front of a mirror so that he can play a sort of peek-a-boo game with himself at the same time.

WORDS

Your baby often understands a lot more than you think, and he loves being able to demonstrate this. He will now start to expand the range of words and phrases he understands with pleasure.

Naming

Name the things your baby looks at or listens to. When your baby expresses with gestures what he wants, translate his question for him by putting it into words. This will teach him that he can use words to express himself.

Let your baby choose a book and hand it to him. Take him on your lap or seat him close beside you. This way he can turn the pages by himself. Point to the picture he is looking at and name the object. You can also make the appropriate sounds for the particular animal or object you are pointing to. Encourage your baby to make that word or sound as well. Don't try to continue if your baby loses interest. Some babies need a momentary cuddle or tickle after each page to keep their attention focused.

Tasks

Ask your baby if he will give you whatever he is holding by saying, for instance, "Give it to Mommy." Ask him to give it to Daddy as well sometime. You can also ask him to get something for you—for instance, "Pass me the toothbrush," and "Get me the ball." Also try calling him sometime when you are out of sight:

(continued)

Top Games for This Wonder Week (cont.) --------------

"Where are you?" and have him answer. Or ask him to come to you, "Come over here." Praise him if he participates, and continue only as long as your baby still enjoys it.

COPYCAT

Many babies study other people with great interest and love imitating what they see other people do. If your baby does this as well, mimic him and encourage him to mimic you.

Do This

First, challenge your baby to imitate whatever you are doing, then imitate him again. Often he will be able to go on forever, taking turns doing the same thing over and over. Try alternating your gestures as well. Make the gestures a little faster or slower. Try making them with the other hand, or with two hands. Try making them with sound or without, and so on. Try doing this game in front of a mirror as well. Some babies love repeating gestures in front of a mirror while watching themselves to see how everything is done.

Talking to the Mirror

If your baby is interested in the positions of the mouth, try practicing them sometime in front of a mirror. Turn it into a game. Sit down in front of the mirror together and toy with vowels, consonants or words, whatever your baby likes best. Give him time to watch and copy. Many babies love watching themselves imitating gestures as well, such as movements of hand and head. Try this sometime, too. If your baby can see himself while he is imitating you, he will immediately be able to see whether he is doing it just like you.

Pat a Cake

Sing *Pat a cake, pat a cake, baker's man,* and let your baby feel every move that goes with the song. In order to do this, take his hands in yours and make the movements together. Sometimes babies will imitate the clapping of their own accord. Or they will raise their hands. They are still unable to imitate all the movements in sequence at this age, but they are able to enjoy them.

ROLE SWITCHING
Encourage your baby to take up a role he has seen you or an older child perform. Then try to switch roles.

Chase

You can consider this the first game of tag. It can be played crawling or walking. Try turning the game around sometime as well—crawl or walk away, and clearly indicate that you expect he will come after you. Try to escape if your baby makes attempts at catching you. If your baby does catch you, or you have caught him, then cuddle him or raise him up high in the air.

Hide-and-Seek

Hide yourself in such a way that your baby sees you disappear, then let him look for you. Also try pretending sometime that you have lost him and are looking for him. Sometimes babies are quick to hide and will stay behind their beds or hide in corners very quietly. Usually, they will pick the spot you were just hiding in or one that was a smash hit the day before. React with enthusiasm when you have found each other.

How to Help Your Baby Explore the New World through Play-acting

If your baby is very bright socially, she will be able to pretend that she is *sad*, *sweet*, or *distressed* from this point on. Such emotional states are categories, too. This means that she can start manipulating or taking advantage of you. Usually, mothers fall for this at first. Some simply refuse to believe that their children, still only babies, could be capable of doing anything like this deliberately. Others are secretly a little proud. If you see your little one is putting on an act, allow her to have a taste at success, if possible. But at the same time, let her know that you know what she is doing. This will teach her that the use of emotions is important, but that she can not use them to manipulate you.

> "During the day, my girl is very troublesome, really pesky, but when it's time for her to go to bed in the evening, she plays like a little angel. It's as if she thinks, 'As long as I behave myself, I don't have to go to bed.' It's useless, anyway, trying to put her to bed when she isn't tired yet, because she'll refuse to stay lying down. Last Friday, she went to bed at 11:30 P.M."
>
> **Jenny's mom, 37th week**

> "If I'm talking with someone, my son will suddenly need instant help, or he'll pretend that he injured himself on something."
>
> **Matt's mom, 39th week**

Sometimes a baby will take up a role she has seen her mother or an older child perform. This is possible now because she knows that she is a person, the same way other people are. In other words, both she and other people belong to the same category. As a result she is able to do the same things that other people can do. She can hide, just as her mother used to, and make her the seeker. She can go get her own toys when she feels like playing with them. Always respond to this, even if only for a short while.

Top Toys for This Wonder Week

Here are toys and things that most babies like best as they explore the world of categories.

- Anything that opens and closes like doors and drawers
- Pans with lids
- Doorbells, bus bells, elevator buttons, traffic light buttons
- Alarm clocks
- Magazines and newspapers to tear
- Plastic plates and cups with plastic silverware
- Things that are larger than he is, such as boxes or buckets
- Cushions and duvets to crawl over and under
- Containers, especially round ones, pots, and bottles
- Anything that he is able to move, such as handles or knobs
- Anything that moves by itself, such as shadows or branches
- Balls of all sizes, from ping-pong balls to large beach balls
- Dolls with realistic faces
- Blocks in all shapes and sizes, the larger the better
- Baby pools
- Sand, water, pebbles, and plastic tools
- Swings
- Picture books with one or two large, distinct pictures per page
- Posters with several distinct pictures
- Toy cars

But beware of other things they are attracted to like: electrical plugs and switches, washing machines, dishwashers, vacuum cleaners, hair dryers, other appliances and stairs.

This will teach her that she is making herself understood and that she is important.

> "This week, another child a little older than my son visited our home. My son and the other little girl each had a bottle. At a certain point, the little girl stuck her bottle in my baby's mouth and started feeding him. She kept holding the bottle herself. The next day, I had him on my lap and was giving him a bottle. Suddenly, he took the bottle and stuck it in my mouth, then started laughing, drank some himself, then stuck it back in my mouth. I was amazed. He'd never done anything like that before."
>
> — Paul's mom, 41st week

> "My daughter stood by a stroller with the neighbors' little boy in it and started playing peek-a-boo with him. Together, they thought it was the funniest thing."
>
> — Emily's mom, 40th week

Some little ones love to play the role of giver. It doesn't matter what things they give, just as long as they can keep giving and receiving—preferably the latter. If your baby gives anything at all, it goes without saying that she expects to get it back immediately. She will often understand the words "Can I have . . . ," as well as "please." So you can combine the giving-and-receiving game with speech, helping her to understand things even better.

> "My daughter likes to show everyone her biscuit with a big smile on her face. Of course, one is not expected to take the biscuit. She quickly retreats her hand when she thinks this would happen. The other day, she proudly reached out to show granddad's dog her cookie, but he wolfed it away in a flash. Flabbergasted, she looked at her empty hand and then she cried of anger."
>
> — Hannah's mom, 41st week

Show Understanding for Irrational Fears

When your baby is learning a new skill, she may also discover a new danger and develop fear. One of these is the fear of the category *heights*. Another one is the fear of *being confined*. When your baby suddenly acts

The Importance of Consistency

Mothers are always proud of their babies' progress and accomplishments, and they automatically react with excitement and surprise. But some of those accomplishments can be mischievous. At first, a mischievous accomplishment may be amusing and your baby may take your delight or surprise as approval. She thinks she is being funny and will repeat the behavior time after time, even when mother tells her "no."

You will now need to be more consistent with your baby. When you disallow something once, it is better not to condone it the next time. Your baby loves putting you to the test.

"My baby's getting funnier and funnier because she's starting to become mischievous. She says *brrr* when she's got a mouth full of porridge, covering me with the stuff. She opens cupboards she's not allowed to touch and throws the cat's water all over the kitchen."

Laura's mom, 38th week

"My daughter won't listen to me. When I tell her 'no,' she laughs, even if I'm really angry with her. But when her babysitter says 'no,' she cries. I wonder if this is because I work. Perhaps I give in too much when I'm home, out of guilt."

Laura's mom, 39th week

scared, sympathize with her, try to find out what is bothering her, and help her. Babies tend to be wary of new things until they are sure they are harmless.

> "My baby always used to like walking when I would practice with her. Now, suddenly, she's stopped. She seems scared. If she even suspects I might let go of one hand, she'll sit down right away."
>
> **Ashley's mom, 46th week**

> "My son can't stand being confined now. When he's strapped into a car seat, he becomes absolutely hysterical."
>
> **Paul's mom, 40th week**

Between 40 and 45 weeks, another relatively easy period sets in. For the following 1 to 3 weeks, many babies are admired for their progress, independence, and cheerfulness. A wide range of things is interesting to them now, from people on horseback to flowers, leaves, ants, and mosquitoes. Many children wish to spend more time outdoors now. Other people suddenly start to play a much more important part in their lives, as well. They make contact with them much more often and are sooner prepared to play games with them. In short, baby's horizon is broader than ever.

> "At the moment, my boy's a doll. He laughs all day long. Sometimes, he'll play by himself sweetly for an hour. He seems like a completely different child this past week. He doesn't look as bloated anymore, and he feels very lithe. He was always a little unwieldy, but now he seems to have loosened up a lot more. He's much livelier, energetic, and adventurous."
>
> **Frankie's mom, 42nd week**

"My son understands much more, so he's getting to a new place, somewhere with more possibilities. I have to make it easier to talk to him. He needs to be where he can communicate with everyone, at the table for instance. It's important now. He's focusing on other people much more outside of the house as well. He makes contact with them right away by blowing bubbles, making certain calling sounds, or by tilting his head questioningly."

Bob's mom, 40th week

Place Photo Here

After the Leap

Age: _____

Reflections: _____

chapter 9

Wonder Week 46: The World of Sequences

Babies are natural mess makers. During the last leap in your baby's mental development, this talent probably seemed at its peak. You may have marveled at your baby's knack for destruction as he disassembled, tossed around, and squished everything in his path. If you are alert for newly developing skills in your baby, at around 46 weeks you may suddenly notice him doing things that are quite the opposite. He will begin, for the first time, to try to *put things together*.

Your baby is now ready to discover the world of sequences. From this age on, he can begin to realize that to reach many of his goals, he has to do things in a certain order to be successful. You may now see your baby looking first to see which things go together and how they go together before trying to put them in each other, pile them on top of each other, or piece them together. For instance, he may concentrate on aiming as well as he can before trying to pile one block on top of another. He may push a peg through a hole in a peg board only after he has compared the shape of the peg to the hole.

This world offers whole new areas of exploration for your baby. You will notice that for the first time, he really seems to be able to put two and two together. He is sometimes able to put one action after another quite spontaneously. It may become apparent that the baby is more conscious of his actions than ever before—that he is aware of what he is doing now.

The onset of this new leap in his mental development begins at around 42 weeks, or between 40 and 44 weeks. While he grows into his new skills and learns to be comfortable in this new world, your baby will tend to be fussy and demanding once again. After all, it's a lot harder to figure out how things go together than to take them apart. The sudden alteration in his thinking can understandably be upsetting. This fussy period will often last for 5 weeks, but it may last anywhere from 3 to 7 weeks. If your baby is cranky, watch him closely to see if he is attempting to master new skills.

Your baby may cry more than he did during the past weeks. Most babies do. They may be fussy, cranky, whiny, weepy, grumpy, bad-tempered, unmanageable, and restless. They will do whatever they can to be able to be with their mothers. Some are preoccupied by this all day long. Some little clingers are more frantic at the prospect of separation than others. They will use every possible means they can think of to be able to stay with their mothers.

"Whenever my baby's brother comes anywhere near him and touches him, he'll start to cry immediately because he knows it will get a reaction out of me."

Kevin's mom, 41st week

Your baby may cry less when she is near you. Most fussy babies cry less when they are with their mothers. And they complain even less when they have their undivided attention.

> "Because I want to keep my baby's sniveling down to an absolute minimum, we do everything together. I do my housekeeping carrying her on my hip or my arm because otherwise I can't move an inch with her clinging to my leg. I explain to her what I'm doing, for example, how I'm making tea or folding towels. We also usually go to the bathroom together. When I do go on my own, I leave the door open. I do this first so that I can see if she's doing anything dangerous, but also because then she can see me and follow me to her heart's content. And she always does. This way of going about things is the only way either of us will get any peace of mind."
>
> Emily's mom, 43rd week

How You Know It's Time to Grow

She May Cling to Your Clothes

Your baby may go to great lengths to be able to stay as close to you as possible. She may literally wrap himself around you, even when there are no strangers present. Some babies do not necessarily cling to their mothers but do want to stay remarkably close to them so that they can keep an eye on them at all times. And there are those who keep coming back to their mothers, as if they need a "mommy refill," to be reassured when they leave her again.

> "My son wants to sit on my lap, ride on my arm, crawl all over me, sit on top of me, or cling to my legs all day long, like a parasite clings to a fish. When I put him down, he bursts into tears."
>
> Bob's mom, 41st week

"My daughter will sit on my shoe and wrap her little arms round my leg. Once she's hanging on, she won't let go if she can help it. I really need to think of some kind of diversion to get her to let go."

> **Emily's mom, 43rd week**

"At the moment, my daughter tends to stay near, but she still does her own thing. It's almost as if she's circling around me like a satellite orbits the earth. If I'm in the living room, she'll be doing something next to me, and when I go to the kitchen, she'll be emptying a cupboard next to me there."

> **Jenny's mom, 47th week**

"Often, my son comes to me to rub tummies, and then he runs off again. I tend to notice it particularly when I'm sitting somewhere doing something."

> **Matt's mom, 41st week**

She May Be Shier with Strangers

When there are strangers near her, looking at her, talking to her, or, worse still, reaching a hand out toward her, your little one may become even clingier with you than she already is. Many babies are shy now.

"My son is a little shy. When he sees new people, or if someone suddenly enters the room, he'll bury himself in my neck. It doesn't last long, though. He just needs to get used to them."

> **Matt's mom, 42nd week**

"My son is shier than he ever was before. Even his grandfather isn't allowed to look at him."

> **Kevin's mom, 43rd week**

"I noticed this week that my baby was really starting to cling to me a lot. Now, whenever a stranger reaches out to embrace her, she'll grab me. But if people give her some time, she often ends up going to them by herself in the end. They just have to make sure that they don't pick her up too soon."

Ashley's mom, 47th week

She May Want Closer Physical Contact with You

Some little worriers hold on to their mothers as tightly as they can once they have a hold on them or when they are sitting on their laps, as if they do not want to give their mothers the chance to let go. Other babies react furiously when they are set down or when their mothers walk across the room.

"If we're apart for even a moment, my daughter cries with rage. When I return, she'll always hit, claw, pinch, and push me for a moment first. If the dog's around, she'll immediately go for him. Once, I came back to find her with a whisker in her hand."

Emily's mom, 43rd week

She May Want to Be Kept Busy

Most babies start asking for more attention now. Your baby may do the same. Even an easy little one usually prefers doing things with you. A demanding little person would, if she could have her way, keep you busy keeping her busy night and day. She is often not satisfied until she has her mother's undivided attention. She can have eyes only for her and only be focused on her.

"My son keeps coming up to me to read a book. He sits with me much more patiently, too. It's just what I've always wanted. He's usually busy as a bee. So when he finally does want to spend some time with me, it makes up for all the arrears."

Paul's mom, 44th week

"My son is becoming less lively in general. His motor development is starting to grind to a halt. He's paying less attention to it now. His toys aren't particularly popular now either. Even when I play along, he has a very short attention span. He'd rather have me than his toys."

Bob's mom, 41st week

"When my son is nursing, if I do anything or talk to anyone, he wails. I have to look at him, fidget with him, or stroke him. As soon as I stop for a second, he'll wriggle uncontrollably and kick furiously, as if to say: 'I am here.'"

Matt's mom, 43rd week

She May Be Jealous

Your little one can be extra cranky, naughty, or sweet when you pay attention to someone or something else. This change in behavior usually makes a mother wonder if her baby might be jealous. This discovery usually comes as a surprise.

"I babysit a 4-month-old baby. My son always finds it very interesting when I give her a bottle. But this week, he was impossible. He kept doing things he normally never does. He was really causing trouble, being obnoxious. I think he was a bit jealous."

John's mom, 44th week

She May Be Moody

Your baby might be cheerful one day and the total opposite the next. Her mood can also change suddenly. One moment, she may be busy and happy doing something, the next she could start whining and complaining. The mood swings come out of the blue for no apparent reason as far as her mother can tell. At times this can make a mother feel insecure.

> "My baby would cling and cry her eyes out one moment and seem to be having the greatest fun the next—as if she could turn it on and off at the flick of a switch. I just don't know what to do. I wonder if something could suddenly be hurting her."
>
> Nina's mom, 43rd week

She May Sleep Poorly

Your baby may sleep less well. Most babies do now. They either refuse to go to bed, have more difficulty falling asleep, or wake up earlier. Some are particularly troublesome sleepers during the day. Others are worse at night. And still others are reluctant to go to bed at any time.

> "My daughter doesn't need much sleep. She stays up hours later in the evening, playing happily."
>
> Hannah's mom, 43rd week

> "My baby wakes up 2 or 3 times a night and doesn't sleep well in the afternoon either. Sometimes it takes me 3 hours to get her to go to sleep."
>
> Jenny's mom, 48th week

> "My son is more restless now. When it's time for bed, I have to force him to calm down. Then, he wakes up a few times during the night."
>
> Frankie's mom, 45th week

> "My son used to sleep in wonderfully long. Unfortunately, he doesn't anymore."
>
> Matt's mom, 41st week

She May Have "Nightmares"

Your baby may turn into a restless sleeper. She could even toss and turn so much that you suspect that she is having a nightmare.

> "My baby woke up screaming at the top of her lungs, like she does when she's angry. I think she must have dreamed something she didn't like."
>
> Emily's mom, 45th week

She May Be Listless

Your baby may temporarily be a little apathetic. Sometimes babies are. They are less active or babble a little less. They may even stop all activity for a while and simply lie and stare. Mothers do not like to see this happen. They think that it is abnormal, and they may try to get the little tykes moving again.

> "My daughter is not as active anymore. Often she just sits there, wide-eyed, looking around."
>
> Hannah's mom, 45th week

> "Occasionally, my son will just sit there, gazing into thin air. This is a change because he always used to be doing something."
>
> Matt's mom, 43rd week

> "My son is more passive, quieter. Sometimes, he'll sit there, staring off into the distance for a few moments. I don't like it one bit. It's as if he's not normal."
>
> Bob's mom, 41st week

She May Refuse to Have Her Diaper Changed

Your little one may become more impatient and unmanageable when she is being dressed, undressed, or changed. She may whine, scream, and writhe as soon as you touch her. Sometimes mothers become aggravated with or concerned about a troublesome squirmer.

"My son won't stay still for a minute. Sometimes, getting his diaper off is like being in a wrestling match. I love the fact that he's become more active, but I don't see why he can't lie still for a few seconds."

Frankie's mom, 43rd week

"Dressing, undressing, and changing are a nightmare. This happened a while ago as well. Back then, I thought the lower part of her little back might be troubling her. I started to worry more and more. So I took her to the pediatrician, but he said that her back was perfectly fine. He had no idea what could be causing it, either. But then, it cleared up by itself."

Juliette's mom, 46th week

She May Lose Her Appetite

Many babies seem less interested in food and drink at this time. Your baby may lose her appetite, or she may be very choosy, eating something only if, and when, she feels like it. Mothers are often worried and aggravated by poor appetites and fussy eating.

"My son is not eating well. But all of a sudden he does want to breastfeed in the middle of the day, and he'll start whining and pulling at my blouse to get what he wants. He wakes up a lot during the night as well, wanting to breastfeed. I wonder whether he's getting good nutrition this way."

Matt's mom, 43rd week

She May Behave More Babyish

Sometimes a babyish behavior that you thought was long gone suddenly reappears. Mothers do not appreciate such revivals. They see them as backward steps and would put a stop to them if they could. Yet a relapse during fussy periods is perfectly normal. It simply means that another huge leap forward is about to happen.

> "My daughter relapsed into crawling this week. I just hope it's nothing to do with her hips or because she started walking so early."
>
> **Jenny's mom, 44th week**

> "My son doesn't want to hold his bottle himself anymore but prefers to lie back in my arms and be fed like a tiny baby. A while ago, however, he insisted on holding the bottle himself. His relapse is actually bothering me quite a bit. I kept thinking, 'Cut it out, son, I know you can do it yourself.' A few times I put his hands on the bottle, but he wouldn't budge."
>
> **Bob's mom, 41st week**

> "Very often, I have to rock my son again before he will go to sleep."
>
> **Steven's mom, 41st week**

> "My son doesn't want to stand anymore and immediately slumps to the floor. He's also become a lot more sluggish."
>
> **Bob's mom, 41st week**

She May Act Unusually Sweet

A fussy baby can now also find nicer ways of asking for more physical contact or attention. This happens more and more often and in increasingly sophisticated ways. She may bring her parents books or toys "asking" that they play with her. She may charm you into playing games with her with a variety of ploys, such as laying her little hand on your lap, snuggling up to you, or resting her head against you. Often, she may alternate between being troublesome and sweet, whichever works best at the time, to get the desired touch or attention.

Mothers of independent babies who don't usually seek much physical contact are overjoyed at the prospect of finally being able to give them a cuddle again.

> "My daughter would come up to me now and again for a cuddle. She was extremely charming this week."
>
> > **Ashley's mom, 46th week**

> "My son was very cuddly and kept clinging to me this week."
>
> > **Matt's mom, 42nd week**

> "When my son is in the bicycle seat or stroller, he keeps looking back to check if I'm still there, and then he'll give me his tiny hand."
>
> > **Paul's mom, 44th week**

> "My daughter wants to sit on my lap with a book more often. When she does, she'll stay there, snuggling up wonderfully close to me."
>
> > **Jenny's mom, 47th week**

> "My daughter keeps crawling after me. When she rounds the corner by the door, she'll give me a big smile and quickly crawl back in the other direction again. We love this little game."
>
> > **Ashley's mom, 43rd week**

She May Be Mischievous

Some mothers notice that their babies are more naughty than they used to be. It may seem your baby does everything that he is not allowed to. Or he may be especially mischievous at times when you are rushing to finish something and can least spare the time to deal with him.

> "We're not allowed to attend to our own business. If we do, then every-thing we told our daughter not to touch suddenly becomes extremely in-

My Diary

Signs My Baby Is Growing Again

Between 40 and 44 weeks, your baby may show signs that he is ready to make the next leap into the world of sequences.

❏ Cries more often and is bad-tempered or cranky

❏ Is cheerful one moment and cries the next

❏ Wants to be kept busy, or does so more often than before

❏ Clings to your clothes, or wants to be closer to you

❏ Acts unusually sweet

❏ Is mischievous

❏ Throws temper tantrums, or throws them more often than before

❏ Is jealous

❏ Is shier with strangers than before

❏ Wants physical contact to be tighter or closer

❏ Sleeps poorly

❏ Seems to have nightmares, or has them more often than before

❏ Loses appetite

❏ Babbles less

❏ Sometimes just sits there, quietly daydreaming

❏ Refuses to have diaper changed

❏ Sucks thumb, or does so more often than before

❏ Wants to cuddle toys, or does so more often than before

OTHER CHANGES YOU NOTICE

_____

_____

teresting, such as the telephone and the knobs on the stereo. We have to watch her every second of the day."

Jenny's mom, 47th week

"My daughter keeps crawling after me. I think that's adorable. But if she doesn't do that, she makes a mess of things. She'll pull the books off their shelves and scoop the dirt out of the flower pots."

Ashley's mom, 43rd week

"Whenever my baby sees I'm busy, she crawls over to things she's not allowed to touch."

Nina's mom, 43rd week

"My son clings to me all day long, and when he doesn't, I have to keep disciplining him and taking things away from him."

Kevin's mom, 43rd week

How This Leap May Affect You

As your baby's new world expands to include sequences, his fussiness and changes that follow will affect you, too. Here are some feelings you may encounter.

You May Feel Insecure

Mothers often worry when their baby is upset. They try to find a cause for his more frequent crying. As soon as they have found one, it puts their mind at ease. At this age, they are often inclined to decide it is cutting teeth.

"I think that my son's mouth was troubling him. He wasn't his normal, easygoing self."

John's mom, 43rd week

"My son cried a lot. I don't think he had enough sleep."

Frankie's mom, 43rd week

"My daughter is whiny and fussy whenever I'm busy doing something. Perhaps she's having more difficulty dealing with her sisters at the moment."

Juliette's mom, 42nd week

You May (Yet Again) Be Exhausted

Mothers of babies who demand a lot of attention and need little sleep feel thoroughly exhausted toward the end of a fussy period. Some complain of headaches, backaches, nausea, and lack of concentration, as well.

"I feel that I've broken down completely because I'm not getting any support or recognition. I'd really love to have one evening of rest. At night, I keep running upstairs to the nursery and back down again. Often, this goes on into the middle of the night. To me, this is the most difficult age so far. I even kept putting off writing this diary. I just couldn't concentrate on it."

Emily's mom, 46th week

You May Become Annoyed

Toward the end of this fussy period, mothers become increasingly aggravated by their fretful little clingers. They are annoyed that they are constantly preoccupied with their demands and do not seem to have a life of their own anymore.

"It's tedious, literally not being able to move an inch. My son constantly demands attention, or else he throws a temper tantrum, and it's slowly but surely becoming very irritating. Sometimes, I feel like he's pulling my strings, and that makes me feel rebellious. Then I get fed up. I keep contemplating if I should take him back to the day care, after all. I've kept him at home for a few weeks now. In the beginning it felt better, but now, once in a while, I can feel myself getting slightly aggressive again."

Bob's mom, 46th week

"I'm very busy, and I can't have my daughter clinging to my legs or sitting in front of the sink anymore when I'm working. Now, when I've had enough, it's off to bed with her. Perhaps I'm starting to lose my patience."

Juliette's mom, 45th week

"Even though I have the easiest baby anyone could ever wish for, when he starts crying hysterically, I notice I do get a bit impatient with him and whisk him off to bed."

John's mom, 43rd week

Sometimes a mother is annoyed because deep down she knows that her baby is capable of more than he is showing and suspects that his behavior is just too babyish for his age. She thinks it's time for him to start behaving more independently.

"When I set my son down for a clean diaper, he always starts to yell. It's the same with clean clothes, as well. This is starting to annoy me more and more. I think he's too old for that kind of behavior. In fact, it's about time he started cooperating a little."

Bob's mom, 47th week

You May Start to Quarrel

Toward the end of every fussy period, many mothers who are still breastfeeding think about whether it might not be time to stop. One of the reasons is that the baby wants to nurse all day long. This is annoying and exhausting, and mothers begin to refuse babies sometimes. The little one, however, finds this unacceptable and before you know it, he and his mother argue.

> "I keep getting more and more annoyed because I have to lull my son to sleep at my breast. I had to start doing it again when he was having so much trouble falling asleep. Now it's starting to become a habit again. Besides, he wants to nurse an awful lot and starts screaming when he doesn't get his way. I just don't feel like doing it anymore."
>
> Matt's mom, 47th week

The good news is that for the mothers who do persist with breast-feeding, the normal feeding pattern will restore itself as soon as the fussy period is over. Once everything has settled down again, mothers seem to forget their irritations.

Another battleground is the familiar territory of negotiating a deal between mother and child about the amount of physical contact and attention.

> "I'm aggravated by my son's continuous crying just so he can sit on my lap. I get terribly angry when he bites me, if I don't respond to him fast enough. It hurts so much that I automatically give him a shove. Once, he fell and hit his head really hard. That wasn't my intention, but I was so furious it just happened."
>
> Kevin's mom, 44th week

It's critical to remember that having feelings of anger and frustration at times is not abnormal or dangerous, but acting on them is. Try to get help long before you lose control.

How Your Baby's New Skills Emerge

At about 46 weeks, you will see your baby growing calmer and attempting to do things that are brand new for him. You will see him handling his toys in a different way and enjoying new activities. He will be more precise about his actions than ever before and will pay even more attention to detail.

Your baby can now understand that sometimes one thing must follow another to make a sequence. He will realize that he can find and construct sequences in all of the senses, and as usual, your baby is unable to explore them all at once. His inclinations, preferences, and temperament will help him to select the aspects of the world that he finds most interesting and the skills that he will develop. Help him to do what he is ready to do, rather than trying to push him.

During the last leap forward, your baby realized that certain things have so much in common that they belong to one group or category. In order to categorize things, she would often examine them by breaking them down and taking them apart. For instance, she might have taken a tower of blocks apart one by one, removed a key from a lock, or loosened a handle on a chest of drawers. This paved the way for the current leap where the very opposite takes place, and she begins to experiment with putting things back together. Every baby needs to learn how to take a tower apart before she can build one. Even the seemingly simple activity of choosing the next block and then deliberately placing it in position requires a mental leap that, until this point, your baby was not prepared to take.

As her new skills begin to take wing, your little one becomes involved for the first time in *constructing*, in *putting things together*, and *linking* things. For instance, she may now take a key off a table and try to put it in a lock. She can learn to dig sand up with a spade and then put it in a bucket. She can learn to aim a ball first and then throw it. While singing a song, such as *Pat a cake, pat a cake, baker's man*, she can begin to make

(continued on page 251)

 **My Diary**

How My Baby Explores the New World of Sequences

Check off the boxes below as you notice your baby changing. Stop filling this out once the next stormy period begins, heralding the coming of the next leap.

    This world is just as multifaceted as all of the others that your baby has entered in her short life. Each baby has her own ideas about what is interesting. Your baby can't experiment with everything at once. If she has always been a listening and looking baby, this may continue at the expense of more physical activities. It is perfectly normal if most of these skills do not become evident until several months later.

POINTING AND TALKING

❑ Follows and points to a person, animal, or object that you have just named, whether in real life or a picture

❑ Points out one or two items for you to name, such as persons, animals, or objects

❑ Points out and names one or two items in turn

❑ Deliberately looks through a book, making different sounds to go with one or two pictures

❑ Points to his nose when you ask, "Where's your nose?"

❑ Points to a body part, for instance, his nose or your nose, wanting you to name it

❑ Imitates the sound when you name an animal, for instance, when you ask, "What does the cat say?" he says, "Meow"

❑ Raises his arms when you ask, "How tall are you going to be?"

❑ Says "yum" when he wants the next bite

❏ Says "no, no" when he does not want to do something

❏ Uses a word in an extended way, for instance, says "yuck" for something dirty but also when he has to be careful of something because "yuck" has come to mean "don't touch" for him

WHAT GOES TOGETHER AND WHAT COMES NEXT

❏ Knows that he can push a round peg through a round hole; for example, he will choose the round peg from a pile of pegs and try to push it through the round hole of a peg board

❏ Tries to put together three pieces of a simple puzzle

❏ Tries pushing coins through a slot

❏ Tries fitting two different sizes of containers inside each other

❏ Takes a key from somewhere else and tries to insert it into a keyhole

❏ Looks at the lamp and reaches for it when you flick the light switch

❏ Tries to talk into a telephone receiver

❏ Puts objects in a container, covers it, removes the cover, removes the objects, and repeats the cycle again

❏ Tries to put a "doughnut" ring over an upright rod

❏ Pushes toy cars around, making a *vrrrm* sound

❏ Scoops up sand with a spade and then empties it into a bucket

❏ Fills bath toys with water and empties them again

❏ Takes a good look at two Primo blocks and then tries fitting them together

(continued)

My Diary (cont.)

❏ Tries scrawling on a piece of paper with a pencil or crayon

MAKING AND USING TOOLS

❏ Helps herself learn to walk by finding an object to push

❏ Finds something to use as a step to reach a desired place or object

❏ Points with her finger in the direction she wants to go when being carried

LOCOMOTION

❏ Clambers down the stairs or off a chair or sofa backward. In the beginning, she sometimes even starts crawling backward toward the stairs before starting her descent

❏ Puts her head down in position to initiate a somersault with help

❏ Bends her knees, then stretches her legs powerfully, so that she jumps off the ground with both feet

❏ Tries to aim before throwing or kicking a ball

❏ Looks first to see whether she can reach another supporting object within the number of steps she can take by herself

PLAYING WITH OTHERS

❏ Plays with you. Clearly expresses which games he wants to play by starting them and then looking at you expectantly

❏ Repeats a game

❏ Entices you to play with him, perhaps by pretending he is unable to do something that you have seen him doing on his own before

HIDE AND SEEK

❏ Looks for something that you have hidden by completely concealing it with something else—either as a game, or because you do not want him to get ahold of it

❏ Hides something that belongs to someone else, waits and watches, then laughs when the other person finds it

COPYING A SEQUENCE OF GESTURES

❏ Imitates two or more gestures in sequence

❏ Studies the way the same sequence of gestures looks in reality and in the mirror

❏ Copies one or two movements while you are singing a song with her

HELPING OUT WITH THE HOUSEKEEPING

❏ Hands you things that you want to put away one by one

❏ Goes and gets simple objects, if you ask her to

❏ Picks up the clothes that you have just taken off her and puts them in the laundry basket

❏ Gets her own bucket with dolls' laundry, and puts it in the washing machine

❏ Gets out a broom and sweeps the floor with it

❏ Gets a cloth out and dusts things off

(continued)

My Diary (cont.)

❏ Imitates you cooking; for example, she bangs a fork in a bowl or stirs with a spoon

---

DRESSING AND GROOMING

❏ Tries to undress himself; for instance, he tries to take a sock off by pulling at his toes

❏ Tries putting on his shoe or sock by himself; for instance, he holds on to his shoe or sock and his foot and puts them together

❏ Helps when you dress him. Leans toward you when you pull a sweater on or off or sticks his foot out when the sock or shoe is coming

❏ Brushes his hair

❏ Uses a toothbrush

❏ Sometimes uses a potty

EATING AND FEEDING

❏ Offers others a bite or sip while eating and drinking

❏ Blows steam off food himself before taking a bite

❏ Sticks a piece of bread on a baby fork and eats it

❏ Can scoop up food with a spoon and put it in his mouth

OTHER CHANGES YOU NOTICE

_____

_____

_____

different gestures successively, without you having to set the example. She can learn to scoop up food with a spoon and then put it in her mouth. She may learn to pick up her clothes from the floor and then put them in the laundry basket. At this age, babies are just beginning to be aware of sequences, and it is quite a feat if they manage to string two actions together. Although they know what belongs together, their attempts may not always succeed. For instance, your baby may try putting on her shoes by getting them out but then sit down and rub them against her feet trying to put them on.

You can also tell by your baby's reactions that she is now beginning to realize how certain events usually follow after another in the normal course of events. You will notice that she now knows what the next step is in any particular sequence. For instance, if she sees you push a doorbell, you may see your baby pause to listen for the bell.

"When a tape is finished, my son now looks up at the cassette player, not at the speaker. He now knows that I have to do something to the player if he is to hear more music."

Bob's mom, 48th week

Your baby can now also start pointing out and naming different people, animals, and objects. When she does this on her own, she may often still say *da* instead of using the proper word. When she does this together with you, she may point things out and want you to name them or have you make the appropriate sound. She might like to play the game the other way around, having you point while she tells you what she calls the object. When you are carrying her around, you may also start to notice that your baby will point in the direction that she wants you to go.

Babies who haven't been doing much in the way of talking may now begin to name people, animals, and objects, or parts of these, for the first time. The very act of naming is a way of relating a spoken word or sound to a person, animal, or object. Pointing or looking followed by a word is a sequence as well. But some babies will still put off talking in favor of other skills, such as walking.

Your Baby's Choices: A Key to His Personality

Babies can now perceive and play with sequences. This opens a new world of possibilities, and your baby will make his own choices according to his mental development, build, weight, and coordination. Some babies are very social and like to focus on skills that involve people; others prefer playthings. Some pick at every little detail and others are more interested in getting an overall impression of many different skills. You may find it irresistible to make comparisons with other babies, but remember that every baby is unique.

Watch your baby closely to determine where his interests lie. Between 46 and 51 weeks, he will select the skills he likes best from this world. Respect his choices. You will find out what it is that makes him unique, and when you follow his interests, you will help him best in playing and learning. Babies love anything new and it is important that you respond when you notice any new skills or interests. He will enjoy it if you share these new discoveries, and his learning will progress more quickly.

what
You Can Do to
Help

Every baby needs time and help to learn new skills. You can help your baby by giving her the opportunity and time to toy with sequences. You can encourage her when she succeeds and console her when she does not. You can try to facilitate her attempts and make her failures easier to bear.

Your baby will find plenty of opportunities to come into contact with sequences herself. Allow her to see, hear, feel, smell, and taste them and indulge in whatever she likes best. The more she encounters and toys with sequences, the better she will learn to understand them. Pay attention, however. She might think she knows it all. It does not matter whether she prefers learning about sequences through observing, handling toys, speech, sounds, music, or locomotion. Soon she will be able to put the expertise she has gained in one area into practice in other areas with no trouble at all.

How to Help Your Baby Explore the New World through Experimentation

When your baby enters the world of sequences it dawns upon him that he has to do things in a certain order, if he wants to succeed. He has observed how adults perform a particular sequence, but he has to master it himself by trial and error. Often his "solutions" are peculiar. The sequence he performs may be correct (grabbing something and putting it into something else), but he may apply the wrong objects to the wrong targets. He knows that dirty cloths go into a container. So why only in the laundry basket and not in the dustbin or the toilet? The sequence is much the same, after all!

"My son pulls plugs from their outlets and then tries putting them into the wall. He also tries sticking other objects with two protrusions in the outlets. I have to watch him even closer now and take safety precautions."

Bob's mom, 48th week

"When my daughter wants to climb onto our bed, she opens a drawer of our nightstand, stands on it, and then climbs onto the bed. If she opens the drawer too far, the whole nightstand starts swaying back and forth. She makes me very nervous."

Jenny's mom, 49th week

Or the sequence itself may be peculiar. For instance, your baby knows how his mother walks up the stairs. But the steps are too high for him, so he has to crawl. However, on every step he stands up.

"My son desperately wants to climb the stairs on his own, but he behaves dangerously. He crawls on his knees to the next step, stands up,
then continues upwards on his knees, stands up again, and so it goes. I
don't like it one bit. I have to keep a sharp eye on him."

Steven's mom, 45th week

Once he is of the opinion that he has mastered a particular sequence,
it is "fixed." He will not accept it to be done in any other way and he
may be quite stubborn if you try to change his mind. So always pay close
attention. Your young wiseacre does not yet know the meaning of
danger.

How to Help Your Baby Explore the New World through Independence

Many babies refuse to be helped and resist any form of interference by
others. These babies want to do everything they can, or think they can, by
themselves. If yours is this type of baby, try to have as much consideration
for his feelings as possible. This is just the age when many little ones like
to start asserting their independence.

"My son always liked practicing walking together. But if I hold his hands
now, he'll immediately sit down. Then when I leave he'll give it another
try. At every successful attempt, no matter how slight, he'll look at me tri-
umphantly."

Paul's mom, 46th week

"My son keeps trying to scribble something on paper with a pencil, just
like his older brother does. But whenever his brother tries to guide his
hand to show him how it's supposed to work, he'll pull his hand away."

Kevin's mom, 48th week

"When we push pegs through my son's peg board together, he'll start throwing them. But as soon as he's on his own in the playpen, he will try to copy it. To tell the truth, it annoys me."

Paul's mom, 53rd week

"My daughter will eat only if she can put the food in her mouth herself. When I do it, she'll take it out again."

Laura's mom, 43rd week

At this age, many mothers spend huge amounts of time taking things away from their children and disciplining them. It's important to consider that your baby isn't necessarily disobedient. She just wants to do things by herself.

Show Some Understanding for Frustrations

Many mothers see their babies' striving for independence as rebellious. But if you stop to think, it is not. Your baby simply wants to do things by himself. After all, he is becoming aware of what belongs together and the order in which things need to be done. He is convinced that he knows it all and is capable of doing anything. He no longer wants you to interfere or to tell him how things should be done. He wants to make his own decisions. But, as his mother, you are not really used to this. You naturally help him as you always have, without giving it a second thought. You know perfectly well that your baby is still unable to carry out the things he wants to do properly. And you know that he will inevitably make a mess of things if he tries.

Mother and baby often may have different views of things. This can lead to conflicts. Mother sees the baby as being difficult, and the baby feels his mother is causing all the trouble. Adolescents may go through the most difficult phases, but babies and toddlers run a close second.

"My daughter is being troublesome and wants her own way with everything. She gets angry when I refuse her something. It's really tiresome."

Jenny's mom, 50th week

"My son tries to get things done by screaming and throwing temper
tantrums."

Matt's mom, 46th week

"When I complain, my daughter screams and lashes out at everything
and everybody around her, or pulls a plant from its pot. This annoys me
to no end. She behaves much better with her babysitter."

Laura's mom, 49th week

"We're stuck in one of those 'no, don't touch that' and 'no, don't do that'
phases now. But my son knows exactly what he wants, and he can get
very angry when he doesn't agree with something. Recently, he got so
upset that he didn't even notice he was standing on his own."

Frankie's mom, 49th week

How to Help Your Baby Explore the New World through Feedback

At this age, babies start testing the limits of how far they can go before
someone stops them. If you let them know clearly when they are doing
something wrong and just why it is bad or dangerous, they can learn a lot
from it.

Similarly, you should let your baby know what she is doing right by
praising her. This will teach her what is good and what is bad behavior.
Most babies ask for praise themselves, anyway. When they do something
right, they ask to be rewarded all the time. They look at you and laugh,
full of pride, or call for attention. They can keep repeating behaviors many
times as well, asking for a reward after each time.

"Every time my daughter puts a ring around the cone she'll look at me, grinning like mad and clapping."

Eve's mom, 49th week

If your baby is frustrated by things he is not able or allowed to do, you can still quite easily distract him with a favorite toy or game. Naturally this is different for every baby.

"This week, my son loved playing football. He'd kick really hard at the ball and then we'd run after it really quickly while I held his hands. It made him laugh so hard sometimes he had to lie down on the ground for a moment to stop laughing."

Paul's mom, 48th week

"My son keeps wanting to help out. He thinks that's the best thing ever and starts beaming. I do have to take my time with him, though. It takes me 10 times longer to put a pile of diapers away in the cupboard with his help. He'll hand me each diaper separately, but before he lets me have each one, he'll put it on his shoulder and rub the side of his chin against it."

Matt's mom, 48th week

Help Your Baby Explore the New World through Language

A baby who lives in the world of sequences may start pointing out and naming different people, animals, and objects. Pointing or looking, followed by a word, is a sequence. If you notice your baby doing this, listen to her and let her know that you understand her and that you think she is wonderful. Do not try to improve her pronunciation. This will spoil your baby's fun and will make no difference to the way she speaks.

Do make sure that you use the correct words all of the time. This way,

Understand Your Baby's Fears

When your baby is learning new skills, she may also perceive things that she does not fully understand yet. In a way, she discovers new anxieties—dangers that up until now she didn't realize existed. As soon as she recognizes these dangers and until she can be sure they are harmless, her fears will stay with her. So show her a little understanding.

> "My daughter keeps wanting to sit on her potty. Even if she hasn't done anything, she'll take the potty into the lavatory to empty it and flush the toilet. But while she seems fascinated by flushing, at the same time she's also scared of it. She doesn't get as frightened when she flushes the toilet herself, only when someone else does. Then she doesn't like it at all."
>
> **Jenny's mom, 50th week**

> "My daughter is fascinated by airplanes. She recognizes them everywhere: in the air, in pictures, and in magazines. This week, she suddenly became frightened by the sound, even though she's heard it before."
>
> **Laura's mom, 46th week**

your baby will automatically learn the right pronunciation in due time. For a while they will "translate" what you say into their own baby pronunciation.

"My daughter is starting to use words and point at whatever she's talking about. At the moment, she's in love with horses. When she sees a horse, she points to it and says 'hoss.' Yesterday at the park, a large Afghan dog ran past her. She called that a 'hoss,' as well."

Hannah's mom, 48th week

"My son suddenly said 'nana' to a toy cat. We have never used that word. He has a lot of toy animals. When I asked, 'Where's nana?' he kept pointing to the cat."

Paul's mom, 48th week

Some babies can tell you that they remember certain situations or that they have seen certain people before by using body language and sounds. If you notice your baby doing this, talk to him a lot, explain to him what you are seeing, and react to what he tells you about it later on.

"We go swimming every week. Usually, we see the same people there. One day, we saw one of the mothers on the street. Immediately, my son called out 'Oh oh' and pointed to her as if he recognized her. Then, he saw a girl in the swimming pool who lives near us and whom he's seen only a couple of times, and he reacted the same way."

Paul's mom, 49th week

"On our way to the store, we saw a large pile of stones. I said, 'Look at all of those stones.' My son gazed at them intently. The next day, he began pointing at the stones from a distance, looking at me and shouting 'eh, eh.'"

Steven's mom, 51st week

The Virtue of Patience

It's important to keep your patience with your baby as he tries to learn new skills. When you see he is not interested, stop. He will be occupied enough with other things that are more interesting to him at that moment.

(continued on page 264)

Here are games and activities that most babies like best now. Remember, all babies are different. See what your baby responds to best.

HELPING OUT GAMES

Your baby likes to feel needed. Let her know that you can certainly use some help from her. At this age, she will not be of any real help, but she will be able to understand the actions involved in many common activities. Plus, it is a good way of preparing her for the next leap.

DOING HOUSEWORK

Show your baby how you cook and clean. Involve him. Explain what you are doing. Give him one of your dusters. This will be much more interesting than using his own cloth. When you are baking a cake, give him his own plastic mixing bowl and spoon.

DRESSING

This is the most fun in front of a mirror. Try undressing your baby, toweling her down, and dressing her while she can watch herself sometime. Name the parts you are drying. When you notice her starting to cooperate, ask her to help out. Ask her to raise an arm or stretch her leg when you are about to put a jumper or sock on her. Praise her when she does it.

GROOMING HIMSELF

Allow your baby to groom himself. This is most fun in front of a mirror, too. This way, the baby can see for himself what he is doing, learn faster, and have more fun. Brush his hair in front of a mirror, then let him try it himself. You can do the same with brushing his teeth. You can also see if he will wash himself. Give him a washcloth when he is in the bath, and say something such as, "Go on, wash your face." Respond with enthusiasm at every attempt. You will see how proud this makes him.

FEEDING HERSELF WITH A SPOON

Allow your baby to eat by herself with a spoon. Or give her a baby fork to eat cubes of bread or pieces of fruit. Lay a large sheet of plastic under her chair so that afterward you will easily be able to clean up the mess she makes.

NAMING GAMES

Your baby often understands a lot more than you think, and he loves being allowed to prove it.

THIS IS YOUR NOSE

Touching and naming parts of his anatomy will help your baby to discover his own body. You can play this game while dressing or undressing him or while you are sitting together. Also see if he knows where your nose is.

POINTING OUT AND NAMING

For many babies, pointing out and naming things, or making the appropriate sounds, is a fun game. You can play this anywhere: outside, in a store, or with a book. Enjoy your baby's misnomers as well.

(continued)

SONG AND MOVEMENT GAMES

Now your baby may want to participate actively in songs. She may start to make one or two movements that go with them by herself, as well.

PAT A CAKE, PAT A CAKE, BAKER'S MAN

Sit facing your baby and sing:

> *Pat a cake, pat a cake, baker's man*
>
> (Clap your hands, and let your baby follow.)
>
> *Bake me a cake as fast as you can*
>
> *Prick it and pat it, and mark it with "B"*
>
> (Make pricking and patting movements, and let your baby follow.)
>
> *And put it in the oven for baby and me.*
>
> (At the word "baby," point to her or poke her in the stomach.)

ITSY BITSY SPIDER

Sit facing your baby and sing:

> *The itsy bitsy spider*
>
> *Climbed up the water spout*
>
> (Walk your fingers up in the air or on the baby like a spider.)
>
> *Down came the rain and washed the spider out.*
>
> (Mimic raindrops coming down and make an action of washing water away.)
>
> *Out came the sun and dried up all the rain.*
>
> (Draw the sun in the air.)
>
> *And the itsy bitsy spider climbed up the spout again.*
>
> (Walk your fingers up in the air or on the baby like the spider coming back again.)

ROW, ROW, ROW YOUR BOAT

Sit on the floor opposite your child. Place your baby in between your legs. Take his hands in yours and sing while gently rocking back and forth:

> Row, row, row your boat
> Gently down the stream
> Merrily, merrily, merrily, merrily
> Life is but a dream.

HIDE-AND-SEEK GAMES

Many babies like uncovering playthings that you have made disappear completely.

UNWRAPPING A PARCEL

Wrap a plaything in a piece of paper or crackly crisp bag, while your baby watches. Then give her the parcel and let her retrieve the plaything, as if by magic. Encourage her with each attempt she makes.

UNDER THE CUP

Put a plaything in front of your baby and place a cup over it. Then put an identical cup next to the first one and ask your baby where the plaything is. Admire him every time he looks for the hidden plaything, even if he does not find it immediately. If this game is still a bit too complicated, try playing it with a cloth instead of a cup. He will be able to see the contour of the plaything through the cloth. Play this game the other way around, too—let your baby hide something that you have to find.

"I'm very busy practicing saying 'daddy' with my boy and playing games like 'Where's your nose?' But so far, we've had little result. He just laughs, jumps around, and would rather bite my nose or pull my hair. But I'm happy enough that he's become such a lively little fellow."

Frankie's mom, 49th week

Top Toys for This Wonder Week

Here are toys and things that most babies like best now.

• Wooden trains with stations, bridges, and sidings

• Toy cars

• Dolls with toy bottles

• Drum, pots, and pans to beat on

• Books with pictures of animals

• Sandboxes with bucket and spade

• Balls of all sizes, from Ping-Pong balls to large beach balls

• Giant plastic beads

• Stuffed animals, especially the ones that make music when you squeeze them

• Bicycles, cars, or tractors that he can sit on himself and move around

• Primo blocks

• Small plastic figures of people or animals

• Mirrors

Remember to put away or take safety precautions with electrical outlets, stairs, stereo equipment, televisions, vacuum cleaners, washing machines, pets, and small objects such as knickknacks, pins, or little pieces of colored glass.

"I try to sing songs with my son, but I don't feel as if they are doing much good. He doesn't seem particularly interested. He seems to be preoccupied by his surroundings."

John's mom, 47th week

After the Leap

Between 47 and 52 weeks, another period of comparative ease sets in. For 1 to 3 weeks, you may be amazed by your baby's cheerfulness and independence. She may pay much better attention when you talk. She may seem calmer and more controlled when she is at play, and she may play well on her own again. She may want to be put back in her playpen—she may not even want to be taken out. And finally, she may look remarkably older and wiser. She is growing into a real toddler now.

"My daughter is getting lovelier by the day. She keeps getting better at entertaining herself. She can really keep herself occupied with something now. I got the playpen out again this week. But the thing I found most striking was that she doesn't at all seem to mind spending an hour or so in it anymore, whereas a few weeks ago she'd scream hysterically if I took her anywhere near it. It's as if she's discovering her toys all over again and enjoying the peace and quiet in the playpen."

Ashley's mom, 52nd week

"My daughter has become a real playmate for her older sister. She responds exactly like you'd expect her to. They do a lot more things together. They take their bath together as well. Both of them enjoy each other tremendously."

Hannah's mom, 47th week

"These were lovely weeks. My son is more of a buddy again. The day care center is working out fine. He always enjoys seeing the other children and comes home in a good mood. He sleeps better at night. He understands a lot more and seems fascinated by the toys he plays with. He crawls into another room on his own again, too, and laughs a lot. I'm enjoying every minute with him."

Bob's mom, 51st week

Place Photo Here

After the Leap

Age: _____

Reflections: _____

chapter 10

Wonder Week 55: The World of Programs

*E*very child's first birthday is a significant occasion. The end of the first year means for many parents the beginning of the end of babyhood. Your little cherub is about to become a toddler. In many ways, of course, she is still a baby. She still has so much to learn about her world—which has become such an interesting place to explore. She can get around so much better now, though, and she has become adept at getting into everything that interests her.

Shortly after the first birthday, at around 55 weeks, your little one will have gone through another big change in her mental development and will be ready to explore the world of programs. This will make her seem even more like a little person with her own way of approaching the world. A watchful parent will begin to see the blossoming of a new understanding in the toddler's way of thinking.

The word "programs" is very abstract. Here's what it means in this context. In the past leap in development, your baby learned to deal with the notion of sequences—the fact that events follow one after another or objects fit together in a particular way. A program is a degree more complicated than a sequence since it allows the end result to be reached in any number of ways. Once your child becomes capable of perceiving programs, she can begin to understand what it means to do the laundry, set the table, eat lunch, tidy up, get dressed, build a tower, make a phone call, and the millions of other things that make up everyday life. These are all programs.

The main characteristic of a program is that it has a goal but that the steps taken to accomplish it are flexible. This is how it differs from a sequence, which is the same every time. An example of a sequence is counting from 1 to 10. You do it the same way each and every time. Dusting is an example of a program. You do not necessarily have to dust an object in the same way each time—you can dust the legs of a table first and then the top, or the other way around. Every time that you dust, you can choose the sequence that you feel is best for that day, that room, that chair, and your mood. However you choose to do it, the program you are working with remains "dusting." So a program can be seen as a network of possible sequences that you can carry out in a variety of ways. The options may be limited in dusting, but if you think of examples such as "going on vacation" or "changing jobs," the programs become very complex.

Your child can now think of a goal, such as "going shopping," and know that this may mean putting on hats, coats, and boots and getting in the car. Or she may be eager to "help" you—doing the cleaning, taking the dog for a walk, and putting away the groceries. She may insist on doing things herself—washing her hands, feeding herself, even undressing herself.

As your child changes, you may feel that she is more unpredictable than ever. Interpreting her actions used to be easy when they were part of simple sequences, because one thing always led to the next in a familiar pattern. Now her world is much more flexible and any action can form part of any program. This is confusing for you both. Until you get used to the way she is operating, some of her actions may be hard to understand because you can't guess what she's trying to achieve any more. This leap will also be apparent in her play. She will begin to be interested in some of her toys all over again, and you may notice for the first time a budding imagination and more complex play.

Between 49 and 53 weeks, your child begins to perceive that her world is changing again. While she is sorting out this new complexity, she will need some extra comfort and support, and this makes her appear fussy and demanding for a while. This fussy period will often last for 4 or 5 weeks, but it can be as short as 3 weeks or as long as 6. If your baby is cranky, watch her closely. There's a good chance that she's attempting to master new skills.

Your child may cry more easily than he did during the past weeks. Children are usually quicker to cry now than their mothers have been used to. They want to be near their mothers, preferably all day long. Some children are much more insistent about this than others are, of course. They may also seem cranky, unmanageable, and temperamental.

> "My son could be pretty bad-tempered at times. Not all the time—he would play on his own for a while, but then suddenly it was all over and he would be terribly weepy for quite some time. Then he would want me to hold him. And all of this commotion would take place in just one morning."
>
> **Bob's mom, 52nd week**

> "My daughter was very quick to cry. All I had to do was say 'no,' and she'd have an immediate crying fit. It was not like her at all."
>
> **Eve's mom, 52nd week**

Children usually cry less when they are with their mothers or when their mothers are somehow occupied with them, playing with them, or watching them.

"While my little girl is doing things, I'm supposed to stay sitting on the sofa, preferably not doing anything myself. I long for the day when I'll be able to knit something quietly while I'm sitting there."

Emily's mom, 53rd week

"Whenever I'm busy doing something, my son wants to be picked up. But once he's on my lap, he wants to get off quickly again, and he expects me to follow him around. He's absolutely impossible."

Frankie's mom, 52nd week

How You Know It's Time to Grow

It's still too early for your little one to tell you in words how he's feeling. But still, he is able to express the turmoil he feels inside. Here's how.

He May Cling to Your Clothes

Your little one may start clinging more to you again—many children do at this age. He may want to be carried around or cling to your legs to prevent you from walking away and leaving him behind. Others do not necessarily need physical contact, but they may keep coming back to be near their mothers for only brief moments or to touch them. Every child comes back for his own brand of "mommy refill."

"My daughter stays around me more again, plays for a moment, and then comes back to me."

Hannah's mom, 54th week

"I can't do a thing as long as my son is awake. When he's out of his playpen, he is constantly underfoot, and when he's in the playpen, I have to stay near him. Otherwise, he'll throw a screaming fit."

Frankie's mom, 55th week

"When I stand up and walk into the kitchen, right away my daughter will come after me and want to be carried. She'll really make a scene. It's all terribly dramatic. You'd think something awful was happening."

Emily's mom, 53rd week

He May Be Shier with Strangers

When there are strangers near, your little one may cling to you even more fanatically than he often already did. Once more, many children suddenly want to have less to do with strangers now. Sometimes, this even includes their own family members.

"This week, my daughter would suddenly become extremely upset, and she'd want only to be with me. If I put her down or gave her to my husband, she'd panic."

Jenny's mom, 56th week

"My little girl won't accept anything to eat from strangers, not even a slice of bread or a cookie."

Nina's mom, 54th week

But there are also children who want only to be with their fathers.

"My daughter was completely crazy about her father for 2 days. She didn't want to have anything to do with me then, even though I hadn't done her any wrong. If he didn't pick her up right away, she'd start crying."

Juliette's mom, 53rd week

He May Want Physical Contact to Be as Close as Possible

Some children hold on as tightly as they can, even when they are being carried. They do not want to be put down—and very likely yours doesn't either. There are also little ones who do not mind being put down, as long as their mothers don't walk away. If anyone leaves, it is allowed only to be the little tyrant himself.

> "One evening I had to go away. When I set my son down to put on my coat, he started crying, grabbed me, and tugged at my hand, as if he didn't want me to leave."
>
> Paul's mom, 52nd week

> "I really have to keep a close eye on my daughter. If I want to set her down to go into the kitchen for a second to get something, she'll go for the dog, pretend to pet him, while at the same time she pulls out whiskers and tufts of fur."
>
> Emily's mom, 53rd week

He May Want to Be Entertained

Your little one may start asking for more attention. Most children do. Demanding ones do this all day long. But even easy, even-tempered children prefer doing things together with their mothers.

> "My daughter keeps coming to get me, pulls me along by my hand so we can play together, with her blocks or dolls or to look at a book together."
>
> Jenny's mom, 53rd week

He May Be Jealous

Some more possessive children seem to put on an act when their mothers pay attention to someone or something else. They pretend to be cranky, mischievous, or determined to hurt themselves. Others act sweetly and cuddly in an exaggerated way in order to get their mothers' attention.

"My son gets jealous when I give something to the tiny baby I look after."

Matt's mom, 53rd week

"My friend came over with her baby. Every time I said something to her baby, mine would step in between us with this big grin on her face."

Jenny's mom, 54th week

He May Be Moody

Your little one may be happily occupied one moment, then become sad, angry, or infuriated the next, for no apparent reason. You may not be able to pinpoint a particular cause.

"Sometimes, my son will sit and play with his blocks like a little angel, but then suddenly he'll become furious. He shrieks and slams his blocks together or throws them across the room."

Steven's mom, 52nd week

He May Sleep Poorly

Your child may sleep less well. Most children resist going to bed, have difficulty falling asleep, and wake up sooner. Some sleep less well during the day, others are restless at night, and still others simply refuse to go to bed quietly at any time.

"This week, I noticed for the first time that my toddler often lies awake for a while at night. Sometimes, she'll cry a little. If I pick her up, she goes back to sleep in seconds."

Ashley's mom, 54th week

"We'd really like our daughter to make less of a fuss about going to sleep. Right now, it involves a lot of screaming and crying, sometimes almost hysterics, even when she's exhausted."

> Jenny's mom, 52nd week

"My son is awake a lot during the night, terribly distressed. He really panics. Sometimes, it's hard to get him to calm down again."

> Bob's mom, 52nd week

He May "Daydream"

Occasionally, some children can just sit, staring out into nothingness, as if they are in their own little worlds. Mothers do not like this dreaming one bit. Because of this, they will often try to break into these reveries.

"Sometimes, my daughter will sit, slouching and rocking back and forth, gazing into thin air. I always drop whatever I'm doing to shake her and wake her up again. I'm terrified there might be something wrong with her."

> Juliette's mom, 54th week

He May Lose His Appetite

Many little ones are fussy eaters. Their mothers almost always find this troubling and irritating. A child who is still being breastfed usually wants the breast more often, not because he really wants to nurse, but so he can stay close to his mother.

"My daughter is suddenly less interested in food. Previously, she would finish everything within 15 minutes. She was like a bottomless pit. Now it sometimes takes me half an hour to feed her."

> Ashley's mom, 53rd week

"My son sprays his lunch around with his mouth. He dirties everything. The first few days, I thought it was quite funny. Not anymore, I should add."

Bob's mom, 53rd week

He May Be More Babyish

Sometimes, a supposedly vanished babyish behavior will resurface. Mothers do not like to see this happen—they expect steady progress. Still, during fussy phases, relapses such as these are perfectly normal. It tells you that progress, in the shape of a new world, is on its way.

"My daughter crawled again a couple of times, but she probably just did it to get attention."

Jenny's mom, 55th week

"My daughter is putting things in her mouth a little more often again, just like she used to."

Hannah's mom, 51st week

"My son wants me to feed him again. When I don't do this, he pushes his food away."

Kevin's mom, 53rd week

He May Act Unusually Sweet

Some little clingers suddenly come up to their mothers for a few moments just to cuddle with them. Then they are off again.

"Sometimes, my son comes crawling up to me just to be a real sweetie for a moment. He'll lay his little head very softly on my knees, for instance, very affectionately."

Bob's mom, 51st week

"My daughter often comes up for a quick cuddle. She says 'kiss,' and then I get one, too."

Ashley's mom, 53rd week

He May Reach for a Cuddly Object More Often

Your little one may cuddle a favorite object with a bit more passion. Many children do so, especially when they are tired or when their mothers are busy. They cuddle soft toys, rugs, cloths, slippers, or even dirty laundry. Anything soft that they can lay their little hands on will do. They kiss and pet their cuddly things as well. Mothers find this endearing.

"My son cuddles away while I'm busy. He'll hold his toy elephant's ear with one hand and stick two fingers from his other hand in his mouth. It's a sight to see."

John's mom, 51st week

He May Be Mischievous

Your child may try to get your attention by being extra naughty, especially when you are busy and really have no time for him.

"I have to keep telling my daughter 'no' because she seems to do things just to get my attention. If I don't react, she will eventually stop. But I can't always do that because sometimes there's a chance she might break whatever it is she's taking apart."

Jenny's mom, 53rd week

"My son is being a handful at the moment. He touches everything and refuses to listen. I can't really get anything done until he's in bed."

Frankie's mom, 55th week

"Sometimes I suspect that my son doesn't listen on purpose."

Steven's mom, 51st week

My Diary

Signs My Baby Is Growing Again

Between 49 and 53 weeks, your child may show signs that he is ready to make the next leap, into the world of programs.

❑ Cries more often and is more often cranky or fretful

❑ Is cheerful one moment and cries the next

❑ Wants you to keep him busy, or does so more often

❑ Clings to your clothes or wants to be closer to you

❑ Acts unusually sweet

❑ Is mischievous

❑ Throws temper tantrums, or throws them more often

❑ Is jealous

❑ Is more obviously shy with strangers

❑ Wants physical contact to be tighter or closer

❑ Sleeps poorly

❑ Has "nightmares," or has them more often

❑ Loses appetite

❑ Sometimes just sits there, quietly daydreaming

❑ Sucks his thumb, or does so more often

❑ Reaches for a cuddly toy, or does so more often

❑ Is more babyish

OTHER CHANGES YOU NOTICE

_____

_____

_____

He May Have More Temper Tantrums

If you have a hot-headed little tyke, he may go berserk as soon as he fails to get his own way. You may even see a tantrum that comes out of nowhere, perhaps because he is anticipating that you may not allow him to do or have what is on his mind.

> "My son wants me to put him on my lap and feed him his bottle of fruit juice again. If he even suspects it might not happen quickly enough, he'll toss his bottle across the room and start screaming, yelling, and kicking to get me to take it back to him."
>
> Matt's mom, 52nd week

> "If I don't respond immediately when my daughter wants attention, she gets furious. She'll pinch the skin right off my arm, nastily, quickly, and violently."
>
> Emily's mom, 53rd week

> "My son refuses to have anything to do with "bed." He gets so angry that he bangs his chin on the railings of his crib, hurting himself every time. So now I'm really afraid to put him in bed."
>
> Matt's mom, 52nd week

> "I was visiting friends with my daughter and talking with one of them. Suddenly, my daughter grabbed the cup and smashed it on the floor, tea and all."
>
> Laura's mom, 55th week

How This Leap May Affect You

No doubt you're feeling the stress of your baby's changes as well, if only vicariously. Here are some of the signs.

You May Feel Insecure

When a mother is confronted with a little fusspot, she may at first be worried. She wants to know what is wrong with her child. But at this age, irritation soon sets in.

Also during this period, some mothers wonder why their children are not walking as quickly as they expected them to. They worry that there might be something physically wrong with them.

> "We spent a lot of time practicing, and I'm amazed that my daughter can't walk on her own yet. She's been walking while holding my hand for so long now that I feel she should have been walking long ago. Besides, I think one of her feet is pointing inward, so she keeps tripping over it. I showed them at the day care center. They told me that I wasn't the only mother worried about a foot pointing inwards at this age. Still, I'll be happier when she's walking."
>
> **Emily's mom, 53rd week**

You May Become Really Frustrated

Toward the end of the fussy period, parents often become increasingly aggravated by their babies' demands on them. They become increasingly annoyed by seemingly purposeful mischief and the way they use temper tantrums to get their own way.

> "I'm so annoyed by my daughter's crying fits whenever I leave the room. I can't stand the fact that she immediately crawls after me either, clutching my leg and crawling along with me. I can't get anything done this way. When I've had enough, it's off to bed with her, I'm afraid."
>
> **Juliette's mom, 52nd week**

> "My son keeps pulling at the big plant to get my attention. Distracting him doesn't work. Now I get angry and push him away, or I give him a gentle slap on his bottom."
>
> **Matt's mom, 56th week**

"My daughter flies into a rage every other minute whenever she's not allowed to do something or can't manage it. She'll throw her toys and start whining like mad. I try to ignore this. But if she has several tantrums in a row, I put her to bed. When she first started doing this 2 weeks ago, I thought it was very amusing. Now I'm terribly aggravated by it. Her sisters just laugh at her. Sometimes, when she sees them doing that, it brightens her up and she'll start smiling back at them, shyly. It usually does the trick, but not all of the time."

Ashley's mom, 53rd week

You May Argue

During this fussy period, quarrels are usually brought on by temper tantrums.

"I feel myself getting angry when my daughter starts bawling if she isn't getting her own way. This week, she got furious when I wouldn't immediately follow her into the kitchen. So I gave her a good smack on the bottom, after which her rage turned into real tears. I know I shouldn't have done it, but I was fed up."

Jenny's mom, 54th week

Feelings of anger and frustration at times are perfectly normal. But be sure to get help long before you lose control.

During each fussy period, mothers who breastfeed feel a desire to stop. At this age, this is because the baby keeps wanting the breast by fits and starts, or because his demands are accompanied by temper tantrums.

"I've really given up now. My son would throw temper tantrums from just thinking about my breast. It messed up our entire relationship with him tugging at my sweater, kicking, screaming, and me getting angry. Perhaps those tantrums will start to disappear now, too. The last time he nursed was on the night of his first birthday."

Matt's mom, 53rd week

How Your Baby's New Skills Emerge

Around 55 weeks, you will notice that your little one is less fussy. At the same time, you should notice that he is attempting and achieving entirely new things again. He deals with people, toys, and other objects in a more mature way and he enjoys doing new things with familiar toys and household objects that have been there since he was born. At this point, he doesn't quite feel like your little "baby" any more but will seem to be transformed into a little toddler. This is because he is entering the world of programs where he is beginning to see that the world is full of goals and sequences of action leading up to such a goal. This new flexible world is his to discover, but, as usual, he will want to do this in his own way and at his own speed. As a parent, your help will be as vital as ever, although it may not always feel that way when another temper tantrum rolls in.

In the past leap in development, your baby learned to deal with the notion of sequences—where events follow one after another or objects fit together in a particular way. A program is more complicated than a sequence because you can reach the end result in any number of ways.

An adult's world is filled with complicated programs. Fortunately, your child's world is simpler. Instead of dealing with enormous programs like "going on a vacation," your child will be working with programs such as "eating lunch." However, operating a program entails choices at each crossroad—rather like finding your way across town. During lunch, he will have to decide after every bite whether he would rather take another bite of the same food, switch to something different, have a sip of his drink, or perhaps even three sips. He can decide whether to take the next

Your child's brain waves will show changes again at approximately 12 months. Also, her head circumference will increase, and the glucose metabolism in her brain will change.

bite with his hands or use a spoon. He can decide to finish what he has or clamor for dessert. Whatever he opts for, it will still be the "eating lunch" program.

Your toddler will as usual experiment with this new world. Expect him to play with the different choices he can make at every juncture—he may just want to try everything out. He needs to learn what the possible consequences are of the decisions he makes at different points—so he could decide to empty the next spoonful on the floor instead of in his mouth.

He can also decide when to put a program into operation. For example, he can get the broom out of the closet because he wants to sweep the floor. He can get his coat because he wants to go out and do the shopping. Unfortunately, misunderstandings are quick to occur. After all, he can not explain what he wants yet and his mother can easily interpret him wrongly. This is very frustrating for such a young person, and a temperamental child might even throw a tantrum. Even if a mother does understand her child correctly, she may just not want to do whatever he wants at that very moment. This, too, can frustrate such a toddler quite quickly, for he can't understand the idea of "waiting" at this age.

Besides being able to learn how to carry out a program himself, he can now perceive when someone else is doing the same thing. So he can begin to understand that if his mother is making tea, a snack will follow shortly and he can expect a cookie—or not.

(continued on page 287)

 My Diary

How My Baby Explores the New World of Programs

Check off the boxes below as you notice your baby changing. Some of the skills in the list below may not appear until weeks or months later. Your toddler will exercise his own choices in exploring what he can do in his new world.

STARTING A PROGRAM HIMSELF

❑ Gets out a broom or duster and tries sweeping or dusting

❑ Goes to the bathroom and tries cleaning the toilet bowl

❑ Comes to you with things he wants to be put away

❑ Gets out the cookie jar and expects a snack

❑ Comes to you with coat, cap, or bag to go shopping

❑ Gets out his coat and shovel, ready to go to the sandbox

❑ Gets out his clothes and wants to put them on

JOINING IN WITH YOUR PROGRAM

❑ Throws the cushions from the chair in advance to help when you are cleaning

❑ Tries to hang the towel back in place when you are finished

❑ Puts an object or a food item away in the right cupboard

❑ Brings her own plate, silverware, and place mat when you are setting the table

❑ Tells you by word, sound, or gesture that it is time to bring out the dessert when she has finished eating

❑ Puts spoons in cups and usually starts stirring

❑ Grabs an item from you and wants to carry it herself

❑ Tries to put something on by herself while she is being dressed or helps by pulling on her leggings or sleeves

❑ Picks out a tape or CD and helps put it on. Knows which button to press for play or eject

---

EXECUTING A PROGRAM UNDER SUPERVISION

❑ Puts differently shaped blocks through the correct holes in a box when you help by pointing out what goes where

❑ Uses the potty when you ask him to or when he needs to. Then carries the potty to the bathroom by himself or helps you carry it (if he is not walking) and flushes

❑ Gets out pens and paper and scribbles when you help him to

INDEPENDENT PROGRAMS

❑ Tries feeding dolls or cuddly toys, copying her own eating program

❑ Tries giving a doll a bath by copying her own bathing ritual

❑ Tries putting doll on the potty, maybe after she uses it

❑ Eats everything on her plate without help; often she wants to do this while sitting at the table politely like the grown-ups

❑ Eats raisins by herself from a packet

❑ Builds a tower of at least three blocks

❑ Starts and continues a telephone conversation, sometimes dialing at the start or ending the conversation with "bye"

❑ Crawls through the room following "paths" of her own choice, under chairs and table and through narrow tunnels, and often indicates which direction she intends to go first

(continued)

My Diary (cont.)

❑ Crawls through the room with a toy car or train saying "vroom vroom." Follows all sorts of different routes—under chairs and tables, or between the sofa and the wall

❑ Is capable of finding something you hid

WATCHING OTHERS CARRYING OUT A PROGRAM

❑ Watches a cartoon or children's show on television, which manages to keep his attention for about 3 minutes

❑ Listens to a short story on the radio or on CD

❑ Expresses understanding of what is happening in pictures—for example, by saying "yum" when the child or animal in the picture is eating or being offered something to eat

❑ Looks and listens when you play "pretend" games—feeding, bathing and dressing his dolls and cuddly toys, or making them talk and answer

❑ Studies how older children carry out a program with their toys—how they play with a tea set, a garage with cars, doll's bed, or train set

❑ Studies other family members when they are carrying out an everyday program, for instance, when they are getting dressed, eating, drawing, or telephoning

OTHER CHANGES YOU NOTICE

_____

_____

_____

Now that your toddler can learn to perceive and explore this world, he also understands that he has the choice of refusing a program he does not like—at least in theory. If he doesn't agree with his mother's plan, he may feel frustrated and sometimes even have a temper tantrum. You may be seeing a lot of them these days.

Your Toddler's Choices: A Key to Her Personality

All toddlers will begin at this age to understand and experiment with the world of programs, a world that offers a wide range of new skills to play with. Your child will choose those things that interest her, things that she has perhaps watched others do in the world about her, but also those things that most suit her own inclinations, interests, and physique. Every little individual learns about programs in her own way. Some children will be acute watchers, studying with care the way things are done around them. Others may want to "help" all the time. Yet others will want to do it themselves, and they will let you know in no uncertain terms that they do not want any interference.

You are probably getting to know the personality of your toddler quite well by now, and many of her choices will follow patterns that you've noticed previously as she has grown. She is still capable of exploring new skills and interests, however, as the opportunity presents itself. Watch your toddler carefully to determine where her interests lie. Use the list on pages 284–286 to mark or highlight what your child selects. Between 55 and 61 weeks, she will start to choose what she wants to explore from the world of programs. Remember to respect those choices and to let your child develop at her own pace. Concentrate on helping her to do what she is ready to do. Young children love anything new and it is important that you respond when you notice any new skills or interests. She will enjoy it if you share these new discoveries, and her learning will progress more quickly.

what
You Can Do to
Help

Help your toddler as he makes his first tentative steps toward his encounters with programs. Talk about what he's going to achieve and how he's going to do it. If he enjoys watching you, encourage this. Talk about what you are doing as you are carrying out your program. Offer him opportunities to help you. Allow him to try carrying out his own program when you notice that he seems to have one in mind.

Help Your Baby Explore the New World through Independence

If your child is interested in dressing, undressing, and grooming herself, then let her see how you do these things. Explain to her what you are doing as well as why you are doing it. She will be able to understand more than she is able to tell you. If you have a little time, let her toy with washing and dressing herself or, if she wants to, somebody else in the family.

> "My daughter tries pulling her trousers up by herself or putting her own slippers on, but she can't do it yet. Then suddenly I found her walking around in my slippers."
>
> **Jenny's mom, 55th week**

> "My daughter likes walking around with a cap or hat on. Whether it's mine, hers, or a doll's—it's all the same to her."
>
> **Eve's mom, 57th week**

> "This past week, my son kept putting all sorts of things on his head: dishcloths, towels, and, a few times, someone's pants. He'd walk around the

house impervious to his surroundings while his brother and sister were on the floor laughing."

Frankie's mom, 59th week

"As soon as my daughter is dressed, she crawls over to my dressing table and tries to spray herself with perfume."

Laura's mom, 57th week

"Yesterday, when I went into my son's room to get him, he was standing up in his crib grinning like mad. He had gotten almost completely undressed by himself."

John's mom, 58th week

"My daughter feeds her dolls, bathes them, and puts them to bed. When she's used her potty, she'll put her dolls on the potty, as well."

Jenny's mom, 56th week

If your little one wants to eat on his own, let him try it as often as you can. Keep in mind that he is creative enough to want to test different methods of eating—and all of them will probably be messy. If cleaning up gets tiring, you can make cleaning easier by putting a large sheet of plastic on the floor under his chair.

"Since my son has learned how to eat his dinner by himself with a spoon, he insists on doing it completely on his own. Otherwise, he won't eat. He also insists on sitting in his chair at the table when he's eating."

Kevin's mom, 57th week

"Suddenly, my daughter discovered it was great fun to first stir something with a spoon, then stick it in her mouth."

Jenny's mom, 56th week

"My son loves eating raisins from a packet by himself."

Matt's mom, 57th week

"My daughter says 'pie' when she's finished eating her food, so she knows there's more to come. As soon as she's finished her dessert, she has to be taken out of her chair."

Emily's mom, 60th week

Bags, purses with money inside, the television set, the radio, cleaning utensils, makeup—many little persons want to use everything the same way their mothers do. Some children now leave their own toys lying somewhere in a corner. Try to work out what your little one is trying to do, even if he does not always make life easy for you.

"I saw my son pushing phone buttons for the first time today, putting the receiver to his ear, and babbling busily. A few times he said 'dada' before hanging up."

Frankie's mom, 56th week

"My daughter picked up the phone when it rang and I was out of the room for a second and really 'talked' to her grandma."

Emily's mom, 60th week

"My little girl knows exactly which button to press to open the cassette player. When she comes to me with a CD of children's songs, she'd really prefer to be putting it in the CD player herself."

Jenny's mom, 57th week

"My son is in love with the toilet bowl. He throws all sorts of things in it, and cleans it with the brush every 2 minutes, drenching the bathroom floor at the same time."

Frankie's mom, 56th week

"My son brings me newspapers, empty beer bottles, and shoes. He wants me to tidy up and put them away."

Frankie's mom, 56th week

Help Your Baby Explore the New World through Toys

Many children now become interested in more complex playthings that allow them to imitate programs, such as a garage with cars, a train with track, a farmhouse with animals, dolls with diapers or clothes, tea sets with pots and pans, or a play shop with packages and boxes. If your little one shows an interest in such toys, offer him opportunities to play with them. Help him once in a while. It is still a very complicated world for him.

"When I sit next to my son on the floor and encourage him, he'll sometimes build towers as high as eight blocks."

Matt's mom, 57th week

"When my daughter plays on her own and needs help, she'll call out 'Mama.' Then she'll show me what she wants me to do."

Hannah's mom, 55th week

"My daughter is becoming increasingly interested in Primo toys, especially the little people and the cars. She's also starting to try to build things from the blocks. She fits the pieces together properly once in a while. She can continue doing this for quite a long time."

Emily's mom, 57th week

"My son is getting much better at playing by himself. Now he is seeing new possibilities in old playthings. His cuddly toys, trains, and cars are starting to come alive."

Bob's mom, 55th week

Most children are interested in seeing the "real thing," too. For example, if your baby is interested in garages, take him to see cars being repaired. If he is interested in horses, tour a riding school. And if his tractor, crane, or boat is his favorite toy, he will certainly want to see a real one working.

Help Your Baby Explore the New World through Language and Music

When he leaps into the world of programs, your child becomes fascinated by stories. You can let him hear and see them. You could let him watch a story on television, you could let him listen to a tape, or best of all, you could tell him a story yourself, with or without a picture book. Just make sure that the stories correspond with whatever your child is experiencing himself or with his interests. For some children, this will be cars, for others it will be a special flower, animals, the swimming pool, or his cuddly toys. Keep in mind that each story must contain a short and simple program. Most little ones of this age can only concentrate on a story for about 3 minutes.

> "My son can really become absorbed in a toddler show on television. It's very funny. Previously he just wasn't interested."
>
> **Kevin's mom, 58th week**

Also offer a budding little talker the opportunity to tell his own story when you are looking at a picture book together.

> "My daughter can understand a picture in a book. She'll tell me what she sees. For instance, if she sees a kid in a picture giving a treat to another kid, she'll say, 'yum.'"
>
> **Hannah's mom, 57th week**

Be Happy with His Help

When you notice your child is trying to lend you a hand, then accept this. He is beginning to understand what you are doing and needs to learn to do his own share.

> "My daughter wants to help with everything. She wants to carry the groceries, hang the dishcloth back in place when I'm done, carry the place mats and silverware to the table when I'm setting the table, and so on."
>
> **Emily's mom, 62nd week**

> "My daughter knows that apple juice and milk belong in the fridge and runs to the door to open it. For cookies, she goes straight to the cupboard and gets out the tin."
>
> **Jenny's mom, 57th week**

Many little children are eager chatterboxes. They will tell you entire "stories" complete with questions, exclamations, and pauses. They expect a response. If your toddler is a storyteller, try to take his stories seriously, even if you are still unable to understand what he is saying. If you listen closely, you may sometimes be able to make out a real word.

> "My son talks until your ears feel like they're about to drop off. He really holds a conversation. Sometimes he'll do it in the questioning mode. It sounds really cute. I would love to know what he's trying to tell me."
>
> **Frankie's mom, 58th week**

> "My son chatters away like crazy. Sometimes he'll stop and look at me until I say something back, and then he'll continue his story. This past

week, it sounded like he was saying 'kiss,' and then he actually gave me a kiss. Now I pay 10 times more attention."

Frankie's mom, 59th week

Many little ones love listening to children's songs so long as they are simple and short. Such a song is a program as well. If your toddler likes music, she may now like to learn how to make all the appropriate gestures as well.

"My daughter plays *Pat a cake, pat a cake, baker's man* all by herself, complete with incomprehensible singing."

Jenny's mom, 57th week

Some children also have a lot of fun playing their own piece of music. Drums, pianos, keyboards, and flutes seem to be their particular favorites. Naturally, most budding musicians prefer grown-up instruments, but they will be able to do less harm with a toy instrument.

Teach Him to Respect You

Many children are now beginning to understand that you can be in the middle of a program, as well, such as when you are busy cleaning. When you notice your baby starts to comprehend these things, you can also start asking him to have consideration for you so that you can finish what you are doing. At this age, however, you can't expect him to wait too long.

"When my son wants to get his own way, he'll lay down on the floor just out of my arm's reach. That way I have to come to him."

Matt's mom, 56th week

Do Remember

Breaking old habits and setting new rules are also part of developing each new skill. Whatever new rules your baby understands, you can demand from him—nothing more, but also nothing less.

"My daughter loves her toy piano. Usually, she plays with one finger and listens to what she's doing. She also likes to watch her father play his piano. Then she'll walk over to her piano and bang on it with both hands."

— Hannah's mom, 58th week

Help Your Baby Explore the New World through Experimentation

If your toddler is a little researcher, you could see him performing the following program or experiment: how do these toys land, roll over, and

Good to Know

Some children are exceptionally creative when it comes to inventing and trying out different ways to attain the same final goal. Gifted children can be particularly exhausting for their parents. They continually try to see if things can be done some other way. Whenever they fail or are forbidden to do something, they always look for another way around the problem or prohibition. It seems like a challenge to them never to do something the same way twice. They find simply repeating things boring.

(continued on page 298)

Top Games for This Wonder Week

Here are games and activities that most toddlers like best now. Remember, all children are different. See what your little one responds to best.

DOING A JOB BY HIMSELF

Many toddlers love being allowed to do something very mature all by themselves. Making a mess with water is the most popular job. Most children calm down as they play with water.

GIVING THE DOLL A BATH

Fill a baby bath or a washing-up bowl with lukewarm water. Give your child a washcloth and a bar of soap, and let him lather up his doll or cuddly toy. Washing hair is usually a very popular part of this game.

DOING DISHES

Tie a large apron on your child, and put him on a chair in front of the sink. Fill the bowl with lukewarm water, and give him your dish sponge and an assortment of baby-friendly items to be washed, such as plastic plates, cups, wooden spoons, and all sorts of strainers and funnels. A nice topping of bubbles will make him even more eager to get to work. Make sure the chair he is standing on does not become slippery when wet, causing the busy person to lose his footing in his enthusiasm. Then stand back and let the fun begin.

HELPING OUT

Your toddler may prefer to do things with you. She can help prepare dinner, set the table, and shop for groceries. She will have her own ideas about the job, but she will learn a lot by doing it with you. This helps her feel grown-up and content.

UNPACKING AND PUTTING AWAY GROCERIES

Put fragile and dangerous things away first, then let your little assistant help you unpack. You can have him hand you or bring you the groceries one by one, as he chooses. Or you can ask him "Could you give me the . . . , and now the . . . " You can also ask him where he would put it. And finally, he can close the cupboard doors when you are finished. Encourage and thank him.

HIDE-AND-SEEK GAMES

Now you can make these games more complicated than before. When your child is in the right mood, he will usually enjoy displaying his tricks. Adjust the pace to your child. Make the game neither impossibly difficult nor too easy for him.

DOUBLE HIDING GAME

Place two cups before him and put a plaything under one of them. Then switch the cups around by sliding them across the table. This way, cup A will be where cup B was, and vice versa. The object of the exercise here is not to fool your toddler but the very reverse. Make sure that your child is watching closely when you move the cups and encourage him to find the toy. Give him plenty of praise for each attempt. This is really very complicated for him.

SOUND GAME

Many toddlers love looking for a sound. Take your child on your lap and let her see and hear an object that can make a sound—for instance, a musical box. Then close her eyes and have someone else hide the object while it is playing. Make sure that your little one cannot see where it is being hidden. When it has vanished from sight, encourage her to look for it.

bounce? Your little Einstein can go on examining these things for what seems like forever. For instance, he might pick up different toy people and drop them on the table 25 times and then repeat this up to 60 times with all sorts of building blocks. If you see your child doing this, then just let him carry on. This is his way of experimenting with the objects' characteristics in a very systematic way. He will be able to put this information to good use later on when he has to decide in the middle of a program whether to do something this way or that. Toddlers are not simply playing—they are working hard, often putting in long hours, to discover how the world works.

"When my son is doing something, for instance building, he suddenly shakes his head, says 'no,' and starts to do it in a different way."

Kevin's mom, 55th week

"My daughter gets out her little locomotive to stand on when she wants to get her things from the closet. She used to always use her chair."

Jenny's mom, 56th week

"When I ask my daughter, 'Do you need to use your potty?' she'll use it if she really does need to. She pees, carries it to the bathroom herself, and flushes. But sometimes she'll be sitting, then she'll get up and pee next to her potty."

Jenny's mom, 54th week

Show Understanding for Irrational Fears

When your little one is busy exploring his new world, he will run into things that he does not fully understand. Along the way, he discovers new dangers, ones that he never imagined existed. He is still unable to talk

Top Toys for This Wonder Week

Here are toys and things that most babies like best now:

- Dolls, doll strollers, and doll beds
- Farmhouse, farm animals, and fences
- Garage and cars
- Wooden train with tracks, platforms, bridges, and tunnels
- Unbreakable tea set
- Pots, pans, and wooden spoons
- Telephone
- Primo blocks
- Bicycle, car, toy horse or engine that he can sit on himself
- Push-along wagon that he can use to transport all sorts of things
- Rocking horse or rocking chair
- Box with differently shaped blocks and holes
- Stackable containers and rod with stackable rings
- Mop, hand broom, dustpan, and brush
- Colored sponges to scrub with or play with in the bath
- Large sheets of paper and markers
- Books with animals and their young or cars and tractors
- Musical instruments, such as drums, toy pianos, and xylophones
- Cassette tape or CD with simple short stories

Remember at this time to put away or take precautions with closets and drawers that might contain harmful or poisonous things, knobs on audio and video equipment, electrical appliances, ovens, and lights and power outlets.

about them, so show him a little understanding. His fear will disappear only when he starts to understand everything better.

"All of a sudden, my son was frightened of our ship's lamp when it was on, probably because it shines so brightly."

Paul's mom, 57th week

"My daughter is a little scared of the dark. Not once she is in the dark, but to walk from a lit room into a dark room."

Jenny's mom, 58th week

"My son gets frightened when I inflate a balloon. He doesn't get it."

Matt's mom, 58th week

"My daughter was frightened by a ball that was deflating."

Eve's mom, 59th week

"My son gets terribly frightened by loud noises, like jet airplanes, telephones, and the doorbell ringing."

Bob's mom, 55th week

"My daughter is scared of everything that draws near quickly. Like the parakeet, fluttering around her head, her brother chasing her, and a remote control car that belonged to a friend of her older brother. It was just too fast for her."

Emily's mom, 56th week

"My son simply refuses to get into the bathtub. He doesn't mind getting into the baby bath when it's in the big bath."

Frankie's mom, 59th week

After *the* Leap

Around 59 weeks, most toddlers become a little less troublesome than they were. Some are particularly admired for their friendly talkativeness and others for their cute eagerness to help out with the housekeeping. Most are now beginning to rely less on temper tantrums to get their own way. In short, their independence and cheerfulness assert themselves once again. With their new liveliness and mobility, however, many mothers may still consider their little ones to be a bit of a handful. That's because they think they know it all, but you know they still have to learn so much.

"My daughter is painstakingly precise. Everything has its own little place. If I make changes, she'll notice and put things back. She also doesn't hold onto anything anymore when she's walking. She will happily walk right across the room. To think I've been so worried over this."

Emily's mom, 60th week

"My son is perfectly happy in the playpen again. Sometimes he doesn't want to be taken out. I don't have to play along with him anymore, either. He keeps himself occupied, especially with his toy cars and puzzles. He's much more cheerful."

Paul's mom, 60th week

"My daughter doesn't play with toys anymore; she won't even look at them. Watching, imitating, and joining in with us is much more fascinating to her now. She's enterprising as well. She gets her coat and her bag when she wants to go out and the broom when something needs cleaning. She's very mature."

Nina's mom, 58th week

"Now that my son runs like the wind and wanders through the entire apartment, he also does a lot of things he shouldn't. He keeps putting away cups, beer bottles, and shoes, and he can be extremely imaginative. If I take my eye off him for a moment, those things end up in the trash can or the toilet. Then when I scold him, he gets very sad."

Frankie's mom, 59th week

"My daughter is such a lovely little girl, the way she plays, chit-chatting away. She's often so full of joy. Those temper tantrums seem like a thing of the past. But perhaps I'd better knock wood."

Ashley's mom, 59th week

Place Photo Here

After the Leap

Age: _____

Reflections: _____

postscript

Countless Wonders

By now you know that every mom will, at some time, have to deal with a baby who is tearful, cranky, or fussy; a baby who is difficult to please; a baby who, in fact, just needs to touch base.

It's our hope that when you find yourself coping with behaviors like these from your baby, you will now understand that you are not alone. Every mother is facing problems like these. All mothers experience worries and irritations when their infants reach certain ages. All mothers forget—or would like to forget—these trying times as soon as possible; as soon as the difficult period is over, in fact. It's human nature to play down the misery we have to go through, once the dark clouds have parted.

Now that you understand that your child's difficult behaviors and your own anxieties and irritability are all part of a healthy and normal development as your infant struggles towards independence, you can feel more secure and confident. You know what you're doing.

Even without an instruction manual, you know that your baby will explore each "new world" in her own individual way. You know that the best thing you can do is to "listen" to your baby, in order to help him on his way. You know how to have fun with him. You also know that you are the person who understands him best, and the person who can really help him unlike any other. We hope that the information and findings we've shared with you about the Wonder Weeks that mark developmental stages will make it easier for you to understand and support your baby during these traumatic times.

More Wonders Await

Obviously, your baby still has a long way to go. Before he reaches the age of 20 months, he will make two more leaps: one when he is about 64 weeks old, and another around 75 weeks. This still is not the end of it: further leaps occur several more times before he becomes fully independent. There are even indications that adults experience these phases, too.

As the Colombian author and journalist Gabriel Garcia Marquez wrote in *Love in the Time of Cholera,*

> People are not born once and for all on the day that their mother puts them on to the Earth, but . . . time and again, life forces them to enter a new world on their own.

resources

The organizations listed below offer more information on childhood development than could be contained within the pages of any book. They are all excellent resources to turn to for advice and support.

About Our Kids
This site offers research-based, practical information covering topics including sleep, thumbsucking, school, social development, mental health, and medications.

http://aboutourkids.med.nyu.edu

Amazon.com and Barnes and Noble.com
These sites offer wide selections of books on childhood development.

www.amazon.com
www.bn.com

American Academy of Child and Adolescent Psychiatry
This organization offers information such as disobedience, defiance, tantrums, and the symptoms and treatment of oppositional-defiant disorder.

www.aacap.org
(202) 966-7300
3615 Wisconsin Ave., N.W., Washington, D.C. 20016-3007

Brain Connection
This site includes a variety of research-based and practical information on how the brain works and how people learn. It features include an extensive library of articles, online courses, brain facts, book reviews, conference information, and brain teasers.

www.brainconnection.com

Brazelton Touchpoints Center
This organization trains experts based on the word of Dr. T. Berry Brazelton. At their website, families can find information on areas such as how to help kids deal

with catastrophes, lists of hospitals with Touchpoints certified programs, and Dr. Brazelton's national speaking schedule.

www.touchpoints.org

Centers for Disease Control and Prevention
This government agency presents research reports and research-based articles on all aspects of family health.

www.cdc.gov
(800) 311-3435
1600 Clifton Road, Atlanta, GA 30333

ERIC Clearinghouse on Elementary and Early Childhood Education
This Web site includes a substantial amount of research-based articles written for an academic audience. Many topics related to education are covered, including language and intellectual development.

www.askeric.org

Exceptional Parent
This Web site and magazine provide information, support, ideas, encouragement, and outreach for parents and families of children with disabilities and the professionals who work with them.

www.exceptionalparent.com
(877) 372-7368
PO Box 2079, Marion, OH 43306

Children, Youth and Families Education and Research Network
This network offers tools and information geared towards youth, parents, families and communities. It's especially useful for locating experts across the country and providing access to the latest research, statistical, and demographic information.

www.cyfernet.org
(612) 626-1111

Healthfinder
This government site provides health information from A to Z — prevention and wellness, diseases and conditions, and alternative medicine—plus medical dictio-

naries, an encyclopedia, journals, and recommends health Web sites from other government agencies, clearinghouses, nonprofits, and universities.

www.healthfinder.gov

KidsHealth

KidsHealth provides doctor-approved health information about children from before birth through adolescence. The site features separate areas for kids, teens, and parents—each with its own design, age-appropriate content, and tone. There are literally thousands of in-depth features, articles, animations, games, and resources, all original and developed by experts in the health of children and teens.

www.kidshealth.org

La Leche League International

La Leche League Groups meet regularly in communities worldwide to share breastfeeding information and mothering experience. The organization has 8,000 leaders and 3,000 local groups in the United States alone.

www.lalecheleague.org
(847) 519-7730
9616 Minneapolis Avenue, Franklin Park, IL 60131

National Parent Information Network

This Web site provides a large quantity of research-based information on making friends, social development, cooperation, and more.

www.npin.org

Parenting Resources for the 21st Century

This Web site links parents and other adults responsible for the care of a child with information on issues covering the full spectrum of parenting. This site strives to help families meet the formidable challenges of raising children today by addressing topics that include school violence, child development, home schooling, organized sports, child abuse, and the juvenile justice system.

www.parentingresources.ncjrs.org

Perceptual Control Theory (PCT)

This resource site provides literature, videos, simulations, discussions, educators and related sites, for those who are interested in further information on the theory concerning the functioning of the human brain that inspired much of the thinking behind the Wonder Weeks.

www.PCTresources.com

Tufts University Child and Family Webguide

This site describes and evaluates other Web sites that contain information about child development. These sites have been selected from thousands of sites about children, based primarily on the quality of the information provided. The goal of the Webguide is to give the public easy access to the best child development information on the Web.

www.cfw.tufts.edu

Zero to Three

This Web site provides an excellent collection of resources focusing on children from birth to three years. The "Brain Wonders" section offers extensive information about early brain development.

www.zerotothree.org
(202) 638-1144
National Center for Infants, Toddlers, and Families, 2000 M St., NW, Suite 200, Washington, D.C. 20036

index